175 YEARS *of* PERSECUTION

Workmen helping to demolish the dome of Tehran's Baha'i Center, the *Haziratul-Quds*, (May 1955), while Hojjat al-Islam Falsafi, a prominent member of the clergy, looks on. The government, here represented by military personnel, is collaborating with religious leaders in the persecution of the Baha'is.

175 YEARS *of* PERSECUTION

A HISTORY OF THE BABIS & BAHA'IS OF IRAN

FEREYDUN VAHMAN

A Oneworld Book

First published by Oneworld Publications, 2019

An earlier, longer version of this book was first
published in the Persian language as
Yeksad-o shast sál mobárezeh bá á'ín-e Baha'i

This translation by Azita Mottahedeh

A CIP record for this title is available from the British Library

ISBN 978-1-78607-586-4
eISBN 978-1-78607-587-1

Typeset by Siliconchips Services Ltd, UK
Printed and bound in Great Britain by Clays Ltd, Elcograf S.p.A.

Oneworld Publications
10 Bloomsbury Street
London WC1B 3SR
England

This book is dedicated to the memory of the Báb and all his followers, who gave their lives for religious renewal and modernity in Iran.

Iran in the nineteenth century

Contents

Foreword

History tells us as much about the past as it does about the present. An account of bygone ages is not merely a retrieval of objective facts, but also their appreciation in light of contemporary values and priorities. In discerning the sequence of events—continuity and disruption, turning points and progress—we invariably make choices as to the sources and voices, the events and epochs that are worthy of our attention. Do we listen to the victor or the vanquished in war? To the story of the slave or the slave owner? Do we only celebrate the strongmen or also the invisible women behind the scenes? Do we measure evolution by spectacular moments of violent revolution, or the subtle embrace of progress in the daily transactions comprising our culture? Do we imagine time as an inescapable repetition of the past or an invitation to imagine a different destiny? Perhaps the sequence of events is less significant than the importance we attach to their meaning, the so-called lessons of history. From this vantage point, great works of history are themselves history-making, because they transform distant occurrences from the past into a narrative about our current struggle to build a better future.

By this measure, *175 Years of Persecution* by Fereydun Vahman, professor emeritus and renowned scholar of Iranian Studies at the University of Copenhagen, is a history-making work of history, an exceptional book written in an exceptional time in the modern evolution of an ancient nation. Against the backdrop of a grave, historical injustice, it is a narrative rooted in the search for redemption against overwhelming odds. His is a comprehensive and heart-breaking, infuriating but incisive, eloquent yet scholarly account of a virulent, obsessive hatred that has profoundly shaped the construction of Iran's modern identity. It is a masterful weaving of abstract historical events with intimate stories of suffering, demonstrating how the choices made by the wielders of power shape the lives of ordinary people going about their lives. The demonization and scapegoating of Babis and Baha'is, from the inception of this faith in the mid-nineteenth century until the present, the treachery of fanatical religious clerics inciting ignorant mobs against people branded as infidels, the complicity of opportunistic political leaders tolerating such atrocities, the attempted extermination of an entire community with shocking cruelty, this appalling yet undeniable past says much about the plight of Iranians today as they struggle for liberation from the grip of a pernicious and hateful ideology.

In reading this gripping, meticulously documented historical narrative, an epic struggle between humanity and inhumanity, the reader is struck by the continuity between past and present: the toxic seeds of hatred sown in the upheavals of nineteenth-century Iran leading to the bitter fruits of fanaticism and corrosive corruption on display today, the decline of a once great and diverse nation into intolerance, division and despair. The gallery of horrors on display will be familiar to students of history, except that they are still occurring today, in the postmodern world of the twenty-first century. The merciless slaughter of innocent men, women and children at the hands of violent mobs, blind, gullible followers convinced by religious leaders that murdering infidels brings divine blessings, are reminiscent of the anti-Semitic pogroms of the Crusades; the ruthless torture of prisoners to recant their faith or face execution replicates the horrors of the Spanish Inquisition; the burning, looting, and mass expulsion of Baha'i villages evoke images of ethnic cleansing from the Balkans; demolishing sacred places of worship, and even desecrating the dead in cemeteries, call to mind the wanton destruction of the Vandals; entrenching discrimination in law by prohibiting the rights of Baha'i citizens to marriage, employment and education reflects the theocratic equivalent of Nazi Germany's infamous 1935 Nuremberg Laws. This barbaric sentiment is captured in the notorious declaration of the Supreme Leader of the Islamic Republic, Ayatollah Khamenei, in a sermon during Friday prayers, that all Baha'is are *najes* (ritually unclean, untouchables), a derisive term reserved for dogs and pigs. As is the case with other historical instances of scapegoating, these heinous acts are the reflection not of any wrongs committed by the victims, but rather a glimpse into the wicked, perverse imagination of the perpetrators—of their need to dehumanize and destroy others in order to feel powerful.

The surfacing, at long last, of this dark and despicable past, and the awakening of enlightened Iranian leaders of thought to this grave injustice, embody an aspiration to live in a just society in which all Iranians enjoy equal rights, irrespective of belief. The growing chorus of condemnation against anti-Baha'i persecution captures the gradual transformation of theocratic tyranny into a culture of compassion, founded on an unshakeable consciousness that human rights belong to all human beings. At this historical juncture, a time of popular resurgence and reckoning with the past, this book has become a focal point for understanding the catastrophic consequences for all Iranians of systematic inhumanity against a peaceful and progressive community in their midst. Professor Vahman vividly demonstrates how, from the origin story of the revolutionary Babi movement in the mid-nineteenth century, to the genocidal pogroms of the Qajar era, to the improved, but precarious, situation during the Pahlavi years, and the calamitous re-emergence of the ideological extermination campaign following the 1979 Islamic Revolution, the history of anti-Baha'i persecution is characterized by pathologically paranoid conspiracy theories, manufactured by a self-serving, regressive religious caste, portraying an indigenous, modern, and socially progressive community of fellow Iranians committed to the moral renewal of their nation as foreign spies, devil-worshippers, and enemies of Islam, so poisoning impressionable minds with the invention of imaginary demons in order to maintain their grip on power. The projection of every conceivable evil onto Baha'is is, above all, about keeping the religious masses ignorant—pliable pawns at the disposal of the clerics in furtherance of their political machinations.

The Baha'i ideals of democratic and consultative rule instead of authoritarian dogmatism; a peaceful international order in place of aggression; the equality of men and women instead of gender apartheid; social justice and moral transformation aimed at eradication of the pervasive corruption that enriches the few at the expense of the many; modern education and freedom of choice on spiritual matters without the control of meddling, mystical middlemen: these were, and remain, emancipatory beliefs and attributes that pose a direct threat to the purveyors of fanatical and authoritarian ideologies that have caused such desolation for the Iranian people. Today, in heroic scenes being played out in the streets of cities, towns, and villages across the country, in social media posts and YouTube clips, films and books, sculptures and paintings, in the inexorable movement of the masses crying for freedom and justice, we witness the dawning realization that the emancipation of the Baha'is is also the emancipation of the Iranian people.

What is perhaps most remarkable about Professor Vahman's historical account is not the more than a century and a half of relentless cruelty and oppression, but the astonishing resilience of the Baha'i community in the face of such hatred and violence. The image recurs of an innocent man stabbed to death in front of his wife and children, solely because of his religion, with the self-confessed culprit acquitted of wrongdoing because murder of infidels was religiously approved. This outrage could have happened, and has happened, equally in 1850, 1903, 1950, and 2016, to give but one example of the abominations detailed in this book. The anti-Baha'i persecutions are not just about a distant past, but also the persistent reality of the present. It is thus perplexing that despite so many years of unceasing efforts, including the Islamic Republic of Iran's deployment over the past forty years of its formidable power and resources—the Revolutionary Courts and Revolutionary Guards, intelligence operatives and prison torturers, an endless torrent of incendiary hate propaganda in school books and the state-controlled media—the clerical establishment has failed to extinguish either the existence or the spirit of this community. On the contrary, the purveyors of religious hatred are confronted today with the manifest failure of their efforts, in view of an unprecedented outpouring of sympathy and support for Baha'is, as influential Iranians, whether secular or religious, express their remorse for the silence of the past and call for the human rights of this persecuted minority to be respected in the name of a new, emancipatory conception of Iranian citizenship.

The original Persian language version of Professor Vahman's book—*160 Years of Persecution of the Baha'is of Iran*—first published over a decade ago, quickly emerged as a highly influential historical work. Today, it is widely considered the authoritative historical source on the persecution of Iranian Baha'is. It has helped galvanize a much-needed debate among a new generation of Iranian intellectuals and activists, struggling to reckon with the past that haunts their present. At a portentous historical juncture, when the likes of human rights champions Nasreen Soutudeh and Shirin Ebadi, and courageous clerics such as Ayatollah Masoumi-Tehrani and Ayatollah Montazeri, have defiantly stood in solidarity with their fellow Baha'i citizens, this book has inspired groundbreaking, once unimaginable films such as Reza Allamehzadeh's *Iranian Taboo* and Mohsen Makhmalbaf's *The Gardener*, that have helped popularize the plight of this peaceful community. Its painstaking and elegant rendering into English by a team of translators and editors has now made it accessible to a wider global audience at a crucial time for all those interested in understanding the fate and fortunes of the Iranian people in their struggle for democracy and human rights.

Professor Vahman's account of anti-Baha'i persecutions is essential reading; it is at once a historical epic, a labor of love, and a moral challenge. It should not be lost on the reader that the author, though a distinguished scholar of Iranian studies, has himself suffered the tragic loss of family and friends to fanatical violence, and endured decades in exile. His continuing faith in the transformative power of truth, despite this experience, is itself remarkable, as is the painful irony that he cannot set foot in his own country without facing imprisonment and torture. In the face of the persistent lies and calumny of the Islamic Republic's Orwellian hate propaganda, his dignified contribution to historical knowledge is a poignant demonstration of scholarship as resistance against oppression, a reminder that a new and better world begins with the power of words and enlightenment of minds. In this groundbreaking work of history, Professor Vahman has given us a gift for generations to come: a window into a dark past, but also a door to a bright future.

Payam Akhavan
McGill University
Montreal, Canada

Acknowledgements

I owe the publication of the Persian and English versions of this book to many wonderful people who helped me at different stages in its research, drafting, and translation. My sincere thanks go to the Office of Archives and Documents of the Baha'i World Center in Haifa, as well as the Representative of the Baha'i International Community at the United Nations in Geneva, for providing me with copies of official documents (not included in this English version) as well as other materials related to the persecution of the Iranian Baha'is.* I am also indebted to my old friends Gitti and Farhang Vahid, Shokouh Madjzoob and Mehri Mavaddat-Mottahedin for providing me with eyewitness accounts of the situation of the Baha'i community in the early years of the 1979 Islamic Revolution. To Bahram Choubine, and a dear friend who prefers to remain anonymous, I express my gratitude for reviewing the Persian manuscript of the book and offering valuable suggestions for revision. I am also grateful to Abbas Amanat for his support and valuable suggestions. My thanks also to Mouhebat Mahdi and Naser Derakhshan. I further note with appreciation that the Persian version of the book was printed four times thanks to the efforts of my publishers 'Asr-e Jadid in Germany and Baran in Sweden.

The publication of this book in English was made possible with the devotion and sincere commitment of Azita Mottahedeh, who spent

* Many of the documents are now available at: https://iranbahaipersecution.bic.org/.

two laborious years ensuring an accurate and faithful translation. I am also thankful to her husband Houshmand Mottahedeh for his support and encouragement.

My sincere thanks also goes to the team of editors for their superb editorial work and their careful attention to detail during the delicate process of editing.

The publication of both the Persian and English editions of this work would not have been possible without generous financial assistance from different sources. In this regard, I wish to recognize with gratitude the Persian Heritage Foundation in New York, the ADEL foundation in Luxembourg, and Velux foundation in Denmark for their support. I am also thankful to Fereydun Javaheri, Iraj Ayman and Iraj Eshraghi for their ceaseless encouragement and assistance in the publishing and dissemination of the Persian edition.

Through a decade of work on this project, I was privileged by the kind support of my family: Enayat and Ruhi Vahman for their assistance, including providing the photos in Chapter 8; my brother and sister-in-law Manuchehr and Parvaneh Vahman, and their son Ashkan Vahman.

Last but not least I offer my warm thanks to Shomais Vahman, and our beloved daughters Sarira and Nilofar for their support and patience. Shomais assisted me with reading the final proofs of this book and offered valuable suggestions. I am also grateful to Payam Akhavan for sharing with me his valuable experiences of human rights activities, as well as writing the preface to this edition.

Finally, I would like to extend my thanks to Novin Doostdar of Oneworld Publications, and to Jonathan Bentley-Smith for supervising the final editing of the English version.

Fereydun Vahman
University of Copenhagen
Denmark

Introduction

The "Enigma" of the Baha'i Religion in Iran

More than a century and a half have passed since the emergence of the Baha'i faith in Iran, and though it is one of the world's most widespread religions, it is little understood in its home country. At least until very recently, Iranian scholars and intellectuals have often regarded the Baha'i faith as an enigma, and popular misconceptions have been uncritically accepted. A long campaign of propaganda and suppression of information about the Baha'i community in Iran has served to mask a continuing human rights crisis.

Following Iran's 1979 revolution, when the Zoroastrian, Jewish, and Christian faiths were designated as recognized religions, the Baha'is—Iran's largest religious minority, at over 300,000 members—were given no such official recognition. Baha'i institutions were forcibly closed, and Baha'is were barred from teaching and practicing their faith. Individuals who identify as Baha'i are denied access to education, barred from all forms of employment, and have no security in property rights. Social rites within their community, such as marriage, are not officially recognized, leaving couples "unwed" and children illegitimate. Their homes and businesses have been confiscated, their holy sites and historical landmarks destroyed, and their graveyards desecrated. Baha'i leaders are periodically targeted for imprisonment and execution.

The persecution of the Baha'i community in Iran began with the very origins of the religion in 1844, when a spiritual leader who came to be known as the Bab ("gateway") declared himself to be the Mahdi—the hidden Twelfth Imam of Shi'i Muslims, the dominant branch of Islam in Iran—and the beginning of a new, post-Islamic cycle of revelation and justice. The movement spread rapidly and brought an immediate reaction from the government and the Shi'i clergy. The Bab was imprisoned and his followers were denounced as apostates, subjected to mob violence, torture, and public executions. They took up arms to defend themselves, and thousands were killed in several confrontations with government forces.

The Bab himself was publicly executed in Tabriz in 1850. Seeking retribution, two Babis from a radical faction attempted to assassinate Naser al-Din Shah in August 1852. They failed. Brutal reprisals against the entire community followed, and many of the leaders of the Babi community were killed. A few, including Mirza Husain 'Ali—later called Baha'u'llah—were exiled to the Ottoman Empire. Those who remained in Iran faced reprisals from the clergy, civilian mobs, and the military. Rather than face the total destruction of their families, their homes, and their cities amidst the chaos of a fractured movement, the Babis of Iran relented. Baha'u'llah assumed leadership of the remaining community, and the thousands of Iranian Babis who had been living in hiding embraced a new religion committed to a peaceful manifestation that emerged as the Baha'i faith.

Within the framework of its spiritual teachings, the Baha'i faith aimed to establish peace and the unity of mankind, and to empower people through education and intellectual freedom of thought. Their ideals included equal rights for men and women, universal literacy, and the education of girls and women. They preached against corruption, theft, and moral decadence. They demanded the clergy cease to interfere in the affairs of the government, and for the first time introduced the idea of a parliamentary system for Iran.

The early years of the movement were distinguished by a wave of enthusiasm for its new principles and the rapid spread of its ideas throughout Iran, reaching into the shah's court as well as to distant rural villages. Thousands of Muslims joined the new faith. The message of this new religion appealed to both the elite and the common people, and shook the very foundations of the country. Half a century before Iran's Constitutional Revolution (1905–11) constrained the power of the monarchy through a constitution and led to the formation of Iran's first parliament, the Baha'i movement planted the seeds of the principles of freedom of conscience and thought, equality of all citizens regardless of gender and religion, the need for educational advancement and the expansion of justice throughout the nation. The spread of these new ideals left a lasting impression on thousands of Iranians, regardless of whether or not they converted to the Baha'i faith.

An influential Babi theologian and poet known as Tahereh Qurrat al-'Ayn was the first woman among the leadership of the new religion, and she was also one of the first to give her life for the faith. The early enthusiasm of the movement was expressed in her poetry:

> Look up! Our dawning day draws its first breath!
> The world grows light! Our souls begin to glow!
> No ranting shaykh rules from his pulpit throne
> No mosque hawks holiness it does not know
> No sham, no pious fraud, no priest commands!
> The turban's knot cut to its root below!
> No more conjurations! No spells! No ghosts!
> Good riddance! We are done with folly's show!
> The search for Truth shall drive out ignorance
> Equality shall strike the despots low
> Let warring ways be banished from the world
> Let Justice everywhere its carpet throw
> May Friendship ancient hatreds reconcile
> May love grow from the seed of love we sow!

These words (here translated by Amin Banani) were suppressed, and seventy years would pass before similar ideas were expressed by Iranian intellectuals at the time of the Constitutional Revolution. Both the message and its style of expression were unprecedented in their time.[1]

Iran's clergy viewed this burgeoning new faith as a threat to the power they had exercised, directly and indirectly, over the country since Shi'i Islam was established as the state religion under the Safavid dynasty in the sixteenth century. The persecution of the Baha'i community that began in the Qajar period with mob violence, executions, torture, and the seizure of property, has persisted in various forms into modern times, but also served for a century and a half as a political tool for controlling the government of Iran. The clergy succeeded in intimidating the statesmen of both the Qajar and Pahlavi dynasties by threatening them with accusations of Babi and Baha'i affiliations. The suppression of the movement has been a consistent feature on the agenda of reactionary elements in Iranian society, as historian Delaram Mashhouri notes, and the persecution of the Babis and Baha'is "has been used as a pretext to extinguish any spark of progress-seeking activity in any arena whatsoever."[2] As the historian Fashahi puts it:

> The Babi movement was drowned in a sea of afflictions, of suffering and blood; yet it had a tremendous effect upon Iranian society, which was deeply dormant in medieval conditions. The reforms made by Amir Kabir, the emergence of enlightened intellectuals, the Constitutional Revolution, as well as the literary revolution and more—that is to say, the overall appearance of a new and modern Iran—were all born out of this movement and were the logical consequence of its endurance.[3]

The policies of Reza Shah Pahlavi (r. 1925–41) towards the clergy differed from those of the Qajar kings, but when politically expedient, he too allied himself with Shi'i religious leaders by imposing severe restrictions on the Baha'is.

Under the reign of his successor, Muhammad Reza Shah Pahlavi (r. 1941–79), the *mullahs* sought to restore their former power. (In recent decades "*mullah*" has come to carry a pejorative connotation, but throughout this book I make no such implication, using the term only in its traditional sense to refer to a teacher who is knowledgeable in religious matters.) Ayatollahs Boroujerdi and Khomeini had both threatened on separate occasions to depose the shah on the grounds that the Baha'is were exercising an undue influence. On June 3, 1963, Ayatollah Khomeini stated:

> Look at the calendar of the Baha'is of two years ago or maybe three years ago; it is there recorded: The equality of the rights of men and women, [this] is the opinion of 'Abdul-Baha; the men [in charge in the government] are following him. The shah, utterly ignorant of this goes up there, and preaches the equality of the sexes. Man! You have been injected with this idea so that they can accuse you of being a Baha'i, so that I pronounce you an infidel; and that you may be dethroned. Don't do this, you wretched one! Don't do this. Universal compulsory education. . . it is 'Abdul-Baha's view.[4]

Khomeini's threat to dethrone the shah was based on the shah's progressive social stance—equality between men and women, and universal education—rather than corruption or mismanagement of the country. The clergy alleged that the shah himself, his prime minister Hoveyda and other members of his cabinet were Baha'is. These accusations attracted the full vitriol of the general public for a final assault against the Pahlavi dynasty. Historian Mohamad Tavakoli-Tarqi notes the centrality of the anti-Baha'i campaign to the 1979 revolution:

> With the merging of the anti-Baha'i campaigns with the anti-Israel, anti-colonialist, and the anti-imperialist movements, the struggle for the elimination of the Baha'is turned into a struggle for the defeat and overthrow of the Pahlavi regime. The Iranian liberation movement regarded the "civil freedom of the Baha'is" as synonymous with the "captivity of the Muslim people."[5]

When the shah was exiled, the clergy seized the reins of absolute power in Iran. For Baha'is, the regime of the Islamic Republic bore a remarkable resemblance to the brutality of the Qajar period as a second bloody age of imprisonment and executions began. Following the Islamic Revolution, the Baha'i community "witnessed attacks on their physical integrity, community structures, social standing and even their community survival."[6]

The Constitution of 1906, which had been indirectly influenced by Babi and Baha'i teachings current among Iranian intellectuals at the time, was finally buried once and for all after the formation of the Islamic Consultative Assembly, led by the Guardianship of the Islamic Jurists. Since that time, merely mentioning the former constitution has been considered blasphemous. The new constitution gave other religions official recognition, but not the Baha'i faith.

* * *

Presently, even basic facts about the Baha'i religion and its followers are little known to the public in Iran. Any uncensored discussion regarding the Baha'is, their religion, and their place in Iran's history, remains largely prohibited. A targeted program of censorship and disinformation carried out by governmental and religious authorities has created a lasting and overwhelmingly negative perception of Baha'is in the public mind.

That negative perception is in part enabled by the highly stratified social hierarchy defined in Islamic law, which distinguishes between the rights of men and women; *Seyyeds*, or descendants of the prophet, and ordinary Muslims; and between legally permitted non-Muslims, and a category regarded as *najes*, or ritually unclean, to which the Baha'i have been relegated. The label of *najes*, and the harsh enforcement of this distinction at a civic level, has rationalized the marginalization of the Baha'i community, deprived them of their civil rights, and cast them under a constant shadow of doubt and suspicion.

The lengthy duration of the Baha'i persecution has desensitized the general public to the nature of the brutality inflicted upon the religious group, but this disregard has also been fed for generations by deeply inculcated negative propaganda—the phenomenon of "fantasy fabrication" about the Baha'is that has become part of common beliefs. These fallacies became firmly rooted in the early years of the religion's advent, but still linger around discussions of the Baha'i faith today. In each era the mythology generates new rumors and accusations, and the constant dehumanization prepares the ground for fresh abuse. Such conversations start in the family, at home, and at school. Now, under the Islamic Republic, these tales are taught to children as part of their education. Even secular Iranians have rarely been able to free themselves from the influence of such ideas, solidified in their minds during childhood.

Many of the enduring rumors about Baha'is cast them as sexual deviants, bringing the Baha'i community's standards of moral conduct into question. Two examples may suffice.

The first is personal. My own grandmother was a devout Muslim, though her husband and children were Baha'is. The elderly woman came home from the mosque one evening in tears. She explained that the *mullah* had said many terrible things from the pulpit about the Baha'is, including that all Baha'is were illegitimately born. She had confronted him outside the mosque and told him, "Aqa, I have four children, all are Baha'is and none were born out of wedlock." We asked her what his reply was. "Nothing," she said, "he sniggered and left."

Reza Fani Yazdi, author and human rights activist, describes the effect such rumors had on him as a non-Baha'i growing up in Iran:

> For the children of our age group, Baha'ism had only a few characteristics. . . The followers were an unclean (*Najes*) group of people among whom there existed no moral standards. They had free sexual relations; father and daughters slept together, and during their nightly gatherings, following the religious portion of the meeting, they would turn out the lights and anyone could sleep with anyone else. . . The belief in the promiscuity of the Baha'is was not confined to the children and the youth. Many adults and elderly people in our country believed it to be true as well. This notion was

> so strong that some of the Muslim men who were looking for fun used to think that by turning to the Baha'i faith, they would have no problems in having affairs with the women and girls of the community.[7]

Another common accusation leveled at Baha'is is that they are intelligence agents in the service of various foreign powers, whether Russia, Great Britain, the United States, or Israel. In a similar vein it was alleged that the establishment of the Baha'i faith was linked to Western interventionism in Iran. The minority religious community became a scapegoat for fears grounded in Iran's past dealings with Western colonial powers. As historian Tavakoli-Targhi notes, the Shi'i clergy "represented a faith that had emerged from the heart of the religious culture of Iran as a complete product of colonial forces. . . This was in fact a scheme for estranging and purging those of a different religion and ideology from the political and religious life of Iran."[8]

The opponents of the Baha'i faith have never presented evidence for the moral decadence of which they accuse the Baha'is, nor have they documented their claims of the faith's links to foreign powers, or its alleged close ties with the shah's regime and its secret police, SAVAK. The ruling clergy of Iran simply repeat the same unfounded statements in newspapers, books, and online media.

Since the beginnings of the Baha'i faith, the mosques have played a major role in turning public opinion against the Baha'is, with inflammatory sermons that could incite mob violence preached from the pulpit. Thousands of articles and volumes of anti-Baha'i literature aimed at the intellectual elite were penned by Shi'i *mullahs* so that hostile attitudes towards Baha'is became entrenched at all levels of society, including the more secular minded. Various Islamic propaganda institutes aided in the publication and dissemination of anti-Baha'i polemical literature, books, articles, and journals as the only sources of information on the minority faith in Iran. Any rebuttal by the Baha'is in self-defense has been strictly forbidden, and discussion of the "enigmatic" Baha'i issue is routinely censored in publications.

Through decades of fierce antagonism and persecution directed at the Baha'is, only in very rare cases have Iranian writers or intellectuals—including the more secular minded—put pen to paper to defend the Baha'is or demand equal rights for them. A rare few courageously documented incidents where Baha'is were slaughtered, though they focused on criticizing the atrocities and violence rather than advocating for the rights of the Baha'is themselves. Only very recently have the voices of intellectuals, lawyers and artists been raised in defense of the human rights of Iran's Baha'i community.[9]

This atmosphere has also had a detrimental effect on Iran's scholars when it comes to discussing historical events that in one way or another involved the Baha'is. A sense of wariness—scholarly self-censorship—prevents historians from exploring these subjects in any depth. Iranian historians of the Qajar period who needed to mention the Babi and Baha'i movement in their accounts either confined themselves to a passing reference or, more likely, repeated familiar attacks on the group, providing few impartial insights into the movement. The censorship and lack of free speech imposed on Iran's Baha'i citizens have further contributed to the erasure of their role in the nation's history.

A few Iranian intellectuals living abroad have, during recent years, investigated the historic implications of this movement rationally and impartially, but rarely have they looked beyond the sphere of Babi research. The execution of the Bab in the barrack square of Tabriz in 1850, and the suppression of the Babi uprisings during the reign of Naser al-Din Shah, are generally regarded as the end of the story. Rather than exploring the actual aftermath of those events, historians have been more interested in speculating on how an alternative policy toward the Babi movement might have limited the power of the clergy. Some of the more thoughtful analysis available on the Baha'i movement will be introduced in the first chapter, which examines the reasons for Iranian opposition to the Baha'i faith.

This book is an effort to counter the dearth of accurate information on the history of the Baha'i faith in Iran, and to illustrate the nature of the suffering imposed on its followers. Recognition of the systematic discrimination they have endured is long overdue, as is the remarkable role of an unprecedented and significant movement that is essential to our understanding of modern Iran. In the early chapters, we will explore in more detail the reasons for the opposition of the clergy toward the Baha'i faith, and then examine the features of this confrontation during the Qajar and Pahlavi periods, and finally under the Islamic Republic as it continues today.

PART ONE

Persecution During the Qajar and Pahlavi Dynasties, 1844–1979

Chapter 1

Why Were the Babi and Baha'i Faiths Suppressed in Iran?

The hostility of the Shi'i clergy towards the Babi and Baha'i faiths needs to be understood in the context of the sociopolitical conditions of nineteenth-century Iran and the historical awakening of Iranian society during that period.

The ruling Qajar dynasty (1794–1925) was a tribe of Turkic origin with uncertain claims to the throne, whose survival depended on the support of the clergy in guaranteeing public acceptance. The *mullahs* were granted many benefits under this arrangement, enjoying financial support in the form of shares in state properties and endowments. Every so often, however, they demonstrated their power to the Qajar monarchs by inciting rebellion, and they resisted any efforts by more progressive government ministers, such as Amir Kabir or Sepahsalar, to curtail their influence.

As historian Abbas Eqbal notes, the power of the Shi'i religious leaders was at least equal to that of the monarchy, and was rationalized by religious law and their claim to be the representatives of the absent and hidden Imam.[1] It was during the reign of Fath-'Ali Shah Qajar that Mullah Ahmad Naraghi first proposed the concept of *Velayat-e Faqih*, the Guardianship of the Islamic Jurists, which would later form the basis of the rationale for the Islamic Republic's power. The authority of the clergy even reached into the military during Fath-'Ali Shah's reign. In the same letter granting permission to the shah to declare war against Russia, the *mujtahid* Kashef al-Gheta referred to Fath-'Ali Shah as "our servant who confesses to his servitude."[2]

Through a legion of *mullahs*, prayer leaders, preachers, *rowzeh khan* (narrators of mourning ceremonies), and even fortune tellers and geomancers, the clergy controlled not only the population's religious experience but its social conditions. Marriages, divorces, inheritance, and the transfer of property all fell under the jurisdiction of the *ulama*. Religious leaders enjoyed similar lifestyles to the monarchy, possessing harems with numerous wives and concubines. Many employed private armies that robbed ordinary citizens with impunity. During the most arduous droughts of the Qajar period, these same clergymen hoarded large quantities of wheat. In return for bribes, religious leaders extended their protection to the Qajar kings by declaring *fatwas* (judicial decrees) that gave freedom to the court, the army, and corrupt provincial rulers to plunder the nation.

The near absolute power of the ruling class in Iran is described in a contemporary account written by Hajj Sayyah Mahallati:

> In no other country can we find one group of people given such free rein to do whatsoever they choose, and another group under such utter suppression and confinement. None of the great monarchs of Russia, Germany, Britain or any powerful government in the world. . . is so exempt from all obligations, so free to do as it pleases, and so immune from any reprimand, as are the monarch, the ministers, the princes, the chief-lictors, head constables, village chiefs, Seyyeds, the clergy and *mullahs*, and narrators of lamentation meetings in Iran. These religious leaders are armed with a sword of excommunication on the one hand, and an arrow of priesthood on the other with which they eliminate the wealth, life or tarnish the good name of whosoever they may wish, or anyone who does not abide by their requests. The concept of what is lawful or illegal; the notion of heaven and hell; the ruling of ritually clean and unclean, accursed and defiled all depend upon their word and decree. They regard themselves to be the lord of the world and the hereafter, and consider the king and his ministers,

> as well as the rulers and the governors to be assigned to implement their wishes, to which there are no limits. . . The state dignitaries, the governors, their relatives and servants also see themselves as the possessors of the lives, dignity and properties of people.[3]

The court historian of Naser al-Din Shah vividly described the actions of the private army of thugs employed by Seyyed Muhammad Baqer Shafti, who had come to Isfahan as a poor theological student, but amassed incalculable wealth:

> It often happened that the bandits would dip and wash, in the mosque basins, the weapons with which they had murdered the Muslims, and took pride in it. "How numerous the nights" when the thugs raided the homes of the merchants and committed "a shameful act and disgrace" with the "wife and children." If, on the following day, anyone would make mention of the "nocturnal occurrence," "no doubt his head would be severed from his body on the following night."[4]

Shafti's judicial rulings condemned to death more than a hundred persons accused of breaking Islamic laws, and he himself was known to carry out many of the lashings and beheadings he ordered.

Over time, the Baha'i community developed its own identity and distinctive features. The emphasis on values such as honesty and being of service to others gradually established a solid reputation for its members as honest and trusted citizens. The stress on the importance of education created a generation motivated and engaged in the development of their country. The Baha'i world view encouraged association with others, including with the persecuted minority communities of Zoroastrians and the Jews, and the establishment of personal and commercial ties with them. Belief in gender equality, and campaigns encouraging the participation of women in public life, became significant factors in shaping its community life. It functioned without clergy and instead valued individual, independent investigation of issues, and administered its affairs through consultation by its elected representatives rather than rely on a clerical elite. All such changes singled out the community and distinguished the Baha'is as "something different".

But in the climate of corruption and lawlessness that prevailed generally, the Babi and later the Baha'i communities were especially vulnerable targets. Anyone suspected of following the new faith was liable to be accused of random crimes. Even someone who was not a Baha'i could find themselves accused by a personal enemy or simply an opportunist wishing to procure another's property. Progressive ideals behind political and social reforms were also rejected by the clergy on such grounds. The Shi'i *ulama* claimed, for example, that the Constitutional Revolution of 1905, which first emerged as a rejection of the old social order, had in fact been initiated by the Babis.

The government turned a blind eye to Babi and Baha'i killings that were provoked by the clergy. The slightest protection or sympathy extended to members of the faith was sufficient grounds for one to be branded a follower and have one's property seized by the government. Many accusations were opportunistic. The persecution or murder of the Baha'is was considered a meritorious act that would secure entry to paradise through the *mullahs*' intercession. Anything obtained through pillage and looting was considered to be earthly reward for the effort. Historian Fashahi describes the frenzy that was unleashed on the Babis in the early years of the movement:

> They ripped open their bodies, disemboweled them, tied their corpses to a rope and paraded them through the streets and alleys. Others were blown alive from the mouths of cannons, and chopped to pieces. The corpses of the dead were exhumed and burnt and displayed in the city. Some were beheaded in public; the severed heads were then stuffed with hay and sent as gifts to the chief army officers and to those in authority. Men, women, children, old and young were all slaughtered together. . . During the bloodbath of Tehran, Haji Sulayman Khan and Haji Ghasem Nayrizi were chained together from the neck, their bodies were pierced and burning candles were placed in their wounded flesh. But when they intended on cutting up Haji Sulayman Khan into pieces, he

> was dancing and chanting mystical poetry, and requested that his comrade Haji Qasem be the first to attain such a bounty as he believed the latter to rank above him.[5]

The opposition of the *mullahs* towards the Babis and Baha'is has been seen as the familiar resistance of an old religion to the emergence of a new one in its sphere of influence. Such a notion is valid, but should not obscure the unique social and political circumstances surrounding the advent of the new faith. In his book *Resurrection and Renewal*, regarded as the most complete academic analysis of the changes in nineteenth-century Iran, historian Abbas Amanat links the Bab's advent to the modernization movement in Iran, and to the quest for freedom from a culture seen as obsolete and backward: "Babism responded to the changing socio-moral climate by consciously incorporating the notion of recurring renewal into the body of religious doctrine."[6]

While the Bab claimed to be the hidden Twelfth Imam who reappears to bring justice to the world, he did not simply resolve Shi'i expectations for the Mahdi and the impending resurrection. Rather than heralding the end time, he was affirming the beginning of a new age and the belief that one universal faith has been revealed in different forms throughout history. The new religion included a deep acknowledgment of change—an acceptance that nothing, including religion and religious beliefs—remains stagnant in this world.

> This revolutionary step set the Babis on the road to a complete break from Islam and the creation of a new religious dispensation. The mind that conceived this break, and set about to achieve it, though primarily religious, shared the modernity of a secular mind as it traced the stagnation of the community not in the irreversible fate of its members but in their failure to see the incompatibility of their past religious values with the realities of a new era.[7]

The new religion's most fundamental challenges to the social order of Shi'i Iran were its emphases on modern education and the equality of men and women. In the teachings of Baha'u'llah and his eldest son 'Abdul-Baha, education is said to be the key to progress. In hundreds of statements, they emphasize the great value of education. Humanity is compared to a mine filled with gems of inestimable value, which education alone can reveal and extract.[8]

In a time of widespread illiteracy, when learning to read the Quran in Arabic was the only education available to most people, the Baha'i community began to establish schools. It is not known exactly when the first ones opened. A small school for boys was founded in the Sar-e Qabr-e Aqa district of Tehran around 1897. In 1903 it was relocated, renamed the Tarbiyat School, and reorganized along Western educational lines. The Tarbiyat School for Girls started unofficially, perhaps as early as 1899, before being officially established in 1911 with thirty students, and quickly grew to several hundred. Both of these schools gained prominence and attracted students from notable families in the capital who were not Baha'is.[9] Early efforts towards modern education were not limited to the Baha'i community; the pioneering educator known as Hasan Roshdieh founded a number of primary schools at this time.[10] Altogether, around fifty schools for girls, as well as boys, appeared across the country.[11]

Conservative clerics such as Shaykh Fazlollah Nuri, who is seen as one of the founders of political Islam in Iran, associated all such efforts at modern education with the Baha'i faith. He claimed these new schools were contrary to religious law and would draw students away from Islam and towards the Baha'i faith. His writing shows the linkage of themes he considered offensive:

> Ever since the inception of the parliament [Consultative Assembly], the ungodly, careless, and irreligious community who used to be referred to as Babis. . .has been set in sinful motion. . . stating that the laws revealed 1330 years ago must be updated according to the requirements of the time; bringing about the legalization of alcoholic beverages, the diffusion of brothels, founding of schools for girls, the education of women, the expenditure of the income from lamentation gatherings and pilgrimage sites towards the building of factories, roads, railways and other projects."[12]

Historian Soli Shahvar notes that modern schools also threatened the source of income of many clerics who taught the Quran in the traditional manner.[13]

The schools organized by the Baha'i community were careful not to teach the Baha'i faith. All efforts were made to abide by state regulations and to precisely follow the government-set curriculum. Despite these measures, the Baha'i schools faced severe opposition and were often forced to close. In 1921, a mob incited by the local clergy in the town of Sangsar raided and burnt down the local Baha'i school.[14] In the 1930s the Baha'i schools were all closed down at the order of Reza Shah Pahlavi.[15]

Reports on the Baha'i community written by foreign envoys who lived in Iran during that period call attention to the advancement achieved by women in this community and point out the significant differences between Baha'i and non-Baha'i women. The Baha'i concern for the equality of men and women was not limited to education, although education was strongly emphasized. In contrast to the prevailing sharia law and Shi'i custom, Baha'i teachings accepted men and women as legally equal, set the age of maturity for women at fifteen, and required the bride's consent as essential for marriage. Monogamy was universally prescribed, and temporary or short-term contractual marriage—known among Shi'i Iranians as *sigheh* or *nikah al-mot'eh*—was forbidden. Baha'i women were not required to wear a *hijab*.

It should not be imagined that these efforts yielded results easily. The surrounding traditional society exerted intense pressure on the emerging Baha'i community, and the greater freedom given to Baha'i women by their own community was interpreted as a sign of promiscuity.

The role of Tahereh Qurrat al-'Ayn (1817–50), whose poetry was quoted in the introduction, throws light on the view of women in the earliest days of the Babi movement. She was among the first followers of the Bab and worked side by side with other leaders of the community in the expansion and organization of the Babi faith. Her scholarly knowledge was so highly regarded that she led seminars and participated in debates while seated behind a curtain, as Muslim custom considered it unchaste for a woman to sit in the same room with men other than her immediate family. In an act of courage that became legendary, she appeared unveiled in a gathering of Babi leaders in the hamlet of Badasht (June–July 1848), and thus opened the way for the liberation of Iranian women, but also her own martyrdom.

These advancements were not confined to women from urban backgrounds, but were promoted equally in rural villages and hamlets. One story shows how women's advancement was deeply woven into the fabric of change that the Baha'i faith promoted.

Mullah 'Ali Jan, the learned *mullah* of the village of Mahfuruzak, embraced the Baha'i faith in 1876, initially in secret and then openly. Gradually, the 400 inhabitants of his village all followed his example, and eventually some 1,500 people in the area converted. Mullah 'Ali Jan and his wife Alaviyyeh founded two schools in the village, one for boys and one for girls, and taught literacy to adults as well. They educated the villagers in hygiene and improved agricultural practices. They founded a cooperative that helped the farmers to sell their products at better prices, and enabled the high-quality cotton they were now producing to reach Armenian and Russian markets. Poverty in the village was eradicated, and its mud houses were gradually replaced by brick homes.

The clergy in the neighboring villages sent letters to Naser al-Din Shah, accusing Mullah 'Ali Jan of building a fort and preparing a rebellion against the government. Four hundred soldiers attacked Mahfuruzak at dawn on April 29, 1883, looting and burning the village. Most of the inhabitants fled to the woods. Mullah 'Ali Jan and his wife Alaviyyeh were arrested along with several other men, women and children. Alaviyyeh was taken to the lieutenant governor for interrogation, but boldly shamed him into freeing the women and the children. The men, however, were sent to Tehran. The shah referred the decision to the leading *mujtahid*, who issued a death sentence, and Mullah 'Ali Jan was publicly executed.[16] The young widow Alaviyyeh, who also lost her two children shortly thereafter, took over as sole leader of the Baha'i community in Mahfuruzak, and continued with the reforms she and her husband had started. For almost four decades she traveled around the country to promote the advancement of women and the Baha'i faith, until her death in 1921.[17]

THE CONVERSION OF JEWS AND ZOROASTRIANS TO THE BAHA'I FAITH

Less than thirty years after the beginnings of the Babi-Baha'i faith, in the midst of the severe persecution of its followers, large numbers of Iranian Jews and Zoroastrians embraced the new faith, and continued to do so in subsequent decades.

The Jewish and Zoroastrian conversions of the 1880s are of particular social and historical interest, and a subject that has not yet been adequately explored. Both communities were highly conservative and had remained steadfast in their ancestral religions for centuries, despite hardships imposed on them after the Arab conquest of Iran. Neither the efforts of the Muslims to convert the Jews, nor those of Christian missionaries, had yielded significant results.

Converts to the Baha'i faith saw the Bab and Baha'u'llah as the fulfillment of messianic expectations in their own religions, but may also have been drawn by the appeal of modernism and the progressive ideologies of the new faith. The early converts from Judaism and Zoroastrianism were primarily merchants or from the educated class; in later stages, they were joined by farmers, laborers and factory workers.[18]

The conversion of Iranian Jews and Zoroastrians to the new religion was not a flight from their earlier persecutions, and it did not lead to comfort, wealth and a peaceful life. These new converts shared the fate of other Baha'is in being subjected to harassment, persecution, and discrimination. Some gave their lives for their faith.

IRANIAN IDENTITY OR ISLAMIC IDENTITY?

Through much of early history, a relative harmony had existed between the diverse ethnic and religious communities of Iran until this balance was upset by the Arab conquest and the introduction of Islam. After the defeat of the Sassanid Empire in the seventh century, Iranians largely gave up their ancestral religion of Zoroastrianism and converted, at times by the sword and at times willingly, to Islam. But unlike many other lands of the Arab conquest, Iranians preserved their national identity and kept their language and ethnicity distinct.

This was due in part to a flourishing of the Persian language in the centuries following the invasion of the Arabs. Shortly after the Arab conquest (between *c.*977 and 1010 CE), the poet Ferdowsi created his national epic, known as the *Shahnameh* (*Book of Kings*). His recounting of the mythical and historical stories of the pre-Islamic kings of Iran sustained the memory of ancient glory, the remnants of which were still visible in the landscape in the ruins of Persepolis and many other sites. Persian remained the language of Iran, and other languages and dialects such as Kurdi, Luri, and Baluchi also survived and were not replaced by Arabic.

The Arab conquest provoked continued uprisings and nationalist resistance movements such as the Shu'ubiyyeh, the Siyah Jamegan, the revolts of Babak Khorramdin, Mazyar and Al-Moghanna, and the Ustad Sis rebellion, but each of these movements was defeated. Conversion to Islam was also encouraged through exemption from the tax known as *jizyeh,* which was levied on non-Muslims.[19] Over centuries, Persian culture forged an internal reconciliation. The experience of Islam was disconnected from the memory of the Arab invasion, and Iranians gave their hearts to the religion and its ceremonies. Nevertheless, the two opposing poles of religious and national identity remained in a certain tension. Iranians participated wholeheartedly in the mourning ceremonies for Shi'i martyrs, but they also joyously observed the ancient Zoroastrian equinox and solstice festivals, in spite of the disapproval of the clergy.

The *mullahs*' opposition to Iranian nationalism has surfaced most recently during the early years of the 1979 revolution in failed attempts to ban the celebration of Nowruz, and fortunately aborted threats to demolish the ancient ruins of Persepolis. Ayatollah Khomeini blamed "colonialist schemers and their agents" for the persistence of Iranian nationalist sentiments, and Ayatollah Murteza Motahhari called Ferdowsi, the beloved poet of the national epic, a "deprived and vanquished loser" who composed his masterpiece for the sake of the Sultan's coins.[20] Ayatollah Motahhari also articulated a plan for programs designed to gradually eliminate the Persian language and replace it with Arabic. However, in the aftermath of the revolution there has been a revival of interest in the Zoroastrian festivals, a new flowering of Persian literary and spoken expression, and a significant increase in the number of Iranians who identify as not adhering to any religious belief. The tension between religious and national identity remains strong.

For many early followers of the Baha'i faith, the new religion restored a sense of national identity. It was seen as a faith that had emerged from Iran, possessing features in common with Zoroastrianism even as it was a contemporary religion consonant with modernist values. At a time when the Muslim lunar calendar was still in use in Iran, the Baha'i faith adopted the solar year as the basis of its calendar, and designated the ancient festival of Nowruz to mark the beginning of the Baha'i year, and as one of its holy days. The founders of the faith praised Iran's past glory and achievements and made the nation's progress and felicity their declared objectives. 'Abdul-Baha challenged his fellow countrymen:

> O people of Persia! Awake from your drunken sleep! Rise up from your lethargy! Be fair in your judgment: will the dictates of honor permit this holy land, once the wellspring of world civilization, the source of glory and joy for all mankind, the envy of East and West, to remain an object of pity, deplored by all nations? She was once the noblest of peoples: will you let contemporary history register for the ages her now degenerate state? Will you complacently accept her present wretchedness, when she was once the land of all mankind's desire? Must she now, for this contemptible sloth, this failure to struggle, this utter ignorance, be accounted the most backward of nations? Were not the people of Persia, in days long

> gone, the head and front of intellect and wisdom? Did they not, by God's grace, shine out like the daystar from the horizons of Divine knowledge?[21]

But he also offered a remedy for the despondency that is the greatest obstacle to progress and well-being:

> It should not be imagined that the people of Persia are inherently deficient in intelligence, or that for essential perceptiveness and understanding, inborn sagacity, intuition and wisdom, or innate capacity, they are inferior to others. God forbid! On the contrary, they have always excelled all other peoples in endowments conferred by birth. Persia herself, moreover, from the standpoint of her temperate climate and natural beauties, her geographical advantages and her rich soil, is blessed to a supreme degree. What she urgently requires, however, is deep reflection, resolute action, training, inspiration and encouragement.[22]

The Baha'i writings offered assurance that Iran would regain her past glory. Future prosperity was not conditional upon the advent of a promised one, but on the merits of the Iranian people themselves, who could play a decisive part in the well-being of their country and liberate it from the condition that it had been struggling with for centuries.

When the Babi movement was first established, its comprehensive philosophy preceded many of the transformational social, cultural and political shifts that pushed Iran towards modernity. Many new followers held positions of power in Iranian society, and their conversion was not a matter to be taken lightly. The Baha'i faith resonated with their desire for social change in Iran. In this sense, the Baha'i faith was a reflection of the internal development of a modernist sensibility in Iranian society.

> The reforms made by Amir Kabir, the emergence of enlightened intellectuals, the Constitutional Revolution, as well as the literary revolution and so forth; that is to say, the overall appearance of a

> new and modern Iran were all born out of this movement, and were its extension and logical consequence.[23]

Although the Constitutional Revolution is counted as the first victory for parliamentary democracy in Iran, the Constitution's final form abandoned its original spirit and aspirations for liberty. The rewritten laws were to serve as the foundation of Iran's government for the next fifty years, through the reign of the Pahlavi dynasty, and always guaranteed the power and influence of the Shi'i *ulama*. From the very start of the Constitutional Revolution, clergymen such as Shaykh Fazlollah Nuri advocated for Islamic law and regarded the Constitutionalists as a product of the Babi-Baha'i movement:

> The essence of this constitutional plaything comes from the misguided, misleading new sect, who in the name of a delusive freedom attempts to trample over the solid religion of Islam.[24]

The unparalleled power that the Shi'i clergy exercise in Iran today is a phenomenon born of more than two centuries of conflict between them and the country's progressive movements, as historian Homa Nateq explains:

> The uprising of the Babis against the existing order, and the consequent defeat of the movement by the government and religious powers, led to the uncalled-for strength of the clergy and lent them a fresh impetus. It opened the path for the *mullahs* to enter the circle of politics and power. It paved the way for suppression and carnage.[25]

Chapter 2

The Violent Repression of the Babis and Baha'is during the Qajar Period

This chapter will present a handful of contemporary firsthand accounts from the Qajar period of the violent campaigns directed against Baha'is throughout Iran. They are published accounts by widely known and respected Iranian authors, foreign political emissaries, and Christian missionaries. Their observations corroborate the many accounts that were recorded by members of the Baha'i community during this period, which are only very recently becoming available to historians.

NARAQ

Upon arriving in an empty caravansary in central Iran one evening at dusk, Hajj Sayyah Mahallati found that the Naraq of his youth was no more. Instead, the travel writer encountered a village in shambles. As he recalled, it was utterly demolished—not a single house was left standing.[1] The few residents who remained in the area walked around in a grim state of disarray. The writer soon discovered that the ruin of Naraq had begun with a libelous accusation against the Babis of the town—he noted that "the appellation 'Babi' in Iran has become an excuse for the officials, as well as for the bigoted and the narrow-minded mobs, to annihilate the innocent." It was commonly known that being branded a Babi was a dangerous, often fatal, accusation. Mahallati observed:

> Anyone labeled as a Babi will be accused of myriad crimes and even of murder. Many of the clergy whose demands were not met by an individual unhesitatingly accused the poor soul of being a Babi and had him exterminated. . . Whenever the Shah wished to do away with a person or a family, he would announce that they were Babis. The governors throughout the country earned large amounts in this manner, killed numerous souls, and terrorized families. An accusation was all that was needed. No investigation, questioning, witnessing, and proof or evidence followed.[2]

Mahallati learned that a man had come forward with some burnt pages of the Quran, claiming to have found the desecrated holy book in the nearby shrine of an entombed saint. Babis of the town were identified with the help of this accuser, and then rounded up at a central location to be interrogated. A certain Mustafa Quli Khan was appointed by government authorities to lead the investigation. He, along with the local *mullah*, plotted together to accuse most of the inhabitants of being Babis. Citizens of wealth were purposely selected so that their possessions could be divided up among the accusers afterwards. Instead of facing an interrogation, all of the Babis who arrived for questioning were immediately arrested. Mass executions followed. Those who remained, the majority being young children or elderly persons, fled. Some managed to resettle in Hamadan.[3]

The Shi'i clergy of Iran encouraged regular citizens to attack Babis and Baha'is by promoting the idea that their killing was considered to be *sawab*, an act rewarded with spiritual merit. This led to many extrajudicial killings.

ISFAHAN

Another Iranian writer, Ahmad Majd al-Islam Kermani, describes a massacre in Isfahan, where the Baha'is endured similar conditions. What follows is an extract from the account published in his book.

One massacre in the region began with a dispute over a large sum of money owed to two local merchant brothers who were known followers of the Baha'i religion. The debtor in question was a famed preacher—an Imam Jum'eh by the name of Seyyed Muhammad Husain. To avoid repaying his debt he conspired with the governor of the city of Isfahan, Zel al-Sultan, and collected eighty affirmations declaring that the brothers were infidels. He issued their death warrant, which was backed by Shaykh Muhammad Baqer Najafi, another influential clergyman from Isfahan. The debt was revoked and the Baha'i brothers' homes were ransacked.

The incident appeared to open the floodgates for attacks on the Baha'is of Isfahan, as local political leaders and Shi'i authorities such as Shaykh Muhammad Baqer Najafi's son, Shaykh Muhammad Taqi (known as Aqa Najafi), stepped up assaults on the community. The next individual to be identified as a Baha'i was Muhammad Javad Sarraf. He was dragged from his home by an angry mob, in bare feet and uncovered head, while the mob jeered and spat in his face. He was marched to the shah's mosque and detained there. At this point, however, the local government feared that a death warrant against such a respected man would tear the city apart, and sent an urgent message to Aqa Najafi. Under a religious ruling, Muhammad Javad was charged with the consumption of alcohol and sentenced to eighty lashes. He was said to have lost consciousness during his punishment before he was carried home.

Fearing further attacks, the Baha'is of Isfahan invoked the custom of *bast*, pleading for protection within the British and Russian consulates. The former refused, but the Russian consulate agreed to admit a large number of Baha'is from Isfahan and the nearby town of Najafabad. After a period of negotiation, Aqa Najafi finally agreed to the terms outlined by Russia's head consul, which included a guarantee that the Baha'is' lives and possessions would be safe. These terms were also signed by Isfahan's governor.

After two weeks living in the Russian consulate, the Baha'is left to return to their homes. Unbeknown to them, a mob had gathered in the alleyways behind the consulate and descended upon them as soon as they left the safety of the building. Many lost their lives during this assault. Others who had managed to get away fled to Tehran. Mobs under the Imam's command were tasked with rounding up the remaining Baha'is in a series of raids on their homes, using threats of imprisonment and death to collect bribes from them.

Even petty criminals took advantage of the atmosphere of mass anti-Baha'i persecution being stoked by the *mujtahids*. When stopping people in the street at night, muggers detained their victims by authority of Aqa Najafi. The thieves accused their targets of being Baha'i, quickly emptied their pockets of any valuables, and then vanished with their cash, jewelry and cloaks.[4]

One of the children who managed to escape the massacre in Isfahan would grow up to become the renowned Iranian novelist Jamalzadeh, a pioneer in the genre of modern Iranian short stories. Jamalzadeh's father, Seyyed Jamal al-Din Isfahani, known as *Va'iz* or "The Preacher," was a famously outspoken proponent of the Constitutional Revolution and critic of the corruption which gripped the Qajar dynasty. The revolutionary preacher was sympathetic towards the Babi faith and was finally imprisoned and sent to Borujerd by the shah's order. During his separation from his family, Seyyed caught wind of a rash of deadly attacks on Baha'is in Isfahan and Yazd. He acted quickly, sending a message to his wife's brother to flee immediately to Tehran with his family.

Their home and all of their possessions were sold within the space of twenty-four hours. The entire city appeared to be occupied with killing the Baha'i residents, while the young Jamalzadeh, his two brothers, and infant sister set off with their mother and uncle in a rented stagecoach for the capital. Jamalzadeh recalled the despair of the refugees he witnessed on the road:

> I well recall when we arrived at a small village named 'Ali-Abad, near Kashan. The village had nothing but salty and bitter water... We came across a large crowd of men and women—both young and old. They all looked half dead, totally pale, with swollen feet, and in a heartbreakingly pathetic condition. They had collapsed in

> the shades of the walls, moaning with hunger, thirst, pain and misery. We found out that they were from Yazd, where, at the order of the governor Jalal al-Dowleh, the massacre of the Babis had intensified. These poor people, utterly helpless, had fled the cruelty of their heartless fellow townsmen and had set out for the wilderness on foot.

Fortunately, Jamalzadeh and his family survived. Years later, Jamalzadeh would write of his childhood memories and the terror that had descended upon Isfahan during his youth. Though Jamalzadeh's father had managed to save his entire family from being slaughtered, he himself was eventually killed in 1908.

Some thirty-five years later, Jamalzadeh, now an accomplished man of letters, found himself in Geneva on the eve of the Iranian new year festival of Nowruz. He had received an invitation to give a talk on the significance of this traditional celebration at a small feast being organized by the Assembly of the Baha'is. Though he was not Baha'i, he gladly accepted. His audience that evening consisted of a group of Swiss, French, and American men and women, along with one Russian woman—the vice-chair of the Baha'i Assembly. After a round of prayers and well-wishes for the new year following his talk, Jamalzadeh retired from the festivities to the library. There he came across a red leather-bound book entitled *The History of the Martyrs of Yazd*, written in, as he recalls, "exquisite *Nasta'liq*."

> While reading the book, the memory of the heart-rending village of 'Ali-Abad situated between Kashan and Qom was brought to my mind, and the images of those homeless unfortunate people, with their sighs of pain, together with the weeping of my mother all paraded before my eyes.

YAZD

The governor of Isfahan, Zel al-Sultan, and the religious leader, Aqa Najafi, further encouraged the spread of anti-Baha'i violence by writing to leaders in the surrounding towns and villages. This ignited another onslaught of deadly attacks on the Baha'is of the neighboring city of Yazd. The new leading cleric of Yazd was a thirty-year-old *mullah* who had arrived from the holy cities of Iraq after finishing his religious education. While making his way to Yazd, he witnessed the ongoing massacre of the Baha'is in Isfahan and shrewdly seized the opportunity to bolster his own popularity. Before he even arrived in Yazd, word had spread there that the new cleric had obtained strict orders from the *ulama* and religious leaders in the holy cities of Iraq to eradicate all Baha'is.

On June 13, 1903, the day after his arrival, he ascended the pulpit to deliver a rancorous sermon against the Baha'is. This move coincided with an atmosphere of heightened religious anticipation, as the city was preparing to observe the birthday of the Prophet Muhammad. Violence erupted in the city that very afternoon. Baha'i residents were not being brought before the *mujtahids* for judgment and sentencing; instead they were torn to pieces in the streets by angry mobs.

Napier Malcolm, a member of the Church Missionary Society living in Yazd at the time, noted that religious feeling was not the sole motivator for these attacks. The Shi'i clerical authorities had declared that it was "lawful" for anyone to rob Baha'is. Any sense of taboo or revulsion against the act of killing dissolved under the influence of these religious rulings.[5]

During the late-night Babi massacre, a soldier found someone dragging about another man and trying to make out whether he was really a Babi. "You see," he said, "I have been a wicked man all my life, and have never said my prayers or done any other *sawabs*, so, unless I can do a big *sawab*, I shall certainly go to Hell. If this man is a Babi, I mustn't let him go, for if I kill an infidel of course I shall go straight to Heaven."[6]

Malcolm recounted that "holes were bored in the heads of these poor wretches with awls; oil was then poured into the hole and lighted." Shaken by the horrific nature of what he'd encountered, he could not continue his report, stating, "other forms of torture were used about which one cannot write." Baha'i men were tortured and

Report of an eyewitness of the execution of a Baha'i in Tabriz in 1905, printed in an Armenian journal in 1912. Fathollah, the executioner, issues the final ultimatum to Ebrahim a Baha'i, to save his life by denying that he is a Baha'i and by cursing the Bab. Ebrahim says: "I prefer death and not be a liar. Nor will torturing or death worry me . . . I am not punished as a criminal, but I am persecuted because of being just and truthful; loving all people. The forces of all your *mullahs* cannot diminish the love of humanity and goodwill, which has filled my heart."

killed while women and children were driven out to starve on the outskirts of the city. In one of the villages, Baha'i children died within full sight of the villagers, after waiting for days under the trees where their murdered parents had left them.[7]

The city was brought to a halt for a week by violent mobs as Baha'i citizens were brutally hunted down. Known Baha'i-owned shops were overturned and looted by crowds. Their homes were emptied and set ablaze.

An account of one unfortunate Baha'i family from Yazd is described by Haj Muhammad Taher Malmiri in his voluminous book, *The History of the Martyrs of Yazd*. This was the same book discovered

This picture, taken in Yazd in the 1930s, shows a group of Baha'is presenting some of the key principles of their faith. The placards read: Humanity is One, Independent Investigation of Truth, All Religions have a Common Foundation, Religion Must Be the Source of Unity, Harmony of Science and Religion, Equality of Men and Women, Elimination of All Prejudice, Universal Peace, Universal Education, Spiritual Solution to Economic Problems, International Court of Justice, and A Universal Auxiliary Language.

by Jamalzadeh, whose family escaped a similar fate. A Baha'i man named Aqa Muhammad, known to be good-natured, was dragged from his home by a large, aggravated mob to the entrance of the Bagh-e Kundih Mosque, located next to a small bazaar. The crowd disagreed over what to do with their captive—some wanted to bring him to Mirza Seyyed 'Ali to obtain a death sentence, while others saw no need and began attacking him.

Aqa Muhammad was stabbed in the chest by the leader of one faction of the mob, 'Ali Akbar Chavoshha. Aqa Muhammad's brother tried to reach him through the crowd, and he was also critically wounded by Chavoshha's dagger. Aqa Muhammad was butchered by the mob, who finally succeeded in carving his liver out.[8] The well-regarded Baha'i man had two young children—a three-year-old son and five-year-old daughter—who both followed their father out of the house. Aqa Muhammad's wife pulled a *chador* over her head and rushed after her children. The entire family witnessed the father's grisly death. Afterwards, their home was raided and everything of value was stolen. Aqa Muhammad suffered one final indignity:

> Once they were done with the pillage, they came back to him, tied a rope around his leg and dragged him around the area. Finally, he was hauled out of the Kushk-Nou city gate and to the Sayyed Gul-i Surkh plains. There, they took the corpse to the old dry well of Kushke-Nou's mill, flung it into the well, threw dirt and stones over it, and left.[9]

This gruesome pattern of disrespect for the Baha'i dead continues in the twenty-first century. To this day the covert vandalism, bulldozing, and firebombing of Baha'i cemeteries in Iran is still commonplace. These burial sites are also razed and built over through official state-sponsored channels.

TURBAT-E HEYDARIYEH, KHORASAN

Mullahs who sought to gain recognition and power played a critical role in the persecution of the Baha'is throughout Iran during this time. Shaykh 'Ali Akbar, a native of Turbat-e Heydariyeh, was making a pilgrimage to nearby Mashhad in 1896 when Naser al-Din Shah was assassinated. Though the killing was the act of a radical Muslim activist, the Baha'i community suffered the inevitable backlash. The shaykh found it a favorable moment to incite the people of his town against the Baha'is, causing a massive upheaval.

Muhammad Hasan, a well-regarded shoemaker with a workshop in the local bazaar, was the first Baha'i to be killed. He was dragged from his shop by an angry crowd led by a man named Karbalai Reza. Rather than cry out as he was beaten with clubs and chains, he engaged in prayer, only stopping when he finally lost consciousness. The Baha'i shoemaker's shop was looted by his attackers, who encouraged fellow store owners and traders in the bazaar to join in the attack. Afterwards, the mob turned their attention to other Baha'is in the bazaar. The second victim was a nearby shop owner by the name of Muhammad 'Ali Sarrafe Harati, who had been born into a Baha'i family—his father was one of the earliest adherents of the Baha'i faith. The crowd rushed his store and took all of the cash. He was pushed out of his shop by the angry mob, beaten with rods and chains, and led out of the bazaar. He bled heavily before losing consciousness next to the critically injured, unconscious Muhammad Hasan.

Once the melee had begun in the marketplace, it became clear that all the remaining Baha'is in the bazaar were surrounded. Another gang took hold of Mirza Ghulam Reza, who was struck on the head by a brick and immediately fell unconscious to the ground. The mob stuffed handfuls of dirt down his throat and left him for dead. Aqa Yahya, a recent convert to the Baha'i faith, was also brutally beaten.

The violence was not restricted to the bazaar. The gangs stormed the homes of known Baha'is one by one. Ghulam 'Ali, whose brother was attacked in the bazaar, was attacked in his home, along with his nephew Asadollah. They were both dragged from safety, severely beaten, and left for dead. The bodies of Muhammad Hasan, Muhammad 'Ali, Ghulam 'Ali, Aqa Asadollah, and Mirza Ghulam Reza were flung into an empty pool outside the city gates. It is unclear whether they were dead or alive at this point.

At this time, another *mullah* from Yazd, also called Shaykh 'Ali Akbar, was passing through Turbat on his way to pilgrimage in Mashhad, and joined with Shaykh 'Ali Akbar of Turbat in exploiting the situation. Together they issued a death sentence for Haji Sadeq, a well-respected Baha'i merchant, which was announced publicly throughout the town. Haji Sadeq was resting in his room when he found himself face to face with a gunman. The gun jammed, but the drunken assailant drew a dagger and lunged at Sadeq, who was slashed from his mouth to his ear. He died in his room after suffering multiple stab wounds.

The assailant who had broken into Haji Sadeq's home, known as Ya'qub 'Ali, had participated in the massacres of other Baha'is. After he had finished with Haji Sadeq, he went to two shaykhs to request *fatwas* so that he might be permitted to kill the four Baha'is who had already been detained. He sought the backing of the religious authorities to avoid reprisals from Haji Sadeq's family. The two shaykhs granted his request and, armed with a copy of the Quran, they set off to the bazaar.

The Jewish and Armenian residents of the city, small in number themselves, feared for their own safety after hearing the cries of a growing mob ringing out in the streets of Turbat that afternoon. They remained in their homes while the streets became choked with men and women all making their way to the prison grounds. The deputy governor, Prince Muhammad Hasan Mirza, could not quell the mob and sent the chief of police to summon the two leading shaykhs. When they arrived, the shaykhs stood outside the prison door while the prince questioned them as to who was responsible for issuing the death sentence on the four prisoners. While the shaykh from Turbat initially denied his involvement, the shaykh from Yazd became furious, protesting that he himself had issued the death warrant and would accept all responsibility. The shaykh from Turbat consented through his silence.

In an attempt to contain the volatile situation, the prince refused to open the prison doors to the mob. Instead, he asked for the names of the four Baha'i prisoners, ostensibly to protect other prisoners who were not implicated. The four Baha'i prisoners were identified and delivered to a crowd armed with cleavers, axes and knives, who hacked them to death.

The dead Baha'is were then unceremoniously thrown into a trench at the front of the prison and covered in stones. A group of men went to retrieve the corpse of Haji Sadeq who had been murdered in his home earlier that day. They tied a rope to the body and dragged it to the same trench. As the day of terror drew to an end, a man known as Haji Mehdi donated two large containers of Russian petroleum to set fire to the corpses as an act of *sawab*.

The dead Baha'i men were pulled out from under the stones by a crowd who tied ropes to them and dragged them to the outskirts of town. The bodies were piled in a dry riverbed, drenched in gasoline, and set alight. It soon became clear that the two containers of gasoline were not sufficient. Another man donated firewood as a charitable act, which was built into a tower. Two hours after sunset, the half-charred corpses were placed on top of the pyre and once again set ablaze. The next morning, the ashes of the four men were dispersed by severe winds.[10]

Chapter 3

The Baha'is during the Reign of Reza Shah Pahlavi

In the early twentieth century, a skilled military tactician with no ties to the aristocracy, Colonel Reza Khan, ascended to the throne to become one of the nation's most defining and complex political figures. His rule posed a direct challenge to the corruption, conflicts, foreign intervention, and widespread suffering of the late Qajar dynasty. The military leader had witnessed an outpouring of nationalistic protests and the rise of the Constitutionalists, and sought to promote modernization and nationalist culture, using force when he deemed it necessary. The fate of the Baha'i community became entangled with the great social, cultural and institutional transformations of this era, as well as extraordinary political power struggles involving internal factions and foreign powers.

In 1921, the colonel and commander in chief of the army stepped into the role of the nation's prime minister after a nearly bloodless military coup. The last Qajar monarch, Ahmad Shah, fled to exile in Europe in 1923. Though Reza Khan had initially planned to abolish the monarchy altogether in favor of a republic, he quickly encountered fierce opposition from the Shi'i clergy and landed elites. The parliament (*Majlis*) member Seyyed Hasan Mudarres led the parliamentary opposition and launched a vast campaign of propaganda against the new prime minister in the mosques and other religious gathering places. One of the accusations against Reza Khan was that he was a Baha'i who sought to implement the prophecy Baha'u'llah had made in the *Aqdas*, the Baha'i holy book, about the reins of power falling into the hands of the Iranian people.

This prejudicial claim that Baha'is were a powerful, shadowy political force masked the lived reality of this religious minority, and resulted in the now familiar pattern of backlash, opportunistic attacks, and the looting and burning of homes and farms.

Around the same time an oil concession was being quietly negotiated with the American Sinclair Exploration Company, and awaited the approval of the *Majlis*. The American chargé d'affaires, W. Smith Murray, reported on a plot between the Bolshevik Russian and British governments to incite the clergy and the feudal landlords into revolting against Reza Khan. In his detailed reports, Murray does not conceal his surprise that the foreign powers orchestrated a rumor about Reza Khan's affiliation to the Baha'i faith in order to prevent the establishment of a constitutional republic. He noted the huge financial bribes being paid by the two foreign embassies to the clergy and other members of parliament to further their agenda. It was known that Reza Khan was planning to amend the constitution following the announcement of a republic, which would restrict the power of the Shi'i clerics and create a firm separation between the state and religion.

Extensive public demonstrations were staged in front of the parliament. Behind the scenes, bribes succeeded in preventing a majority vote. Reza Khan's plan to establish a new republic collapsed and the Shi'i clergy moved to prevent any further mention of the Constitutional movement in the press.

The United States and Britain both took notice of the unabated tension within the country's leading institutions—their intelligence reports described Reza Khan losing control over Iran's internal affairs as the clerical opposition continued to demonstrate their ability to cultivate a massive public outcry at critical moments. Reza Khan reacted to this defeat with an ostentatious display of piety: he visited the holy sites in Najaf and the shrine of 'Abdul-'Azim near Tehran, and took part in the public mourning rituals during Muharram in commemoration of Shi'i martyrdom.[1]

In early July 1924, Tehran was suddenly abuzz with excitement over a certain drinking fountain. (Public fountains known as *saqqa khaneh* were often religiously endowed, and sometimes believed to produce miracles.) On this occasion, it was claimed that a Muslim who passed the public fountain while uttering the name of Abbas Effendi, Baha'u'llah's son,[2] immediately turned blind. Another version of this rumor stated that the fountain made Baha'is turn blind, while giving sight to blind Muslims. In any event, news of the fountain spread, and the *saqqa khaneh* quickly became a pilgrimage site for devout Shi'i Muslims who hoped to have their prayers answered and their illnesses healed. In the following days, a massacre appeared to be imminent after a rumor spread that Baha'is had poisoned the water fountain in revenge.

On July 14, 1924, the American vice-consul Robert Imbrie and his colleague Melvin Seymour took a carriage to the sacred fountain to photograph the scene, but were warned away on arrival because of the presence of Muslim women in the crowd. As they returned to their carriage someone cried out, "These are the Baha'is who have poisoned the well!" The crowd chased the carriage and dragged Imbrie and Seymour out, kicking and beating them with sticks and stones. Though the *saqqa khaneh* was located near the police headquarters and only a few hundred meters from the Cossack barracks, the police and the military watched the incident unfold and made no attempt to stop the attack.

Major Imbrie suffered severe injuries to his skull and jaw before the police finally intervened and carried him to the nearby police hospital. The mob then stormed the operating room and delivered over forty fatal wounds to Imbrie. Later, the commanding Cossack officer, Jan Muhammad, was found to have struck Imbrie in the face with a saber. When questioned about his motives for leading the charge to Imbrie's hospital bedside, he stated, "We did not know he was American. We thought that we were killing a Baha'i dog." The officer freely confessed that his soldiers had rushed to join in the attack under his orders.

The attack on the American vice-consul further cemented the idea that Iranian Baha'is were linked to foreign interference in the country, no matter how contrived the link was to begin with. The skirmish managed to undermine the inroads being made to court American commercial interests. A war of words ensued between the British and Iranian presses after the latter accused the British of being conspirators who had arranged the incident in order to sabotage American oil interests. After protests and heavy pressure from foreign diplomats, Reza Khan declared martial law and gagged the press in an attempt to regain control over the military and the country. Reza Khan assured the Shi'i clergy, as well as the feudal aristocracy, that he would uphold Islamic law and abstain from any policy decisions that might undermine their position.[3] Such appeasements were a necessary part of his mission to establish a strong centralized government. Finally on December 12, 1925, the Constitutional Assembly voted to depose the last Qajar shah and declared Reza Shah Pahlavi to be the new reigning monarch.[4]

In 1926, there were two anti-Baha'i pogroms, one in Jahrum in the province of Fars, and one in Maragheh in Azarbaijan, both of which were incited by the Shi'i clergy and went largely unpunished. Ismail Khan, the leader of the Qashqai confederation of tribes, incited a riot against Jahrum's sizable Baha'i community after losing an election for the position of deputy. Hoping that violence would overtake the city and thus invalidate the election results, Ismail Khan plotted with the local clergy, in particular a *mullah* named Seyyed 'Ali, who was the son of a *mujtahid* who had led anti-constitutional riots in 1909 in which many Baha'is were slaughtered. The Baha'is, however, did not respond to the provocation.

For several days the *mullahs* preached against Baha'is from the pulpit. On April 7, mobs overran the homes of known Baha'is in the city, killing eight individuals. In one particularly appalling incident, a woman and her fifteen-month-old child were dismembered in the street by a group of killers. Many more Baha'is who fled or were in hiding had their homes looted and set on fire.

The attack had been planned to coincide with the coronation ceremony of Reza Shah, and was seen as a challenge to the rule of law. Governor Qavam Shirazi of Fars dispatched a group of soldiers to Jahrum to arrest the *mullahs* who had provoked the violence, as well as the Qashqai tribal leader. However, they were all freed a few months later, in part on the pretext that it was impossible to assign culpability in a mob action. Ismail Khan was also released after three and a half months through the mediation of the prior and future prime minister, Mostawfi al-Mamalek. The shah and his court had received numerous appeals by telegram from Baha'i communities all over the world, but after the release of Ismail Khan, Reza Shah issued orders instructing the post offices to refuse to accept any further appeals related to the case.[5]

Reza Shah's ambitious plans for Iran included the emancipation of women to enter the arena of social affairs and administrative work, the reorganization of the army along modern lines, restructuring the judiciary into a system of secular courts based on civil rather than religious law, a system of government bureaucracy to manage the nation's administration and finances, and the establishment of a university, as well as major civic developments such as the building of the cross-country railway system and highways. Accomplishing them would be impossible if the clergy were allowed to maintain their influence.

By 1928, Reza Shah had the political stability necessary to shift to a new, tougher stance in pushing his reforms through against the objections of the clergy. In March of that year, the shah traveled to the shrine of Ma'sumeh in Qom and beat a local *mullah* who had disrespected the queen a day earlier for not wearing a veil while there on pilgrimage. The *Majlis* soon passed a dress-code law, declaring that only clerics who had taken a qualifying exam were entitled to wear the attire of the clergy, causing much resentment among those who did not meet the new requirements. Unless they were qualifying clerics, all men—who then still dressed in traditional robes—were obliged to wear Western clothing and a Pahlavi hat. University classes were made co-educational. Women were encouraged to unveil, though it was not yet mandatory. Any movie theater, restaurant or hotel that did not admit women was fined. By 1935, public mourning rituals and religious demonstrations in the streets were restricted, and their duration curtailed. The religious unrest that ensued in Mashhad as a result of these rulings was harshly suppressed by the shah's troops.

The shah's newly adopted policy of strict governance was felt by all of Iran, including the Baha'i community. The establishment of order and security in the country took precedence over all else. Prior to becoming shah, Reza Khan was well known for his military suppression of the Jangali Movement rebellions in the north, and the defeat of the armed Kurds in the west, the Fars nomads in the south, and other rebels such as the Arab nationalists led by Khaz'al in Khuzestan. This strategy continued in the name of national unity after he took power as shah, and all of these separate groups were made to submit to his central government.

Reza Shah needed peace and stability for the advancement of his plans. He would not accept any unrest or rebellion, or even criticism in the press. He outlawed political parties, banned the opposition press, and did not hesitate to eliminate those who might be considered a threat to his power.

Having once displayed his devotion to Islam, even going so far as to perform public lamentations during Muharram, Reza Shah made remarkable changes in his dealings with the clergy as time went on. The modernizing projects which had recently transformed Turkey made a strong impression on him. He attempted to follow the Turkish model by encouraging Iranian nationalism in the place of Islamic sentiment, while also extending greater acceptance towards religious minorities. He respected the Zoroastrians, an ancient religious minority predating Christianity and Islam, who had been living in hardship and poverty in the Qajar period, encouraging them to build their fire temples, to form Zoroastrian societies, and to establish their own schools. This same hand of friendship was extended toward the longstanding communities of Iranian

Christians and Jews. Many Christian churches and Zoroastrian temples were built in his time, and Jewish Iranians were given freedom to work and set up their own businesses.

In the early years of his rule, Reza Shah treated the Baha'i community much the same as other religious minorities. After the violent purges during the Qajar era, the Baha'is found themselves in a period of relative tranquility. Access to higher education, as well as study abroad, allowed religious minorities to join the ranks of a growing educated class and the Baha'i community itself went on to play an important role in improving and expanding the nation's modern education system.

As discussed in Chapter 1, the Baha'i faith places a very high value on education, an ethos which featured prominently in the original teachings of Baha'u'llah and 'Abdul-Baha. Guided by this belief, the Baha'i educational leaders established schools in cities and villages throughout Iran at the tail end of the Qajar period. But until the end of the nineteenth century, no modern schools managed to survive the clergy's opposition, apart from private schools held in people's homes. The systematic establishment of schools that were open publicly did not begin until the first decade of the twentieth century.

The Tarbiyat School for boys and the Tarbiyat School for girls were both founded, about a year apart, in Tehran at the end of the nineteenth century. Around the same time, a Baha'i woman named Munireh Ayadi established the Ta'idiyyeh Dushizigan-e Vatan School. Gradually, the Baha'is succeeded in establishing over fifty schools for both boys and girls in different towns and villages in Iran.[6] Certain Baha'i-run institutions became renowned during the reign of Reza Shah. The Tarbiyat schools in Tehran were both so highly regarded that many non-Baha'is, including statesmen and dignitaries, sent their children to be educated there. Inspectors from the Ministry of Education made regular visits to these schools and praised the discipline, order, and high level of mathematical knowledge among the students.

For the most part, these schools made diligent efforts to comply with state regulations that were part of Reza Shah's efforts to establish a national educational system, and they followed the officially mandated curriculum. They were, however, sensitive to the dominant religious sentiment and deliberately placed a stronger emphasis on Arabic and Quranic teachings than was required, while avoiding any reference at all to the Baha'i faith. Female students and teachers also wore the chador until the law later mandated otherwise. Even with these measures in place, the schools faced intense clerical opposition.

When the newly appointed governor of Fars, Haji Mukhber al-Saltaneh, passed through the town of Abadeh in 1913, the local clergy complained to him about a Baha'i school for girls, which had been running for five years at that point, arguing that such a school contradicted the principles of Islam. The governor summoned the school founder Haji 'Ali Khan and told him, "We have not even been able to establish a girls' school in Shiraz. To do this in Abadeh is premature." The school was forced to close.[7] In 1921, a religiously motivated mob in the town of Sangsar raided and burnt down the local Baha'i school.

The expansion of education became a battleground for another pressing social issue—the role of girls and women in Pahlavi-era Iran. Baha'is were among the first to adopt Reza Shah's policies regarding gender equality—their work in establishing schools for students of both genders provided more entryways for girls and women into the public sphere. However, the Baha'i community would suffer for its efforts to introduce modern education in Iran, and their schools would be sacrificed to political expediency.

On December 8, 1934, the deputy minister of education, 'Ali Asghar Hekmat, sent an official notice to the Tarbiyat School that the institution would be shut down permanently as a penalty for having closed on December 6 in observance of the anniversary of the martyrdom of the Bab. Baha'i leaders attempted to annul the order, but to no avail. One by one Baha'i schools all over Iran were shut down, affecting several thousand students. Muslim pupils (whose parents were often high-ranking officials) attending the same schools were also affected. The closure of over fifty schools was a devastating blow to the Baha'i community, dealt by an administration that was purportedly attempting to raise the nation's educational standards.

The Baha'i School for girls in Saysan (a hamlet in Azarbaijan), 1932. The man sitting in front is the late Mr 'Ali Akbar Furutan and his wife who had gone from Tehran to visit the school.

Even if the Baha'i schools had not observed that holy day, Reza Shah's government would have eventually closed them, with or without a pretext. Their closure was linked to a significant national event at that time: the removal of the veil.

Following Ataturk's reforms as a model for the development of Iran, Reza Shah was eager to ban the *hijab*, but he feared the opposition of the clergy. The removal of the veil was perceived as a challenge to strong religious conviction. Women whose faces had never been seen by anyone other than immediate family would now be expected to enter the streets and bazaars uncovered, and they would be sitting in classrooms side by side with male students. In order to move forward, Reza Shah recognized that he would have to reassure the clergy by demonstrating his devotion to Islam. He achieved this by closing down all Baha'i schools throughout the country and by initiating further restrictions on the Baha'i communities.

The banning of the veil took several years of effort by the government and the royal court, during which time rumors circulated and the topic of women's emancipation came to the fore. In 1926, the feminist activist and journalist Sediqeh Dowlatabadi reported on the Congress of International Women's Suffrage Alliance held in Paris. In 1928, the *Majlis* passed a bill instructing those who worked in government offices to wear European attire. The following year, the king of Afghanistan made an official visit to Iran with his wife Queen Soraya, who did not wear the *hijab*, causing uproar among the clergy. In 1930, ladies' hats imported from abroad were exempted from tax. That same year, the first society for women's emancipation was formed in Tehran, and a number of Iranian feminists attended the Congress on the Emancipation of Muslim Women in Damascus. Marriage laws were changed in 1931 when the *Majlis* approved a bill that gave women the right to seek divorce under certain circumstances, and raised the legal age for marriage to fifteen for girls and eighteen for boys. The Congress of Eastern Women was held in Tehran in 1932, and the next year the resolutions of the Damascus and Tehran Congresses regarding women's emancipation and suffrage were presented in the *Majlis*, and rejected. But, having made an official visit to Turkey that year, Reza Shah remained determined to implement the same reforms as Ataturk.

By the time the Baha'i schools were closed down throughout Iran on December 8, 1934, Mashhad was in turmoil over a proposed ban on the veil. Ayatollah Haj Aqa Husain-e Qomi traveled to Tehran to dissuade Reza Shah from the ban, but he was arrested and sent into exile. In July of the following year, a man named Shaykh Bohlul gathered a crowd in the sanctuary of the shrine of Imam Reza in Mashhad and proceeded to denounce Reza Shah's ban on the veil and the recent bill enforcing a new dress code for men. The shah responded with a show of military might, and a large number of people in attendance were injured or killed.

After this display of force in Mashhad, the banning of the *hijab* was not opposed by the clergy in any other town. Government officials held festivities celebrating the 'Jubilant Feast' for the removal of the veil across the country, and invitations were sent out requesting the presence of invitees in mixed company with their spouses.

Reza Shah considered the veil to be a visual marker of Iran's backwardness in comparison to Turkey and Europe, and unveiling was intended to be part of the integration of women into greater society. Ironically, the shah's militant enforcement of the unveiling law resulted in women being beaten and assaulted in the streets by policemen who tore their veils off. What was meant to be a state-mandated gesture towards women's emancipation led to traumatic experiences for many Iranian women, and reflected Reza Shah's increasingly dictatorial style of governance.

The closure of the Baha'i schools as a penalty for observing a religious holiday was followed by the shutdown of Baha'i administration throughout the country. Horace Holley, an American Baha'i visiting Iran at that time, witnessed the escalation of widespread institutionalized discrimination against Baha'is. In a detailed letter addressed to the American Baha'i community, he relayed that the local board of education in the city of Qazvin had shut down a Baha'i girls' school:[8]

> Information was received from Qazvin through a traveler stating that the local Board of Education had closed the girls' school and that the Police had forbidden Baha'i meetings and gatherings. It was surprising that the local Police had forbidden the Baha'is to have their dead buried in the Baha'i cemetery *Gulestan-e javid*, suggesting that the Baha'is should acquire a piece of ground near the Muhammadan cemetery and bury their dead without performing any rites or ceremonies.
>
> A report was received from Kashan that. . . on December 13th the Chief of Police, accompanied by another official and a number of policemen and an inspector from the Detectives, went to the *Vahdat-e Bashar* school for boys and girls and closed down

the same by order from the capital. Then the party proceeded to the Baha'i center, the *Haziratul-Quds* and ordered that nobody should visit this place. They also confiscated the furniture and articles of the boys' and girls' schools and sent out the gate-keeper of the *Haziratul-Quds* from this building. Then they took Mirza 'Abbas Khan Mahmudi, the Principal of the School, to the police, arrested him there for three days. The Ma'refat school at Araan (a suburb of Kashan) was also closed. The pupils who were studying in the Baha'i schools were left without any decision and are having their time wasted since they will not be admitted in Muḥammadan schools. According to information received, the schools of Ta'id and Mowhebat in Hamadan have been closed by order of the local Education Department and the intervention of the Police, who had driven away the pupils from the schools in a most discourteous and harsh manner.

Similar news was received from almost every corner of the country, but such events had not taken place in Tihran until it was lately heard that the police had issued some circular instructions to its various branches both in the provinces and in the capital to prevent strictly Baha'i activities and suspend all gatherings and meetings and prosecute and arrest everybody who professes his faith openly and also to dismiss from the Government service any Baha'i who declares his faith openly. Since the issue of these instructions the restrictions began to appear for the friends in Tehran: all Baha'i gatherings and meetings, both private and public, which used to be held in the Baha'i center and private houses, and even some of the Character Training Classes of children were suspended and those friends who used to have meetings in their houses were forced to give written assurance that they would not hold any.

Then some of the local papers and magazines in Ṭehran, taking advantage of the occasion, began to write articles attacking the Baha'i schools and the Baha'is. One of the local preachers, Shari'at Sanglaji, referring to the attack made in some of the papers, had, in the course of the speech he had delivered for the

> public, expressed his utmost joy and gratitude at the action taken by His Imperial Majesty in closing up the Baha'i schools which, in the opinion of the preacher, were prejudicial to the good morals of those Muḥammadan students who were studying in the Baha'i schools.

Holley's account is representative of the circumstances of the Baha'i community under Reza Shah's reforms, and typical of the documentation recorded at that time. It is evidence of the sad irony that, in spite of its own progressive values and emphasis on women's emancipation, the Baha'i community paid a high price for Reza Shah's removal of the veil.

It is still too early to be able to pass judgment on Reza Shah's reign, or to evaluate his reforms. After his forced abdication and exile to Mauritius (September 16, 1941), the clerical leadership achieved a heretofore unprecedented level of power and influence, and, together with Iran's Communist Tudeh Party, trampled Reza Shah's reputation. The events of the last several decades have demonstrated that, despite being an authoritarian ruler, Reza Shah was no Stalin, nor can his actions be compared to the cruelty and brutality of the clergy towards those they considered a threat.

Chapter 4

Baha'is in the Reign of Muhammad Reza Shah Pahlavi

Iran's religious and ethnic minorities enjoyed relative well-being and security during the reign of Muhammad Reza Shah, in stark contrast to the brutally violent repression that was to come under the Islamic Republic. Although the Baha'is were still treated as an exception among religious minorities, the oppression under Muhammad Reza Shah's rule was in no way comparable to what the Baha'is have suffered since the revolution. Baha'is were not officially imprisoned or subjected to inhumane torture on the basis of their faith. They were allowed to attend schools and universities, hold government jobs, and engage in business. Indeed, there were highly successful Baha'is in prominent positions. Attacks on Baha'is during this time happened sporadically rather than systematically.

Muhammad Reza Shah, like his father Reza Shah, was neither a fanatical Muslim nor inherently anti-Baha'i, and he saw minorities' security and human resources as essential to his goals for the nation's progress. Yet he, like his father, was dependent on the support of the clergy to maintain his power. Throughout his reign, the clergy continuously tested their own power against that of the government. Many of the ensuing conflicts were unrelated to the Baha'i community, the targets were instead secularist leaders or prominent figures in the shah's government, but at each step, the clergy measured their influence by the extent of the oppression that the government would allow them to inflict on the Baha'is. They pressured the government to drop charges against those who killed Baha'is, to neglect Baha'i appeals, and to close cases after rapidly acquitting the perpetrators of all accusations. The weakness of the judiciary revealed the true balance of power. As did the degree to which the shah felt obliged to display Islamic piety.

In the vocabulary of the clergy during the Pahlavi rule, any justice or clemency granted to the Baha'is was a deviation from the standards of Islam and prompted the clergy's opposition to the government, and eventually to the revolution. Whenever the government or the shah himself remained quiet in the face of Baha'i persecution, censure was subdued and prayers for the long life of the shah would grace the *mullah*'s sermons. The degree to which the shah collaborated with the clergy depended on the strength of his own position and his popularity with the people. During the unstable early phase of his reign, after his father's abdication in 1941 and before the coup d'état of August 1953, he was especially reliant upon their support. Even after the coup, during the period of his absolute rule, that dependency was only slightly reduced.

After Reza Shah's abdication and his departure from Iran in 1941, the structure of his dictatorship collapsed overnight, along with his decades-long modernization project for Iran. Many political factions emerged to vie for power and exiled ayatollahs were welcomed back as heroes. The *mullahs* made great efforts to regain Islam's cultural foothold in the country. Old mosques were restored, and hundreds of new ones were built in towns and villages throughout the nation. The tomb shrines known as *imamzadeh* began to produce miracles during this period. The public mourning rituals commemorating the martyrdom of Imam Husain at Karbala, as well as productions of the *ta'zieh* passion plays, saw a resurgence after having been suppressed under Reza Shah. Ahmad Kasravi, the noted historian and outspoken secularist, paints a vivid picture of how the *mullahs* capitalized on the famine in Iran during World War II to stir up religious fervor:

> They began to address the people from the pulpit-tops in these words: "Can't you see, O you profane people? You stopped your prayers; you did not observe the fast; the mourning ceremonies were abolished; pilgrimage was prohibited; and women appeared veil-less in public! So, the wrath of God was provoked, and He sent you this adversity and disaster." I commented that this statement implied that God is seated in heaven, has turned his attention away from the whole world, and seems to be only scrutinizing Iran.[1]

During the 1940s, young theologians who would later become prominent figures in the 1979 revolution established names for themselves in the Shi'i leadership through anti-Baha'i activities. Ayatollah 'Abdul-Rahim Rabbani Shirazi (1922–81), a follower of Ayatollah Khomeini who, after the 1979 revolution, would sit on the Council of Experts and on the Guardian Council, was noted during his youth for inciting the demolition of the Baha'i Center of Sarvistan. In 1948, he was acquitted of killing a Baha'i man named Habibollah Hushmand after the legal intervention of Ayatollah Boroujerdi and Ayatollah Kashani.[2]

Ayatollah Boroujerdi (1875–1961), the highest ranking Shi'i leader and head of the Qom School of Islamic studies, otherwise known as a quietist who firmly avoided political involvement, declared anti-Baha'i campaigns to be among the non-deferrable duties of Shi'i clerics, and the killing of Baha'is to be a lawful act. He dispatched *mullahs* and young theology students to cities, towns, and villages with the aim of spreading Islam and combating the Baha'i faith. In his memoirs, Ayatollah Montazeri, who would later become a leader of the revolution until his advocacy for human rights put him in conflict with Ayatollah Khomeini, describes Boroujerdi's strong anti-Baha'i views:

> I once asked him a question regarding the advisability of socializing and dealing with the Baha'is. He wrote in reply: "In the Name of God! The Muslims should abandon all kinds of communication, contact, and business dealings with this sect." So what I did was to

> gather together representatives from different classes and professions in Najafabad; and I asked them to all sign a pledge against the Baha'is. For example, the bakers declared that they would not sell bread to the Baha'is; the taxi drivers vowed that they would not carry Baha'i passengers, and so on. . . In brief, I created a situation so that for a trip from Najafabad to Isfahan, normally costing a single tuman, a Baha'i would plead to be taken, offering fifty times the normal fare, and they would still not take him.[3]

Ayatollah Ahmad 'Ali Ahmadi Shahroudi, another student of Boroujerdi, described his teacher's efforts to wipe out the Baha'is during the years 1947–50:

> He assigned me, Montazeri, Mishkini, and a few others to go to the Faridan region in Khansar to spread anti-Baha'i propaganda. He wrote a mandate for each of us to carry out. . . Then together we went to Ayatollah Boroujerdi. Shaykh Mostafa Khansari was also present. Ayatollah Boroujerdi told us: "Go and kill them [the Baha'is]! Whenever it is possible to kill them, do so and rest assured."[4]

In a report on his years as a theological student during this same period, Ayatollah Muhammad Husaini Beheshti describes participating in a propaganda campaign that sent him, along with eighteen other theological students, to the farthest villages for two years to spread the anti-Baha'i message.[5]

The 1940s saw the rise of hundreds of Islamic organizations that would have a far-reaching impact on religious and civil circles in Iran. Many of these arose specifically to fight against the Baha'i faith, other religious minority groups, and secular activists. From political parties and local councils, to youth groups and student associations, to organizations that published Islamic instruction and propaganda, these new groups joined with mosques and neighborhood shrines to create a dense network to spread Islamic thought and teachings. What distinguished the educational gatherings of these newer associations from traditional devotional meetings or recitations of the tragedies of Karbala was their long-term objective. They defined their purpose as preventing the advancement of "Baha'i committees," as well as political parties, civic groups, and any secular system of thought. Their many publications played a significant role in the Islamicization of the public sphere.[6]

When an organization such as the Society for Islamic Education (*Jam'iayyat-e Ta'limat-e Islami*) chose to expand its efforts beyond the capital, its new academies were established in towns and villages where Baha'is were perceived to be actively teaching.[7] The Association for Islamic Propagation (*Anjuman-e Tabliqat-e Islami*) was at the forefront of many anti-Baha'i activities. Among its other more conventional religious publications, it published anti-Baha'i propaganda and an annual compilation of letters of repentance supposedly written by Baha'is who had converted back to Islam that year.[8] A number of journals and newspapers with titles such as *Banner of Islam* (*Parcham-e Islam*), *Islamic World* (*Dunyay-e Islam*), *The Religion of Islam* (*A'in-e Islam*), and *The Call of God* (*Niday-e Haqq*) spread rumors and exaggerated reports of Baha'i activities, as well as the typical letters of repentance.

Those same *mullahs* who were the sworn enemies of the Baha'i faith, and responsible for the harassment of Baha'is during the time of Muhammad Reza Shah, would later come to control the government and oversee the widespread institutional persecution of religious minorities during the Islamic Republic.

THE HOJJATIEH SOCIETY

The secretive Hojjatieh Society, founded in 1953 with the express aim of countering the spread of the Baha'i faith on theological grounds, was the most effective of the anti-Baha'i organizations that originated during the shah's reign. Initially small, it gradually grew into a vast and highly structured organization that would come to have influence in all administrative and political organizations in Iran after the 1979 revolution.

It was founded by a young seminarian in Mashhad named Shaykh Mahmud Zakerzadeh Tavallai, known as Halabi. On the advice of a tutor, Halabi and a colleague of his named Abbas Alavi studied the Baha'i faith for the purpose of disputing its veracity. In the course of their study, Alavi was personally drawn to the Baha'i teachings and converted. Rather than oppose the Baha'i faith, he went on to write a book defending its authenticity.

It seems that Alavi's conversion was an alarming experience for Halabi, as from that time on opposing the Baha'i movement became his central mission in life. A charismatic orator, Halabi created the Hojjatieh Society to train laymen in debating skills and arguments to confront Baha'i beliefs and guide Baha'is back to Islam. Although originally established in Mashhad in the early 1950s, the Hojjatieh Society met with little success until Halabi moved to Tehran and started to recruit high school students and young merchants from the bazaar. He offered a highly structured and systematic training that was conducted largely in secret, with evening and weekend classes initially held in private homes, and literature shared under strict conditions. Teams were formed not only for debating, teaching, and reproducing instructional materials, but also for infiltrating Baha'i organizations, where some members advanced to high levels of responsibility.[9] They monitored Baha'i gatherings in Iran and abroad, and the interaction between Iranian Baha'is and the international Baha'i community, so that they could disrupt them.

The Hojjatieh Society steadily grew and spread widely during the 1970s. It banned its members from becoming involved in politics (which, in the context of the time, implied underground resistance movements), and so was given free rein by the shah's regime, which saw it as a way to divert young people from more threatening activities. The Society quickly flourished and became the only non-governmental organization that had a presence in every city and town, and many villages, as well as in the armed forces. Thus, although it was not explicitly involved in politics, its power was pervasive throughout the country, and exceeded its original aim of countering Baha'i teaching.[10]

However, Abol-Hasan Banisadr, the first president of the Islamic Republic of Iran, saw it as draining energy that otherwise could have supported the movement towards revolution, citing a report that claimed there was an agreement between the Hojjatieh Society and SAVAK, the shah's secret police, for that purpose.[11] SAVAK supported the Hojjatieh Society in their anti-Baha'i activities on the condition that their efforts did not extend into any other sphere, or create disruptions that would be problematic for them. In return, SAVAK ignored any complaints from the Baha'i community about the organization's illegal activities and its rapid growth.

As the Baha'i community reacted to the Hojjatieh Society's attacks by adopting a more reserved posture and avoiding open debate, Hojjatieh members were emboldened and gained confidence in their methods.[12] In some areas, the organization "grew disproportionately to the Baha'i threat and bred resentment among other Islamic organizations that intended to mimic its success or to recruit from the same pool of talented religious youths."[13] To a lesser extent, Hojjatieh members also began targeting Iranian converts to Christianity, who were seen as apostates, unlike the country's Christian Armenian and Assyrian ethnic minorities.[14]

Halabi was sophisticated in the methods he developed and, as a result, sometimes at odds with the more traditional world view of the clergy. The Hojjatieh Society's members were groomed for success in a secular and professional world, and trained to counter progressive Baha'i views on their own turf with "rational, principled, and methodical" argument. During a private conversation with the author, a former member of the Society recalled that:

> On a certain occasion when Mr Halabi had gone to visit Ayatollah Boroujerdi, he challenged the Ayatollah by saying, "I tell my youth to shave their beards, to drink tea at the homes of the Baha'is, and to shake hands with them. What do you say?" Boroujerdi raised his hands three times out of despair and repeated, "What should be done, what should be done, what should be done?" Up until

> that time, the clergy whom Halabi regarded as utterly illiterate and uneducated, had been totally disarmed in the face of the logical and rational reasoning of the Baha'is, and were completely incapable of doing anything.

The Society's methods were often less scrupulous and more thuggish than their emphasis on rational debate would suggest. Members of the organization feigned interest in the Baha'i faith in order to infiltrate the Baha'i community. Hojjatieh members would attend Baha'i gatherings and then initiate disturbances and brawls that would see the host and some visitors end up at the police station. There, the duty officer, who was often a member of Hojjatieh himself, would demand that the host pledge not to hold Baha'i meetings at his home in the future. Another tactic was to hold religious meetings adjacent to homes where Baha'i gatherings were scheduled, using loudspeakers to deliver sermons combined with threats and insults to disrupt the Baha'i meetings. Just the prospect of such disturbances further discouraged attendance at Baha'i meetings. By infiltrating Baha'i meetings, Hojjatieh members were also able to identify individuals who were in the initial stages of interest in the Baha'i faith and target them for later intimidation and threats to prevent conversions.

The Hojjatieh Society produced publications that imitated the language of Baha'i literature, but contradicted its teachings or attacked Baha'i individuals and the Baha'i administration. These materials were distributed to Baha'i homes. Fake recantations by individuals who pretended to be Baha'is were staged in mosques and at other Shi'i religious gatherings. Likewise, fake letters of repentance were published in the name of individual Baha'is, and any denial was refused publication.

Hojjatieh members exerted pressure on the government and police to prevent the distribution of books by Baha'i authors, even on subjects unrelated to the faith. They spread rumors that individuals in high government posts were Baha'is, creating the unfounded illusion of Baha'i power and leading those named to create difficulties for any

Baha'i employees in order to distance themselves from the accusations. Hojjatieh members followed and harassed Baha'is who were traveling for purposes related to their faith. They made anonymous calls to Baha'i homes delivering false bad news to families. They influenced judicial decisions against Baha'is involved in lawsuits. In villages where social pressures could be brought to bear on every aspect of life, people were prevented from having any dealings with Baha'is, including the sale of basic provisions.

During the years between the organization's inception in the early 1950s and the fall of the shah, many of Iran's future elite were at some stage in their ideological development trained by the Hojjatieh Society.[15] Many of the Society's activities foreshadowed policies that would come into full force after the revolution. For example, through the Society's influence in the writing of government regulations under the shah, employment in many government offices was made conditional on belief in Islam, Zoroastrianism, Judaism, or Christianity. Thousands of job advertisements published in newspapers during the shah's regime discriminated on this basis. After the revolution, such practices became the norm and extended into many other spheres of employment. Similarly, through their infiltration of the Baha'i community, Hojjatieh members gained access to local registries in order to identify Baha'is and target them for harassment. These same lists would be used after the revolution for the arrest and execution of Baha'is.

Following the revolution, the Hojjatieh Society fell out of favor due to theological and political differences with Ayatollah Khomeini, and was ostensibly disbanded in 1983. However, many believe that the Society still functions mysteriously behind the scenes today, with particular influence in the military and executive.[16] In any case, many former members of the Hojjatieh Society hold key positions of influence in Iran, though their thinking may have evolved since their active involvement in the organization. At the same time, among prominent dissidents who oppose the current regime on doctrinal matters quite separate from the Baha'i issue, are a number who began their careers in the Hojjatieh Society, and a few have even publicly apologized for the cruelties that they inflicted on Baha'is during their time in the organization.

CONSPIRACY THEORIES

Conspiracy theories have long played an exaggerated role in Iranian political discourse, and have led to the Baha'is being characterized as covert Zionists or powerful Freemasons, as spies in the service of various foreign powers, and as having infiltrated Muhammad Reza Shah's government at the highest levels. The belief that Baha'is are a shadowy, powerful cabal of imperialist stooges is manufactured to support the continued oppression of this minority community in Iran.

The Iranian susceptibility to conspiracy theories is, in some ways, a product of the legacy of semi-colonialism under Russia and Great Britain. Nearly two centuries of political and military interference by these nations (and later the United States) created a deep wariness of Western powers, and a cynical belief that the West's influence over matters large and small throughout Iran was inevitable. Covert foreign plots to capitalize on Iran's natural resources and strategic geopolitical location are a well-documented part of the nation's history and created a lasting perception that important state affairs were conducted through embassy backchannels and by other means hidden from the general public. Many dignitaries of the Qajar period profited blatantly from their relationship with either the British or Russian governments. Thus, accusations of collusion are easily accepted by Iranians.

The awareness of foreign intervention is reflected frequently in popular culture. In literature, it manifests memorably as a farcical portrayal of paranoid delusion in the enormously popular, darkly comic novel *My Uncle Napoleon*, which was published in 1973 just six years before the Islamic Revolution. Sociologist and historian Ahmad Ashraf notes that Iranian conspiracy theories can be traced as far back as the Achaemenid period, and show the influence of both the Zoroastrian view of the universe as the arena of a perpetual struggle between good and evil, and the Shi'i view of the Caliphate as a conspiracy violating the rights of the prophet's family. Conspiracy theories have influenced the interpretation of history in all strata of Iranian society, not least among the ruling and intellectual classes, and the phenomenon intensifies during times of political disruption and social crisis, when all ills are attributed to the unseen hand of foreign powers.

Given this predisposition for conspiracy theories, and the consternation of the Shi'i clergy at the spread of the Baha'i faith internationally, the opponents of the Baha'i faith initially claimed that its very existence was part of a Russian plot to undermine Iran and divide Islam. As Russia's power in Iran waned, the blame shifted to Britain. When the British Empire faded, they became less interesting as villains and the connection shifted to America. More recently, Israel and Zionism have been seen as the masters in control of the Baha'i faith and its spies. No evidence is ever presented for the charges of espionage, but it is possible to trace the flawed logic behind them.

The misapprehension that the Baha'i faith was inspired, instigated and controlled by Tsarist Russia is based on a handful of circumstances that, while true enough, hardly support the story that has been built on them. After the Bab's execution in 1850 sparked a failed assassination attempt on Naser al-Din Shah, a nationwide massacre of the Bab's followers took place, with atrocities so gruesome that they created outrage in the international press. The British and Russian ministers for Iran wrote jointly to advise the shah to stop the torture. This was seen as evidence of their collusion with the new religion, though it was entirely in keeping with the role they had long played in Iranian affairs.

The other issue on which many of the conspiracy theories seem to hang is that the secretary to the Russian Legation in Tehran was an Iranian who was married to Baha'u'llah's sister, and helped to arrange for his exile and safe passage. The Russians had no particular interest in the Babi religion. Their main concern was the security of the border towns that some years earlier had fallen under Russian control. Thus, when the Bab was imprisoned in the fortress of Mahku in Azarbaijan, the Russian minister requested the Iranian government transfer the Bab to a prison further away from the border, fearing that his presence would spark unrest.[17] Following this request, the Bab was transferred to the fortress of Chihriq. He was executed in Tabriz soon afterwards on July 9, 1850.[18]

The supposed links between the Baha'is and the British government have even less grounding in reality than the links to Russia. The smoking gun that is most often cited is a photograph taken in 1920 on the occasion of the conferring of an honorary knighthood, or OBE (Order of the British Empire), on 'Abdul-Baha. The photograph has been published repeatedly in Baha'i books, and the award is an entirely public recognition of an individual's contributions in the arts, sciences or public service. It has often been extended to citizens of the Commonwealth and former British colonies.

'Abdul-Baha was nominated for the award by officers of the British Mandate in Palestine, who were dealing with the catastrophic after-effects of World War I and the fall of the Ottoman Empire on the Palestinian communities under their administration, including Akka, where 'Abdul-Baha was living in exile. His leadership, local knowledge, and respect within the community were instrumental in the organizing of relief efforts and outreach to those in need. London's Foreign Office weighed the recommendation carefully, as it was feared that conferring the honor on 'Abdul-Baha might aggravate the relationship between Britain and Persia, but both the British ambassador in Tehran and the Persian minister for foreign affairs saw no objection, and so they proceeded.[19]

The accusation that the Baha'i faith is tied to Israel and Zionism has been repeated countless times since the Islamic Revolution, though it took hold in the popular imagination under the shah. Two points are offered as proof: references in the early writings of the Baha'i faith to the gathering of the Jews in Palestine, and the presence of the Baha'i World Centre in Haifa, Israel.

In fact, the references in Baha'i writings to the gathering of the Jews in Palestine relate to passages from the Bible and the Quran and have no connection with the aspirations of the Baha'is.[20] The presence of the Baha'i World Centre in Israel goes back to the time when Palestine was part of the Ottoman Empire.

Following the exile of Baha'u'llah and his companions to Baghdad in 1853, the Iranian government became apprehensive about the increasing number of his followers who gathered near the border, and requested the Ottoman emperor to exile the Baha'is to a more distant region. They were first banished from Baghdad to Constantinople (Istanbul), Adrianople (Edirne), and then finally to Akka (Acre) where Baha'u'llah was imprisoned until his death.[21] A few years later, and still during the Ottoman reign, the Bab's remains, which had been kept hidden for sixty years in Iran, were laid to rest on Mount Carmel in Haifa. It is the location of this holiest of sites for the Baha'is that has led the international Baha'i community to build its administrative center in what is now Israel.

The Ottoman Empire collapsed after World War I, and the state of Israel was not established until 1948, in the aftermath of World War II, in the former Ottoman territory known as Palestine. The small number of Baha'is in Palestine at the time had no influence over the formation of the state of Israel, nor did the Zionist movement have any part in the creation or support of the Baha'i faith.

Unlike many other Muslim nations, Iran recognized the state of Israel soon after its formation in 1948, and the two countries had amicable relations during the years before the revolution. While this was frequently a pretext for the clergy's anger at the shah, the relationship between the Baha'is and Israel became a common theme only later. Ayatollah Khomeini's exhortation here, several years before the revolution, shows how the connection was used as an emotional ploy, without argument or evidence:

> Shame upon this country; shame upon this ruling administration! Shame upon this world! Woe betide us! Woe betide the silent *ulama*! Woe betide the quiet Najaf! This Qom is silent. This Tehran is silent. Mashhad silent! This deathly silence will lead our country, our honor to be trampled under the feet of Israel, in

> the hands of these Baha'is. . . If all the Muslim *ulama* agree on one thing [that is] now that a danger has befallen upon Islam, and that danger is Judaism and the Jews – that is the same thing as Baha'ism – that this danger is now near. If the gentlemen, the esteemed scholars, preachers, and seminarians all raise their voice in unison [it is] that we do not want the destiny of our nation to be governed by the Jews.[22]

After the victory of the revolution, despite the fact that all records of the shah's government, including SAVAK and the military, fell into the hands of the revolutionaries, in addition to the records that were confiscated from Baha'i centers, no shred of evidence was ever produced to show how the Baha'is were linked to Zionism or Israel.

Beyond the construction of stories on the flimsiest foundations, there have been deliberate campaigns to concoct and disseminate false documents to feed conspiracy theories about the Baha'is as part of a larger anti-Baha'i propaganda effort. One widely circulated forged document, known as *Memoirs of Dolgorukov*, purports to be the memoir of the Russian minister to Iran who served from 1846 to 1854. The 125-page story, embroidered with lurid detail, describes how he became fluent in Persian, ostensibly converted to Islam, instigated the Bab's claim to leadership of a new faith, bribed people to follow the Bab, and organized Baha'u'llah's settlement in exile. Circulated first in the 1940s as a chain letter, with dire warnings of the misfortune that would befall anyone who failed to transcribe and disseminate it, the document has been thoroughly debunked by historians on the basis of factual errors in the earliest copies that were corrected in later versions. It continues to circulate, and even today is offered as evidence of a plot between Russia and the Baha'i movement.

Even Persian literary works were not safe from the meddling fingers of conspiracy theorists. Naser Khosrou (1004–1088 CE), was among the best-known philosophers and poets of his era. In addition to volumes of philosophy and poetry, he wrote an account of his travels on pilgrimage—a *Safarnameh*—that in its engaging presentation, its flowing style, and the detailed descriptions of all that he witnessed, is considered one of the masterpieces of Persian literature. Incensed by Naser Khosrou's description of Akka, Firuz Mansuri claims in his book, *A New Look at the Safarnameh of Naser Khosrou*, that:

> Hakim Naser Khosrou Qubadiyani, that scholarly man and noble poet, never wrote a travelogue (*safarnameh*). This book has been forged in his name with the intention of presenting some distortions of historical facts as authentic and valid. . . The truth of the matter is that during the middle of the nineteenth century, the British government used Palestine as a center for its political activities, and founded the Zionist Movement and the Jewish Union. During these years and decades, in order to weaken the Iranian central government, and with the purpose of taking hold of the means for threats and provocations for its own colonial ends, and in addition to inciting the local tribes and nomads, the great Majesty's Government of Britain reinforced and consolidated extremist and perverted religious sects. One such sect was the newly founded sect of the Baha'is, towards whom even Colonel Sheil's wife had showed partiality in her memoirs, and had considered their ideologies to be akin to socialism or communism. By lodging Mirza Husain-Ali Nuri (Baha'u'llah) in Akka, the British government turned that place to a centre of pilgrimage and made it the *ka'ba* for the Baha'is.[23]

The so-called evidence, which Mansuri presents at length to support his view, reveals an ignorance of normal methods of textual criticism that verify the authenticity of Naser Khosrou's masterpiece, and has been thoroughly debunked.[24] The reason Mansuri considers the travelogue a forgery is a sentence where Naser Khosrou says he drank from a natural fountain in Akka. Islamic tradition attributes many virtues to Akka, including the merits of drinking from this fountain.

Conspiracy theories are notoriously tenacious and difficult to refute. It is perhaps in part the Baha'is' steady survival of years of persecution that contributes to the idea that there must be hidden forces at work. With each successive political regime, such conspiracy theories are renewed to cast the Baha'i community as enemies of the current moment, and the idea that they are devious, powerful enemies has become entrenched in the culture.

ALLEGATIONS THAT THE SHAH'S GOVERNMENT WAS INFILTRATED BY BAHA'IS

During Muhammad Reza Shah's reign, allegations that Prime Minister Amir 'Abbas Hoveyda and other members of the shah's cabinet were Baha'is were frequently made by the Shi'i clergy—effectively, a new conspiracy theory fitted to the time.

The clergy made the allegations to compel Hoveyda and the cabinet to crack down on the Baha'i community in an effort to deflect the stigma from themselves. They also served as a threat to ensure that the clergy's demands for further privileges would be met. Finally, they fostered the belief among the populace that the Baha'is were in close collaboration with the shah's regime. This tactic had the double benefit of portraying the shah and his cabinet as non-conformists who were profaning the sanctity of Islam, as well as depicting the Baha'is as mysteriously and dangerously powerful in their influence over the nation. Although the shah and Hoveyda are long gone, the clergy still persist with these old trumped-up charges in order to justify the persecution of the Baha'is.

Amir Asadollah 'Alam, the powerful minister of the Royal Court, who was the shah's friend and constant companion, described in his 1973 memoirs attending religious gatherings for the purpose of distancing himself from the Baha'is:

> I attended the celebration held in Gulistan Palace in the afternoon; a celebration marking the birth of the Imam of the Age. I generally avoid the religious gatherings at the Court, as I have no time. . . However, I regularly attend this specific festivity, so to completely separate myself from the band of the Baha'is. These antipatriotic

> Baha'is have infiltrated in all ranks. It is believed that half of the cabinet consists of them, and the people are very put out by this fact. Regrettably, Gen. Ayadi, the Shah's personal physician, is also known to be a Baha'i. The Shah's reputation suffers greatly on this account.[25]

'Alam's fear was no doubt intensified by his awareness that the allegations leveled against the other ministers and dignitaries of the court were all baseless and, as such, he too could as easily be made a target. Yet he could not admit that the rumors were false.

That the allegations are logically impossible has never made any difference. Iranian constitutional law prohibits any non-Muslim from serving as a minister. Indeed, the only non-Muslim members of parliament are those who fill the seats designated in the constitution for the recognized religious minorities.

Because of the rapid spread and diversity of the Babi-Baha'i movement in its earliest phase, there are many Iranians who are not Baha'is, but who have Baha'i relatives, either through marriage or blood relations. With the advent of the Babi-Baha'i movement in the Qajar period, countless individuals from all strata of society—including intellectuals, merchants, and students of religion—were attracted to the movement. Over the course of time, some who were previously Baha'i drifted away from the faith.

According to Baha'i teachings, the mere fact of being born in a Baha'i family does not in itself make someone a Baha'i. The Baha'i faith cannot be inherited, nor is it identified with any ethnic group. It is a belief that must be chosen freely by each individual, and Baha'is are free to convert to any other religion or belief, at which point they are no longer Baha'is. An individual may be born to Baha'i parents; may be married to a Baha'i; may socialize and associate with Baha'is; yet none of this constitutes his membership in the Baha'i faith unless he personally declares himself to be a Baha'i.

For people raised within a religious culture, this may be difficult to grasp. Muslims regard Islam as an inherited and native religion; if even one of a child's parents is a Muslim, that child is also regarded as a Muslim. Baha'is, however, see the distinctive characteristics that define a Baha'i as a collection of individual convictions and social conduct, the lack of which divests a person of his or her identity as a Baha'i. Acts that explicitly conflict with Baha'i principles include political involvement such as running for elected office or membership in a political party. Such involvement would cause a Baha'i to be ineligible to participate in an administrative role in the Baha'i community, and an announcement would be made by the Baha'i community to that effect.

Given that a minister's post is the pinnacle of a political career, if any Baha'i had actually received such an appointment, the Baha'i administration would have made an announcement depriving the individual of their Baha'i administrative rights. This happened only once during the shah's reign, for the simple reason that the many other individuals in the shah's government who were alleged to be Baha'is never considered themselves as such, nor did the Baha'i community regard them as its members.

Nevertheless, the popular belief that Hoveyda was a Baha'i was so deeply rooted and so consequential that historian Abbas Milani dedicates significant effort to investigating the allegations, and denying them, in his biography of Hoveyda. Hoveyda's paternal grandfather was a Baha'i from Shiraz, and was among those banished to Baghdad at the beginning of the movement, and accompanied Baha'u'llah in his exile to Adrianople and Akka. His son, Hoveyda's father, was educated in Beirut and Paris before returning to Iran in 1910. He had a successful career as a diplomat in the foreign service, where his political involvements and his marriage to a Muslim daughter of the Qajar family severed whatever relationship he might have had with the Baha'i community. All evidence indicates that Hoveyda grew up in a family with no Baha'i inclinations. As Milani writes:

> As for religious matters, the father's beliefs, past or present, were a taboo subject in the family—a taboo, incidentally, that lasted long after his death. . . According to Fereydun Hoveyda [Amir 'Abbas's

brother], the Baha'i Faith was never mentioned in the family. "I was fourteen years old," he says, "when I first heard the word 'Bahai' and learned what it meant from a friend." [26]

In 1978, after Hoveyda was dismissed as prime minister and appointed minister of court, SAVAK produced a report on their own investigation into the allegations that Hoveyda was a Baha'i. Their conclusion:

> In relation to the affiliation of the Imperial Court Minister to the Baha'i sect, it is respectfully informed: Prior to the appointment of Amir 'Abbas Hoveyda to Premiership, no mention, not even the slightest debate or rumor about him being a Baha'i ever existed in any of the organizations where he served. No such discussion or word ever circulated among his friends either. After his appointment as Prime Minister, however, his opponents started to spread the word that his father was affiliated to this sect. Based on the investigation that was carried out, Hoveyda's father passed away when he and his brother were at a young age. Hoveyda's mother and his relatives have been and are Muslims. His mother, who has been on pilgrimage to Mecca, is a devout and pious Muslim, and has educated her children accordingly, and they too are pious, scholarly, and possess many human virtues. Amir 'Abbas Hoveyda has never been affiliated to the Baha'i sect. Furthermore, according to the exalted teachings of Islam, there is a tradition current since the time of His Holiness the Prophet, stating that any individual who avows that he is a Muslim and who states the testimony verse. . . is recognized as a Muslim. During the past 15 years, and in various occasions, Amir 'Abbas Hoveyda has continually, explicitly, and clearly testified to his belief in Islam.[27]

Like many Iranian intellectuals of the period, Hoveyda was not religious. One of his close friends, the author Sadeq Chubak, described him as a strongly secular person who in fact shunned religion.[28]

However, so widely spread were the rumors of him being a Baha'i that he went to great lengths to display an affiliation to Islam. He attended lamentation gatherings, visited Muslim shrines, and made a pilgrimage to Mecca, all of which presented opportunities to publish photos. The display of piety was also demanded of him by the clergy.

A SAVAK document dated February 11, 1965, reveals agreements between Hoveyda, the clergy, and SAVAK to acquit him of the charge of being a Baha'i. Hoveyda was required to provide free water and electricity to the mosques; to mention and recall Islam, the Quran, and the Imams in his press interviews; to appoint a person associated with the leading clergy as the director of the Endowment Organization; and finally to ensure that the government would found a religious university.[29] In addition, according to his brother Fereydun Hoveyda who was also a cabinet minister, Hoveyda was obliged to pay eleven million dollars annually from his confidential budget to the clergy.[30] In spite of all this, years later the Islamic Republic produced forged documents and fictive memoirs to prove that Hoveyda was a Baha'i. Oddly enough, during the trial leading to his execution after the revolution, this was not mentioned in the long list of charges in the indictment drafted by the prosecutor general, nor did anyone ever refer to it.[31]

Aside from Hoveyda himself, a number of his cabinet ministers were also accused of being Baha'is, including Farrokhroo Parsa, the minister of education; Mansoor Rohani, the minister of agriculture; Manuchehr Taslimi, the minister of commerce; and Mahnaz Afkhami, the minister of women's affairs. Among them, Farrokhroo Parsa had absolutely no connection to the Baha'i community, other than once having defended two girls who were expelled from school in Sarvestan for being Baha'i. Ministers Rohani, Taslimi, and Afkhami all had family members who were Baha'i, though they themselves either had cut off any relations with the Baha'i community when they first became involved in politics, or else never professed to the faith in the first place.

Only one member of Hoveyda's cabinet was in fact a Baha'i, General Asadollah Sani'i, who was appointed by the shah to the post of minister of defense. Credible sources state that Sani'i demurred because of the conflict with his Baha'i beliefs and was met with the shah's wrath for refusing to comply with the orders of his commander in chief. He reluctantly accepted the post and lost his administrative rights in the Baha'i community.

Houchang Chehabi offers a rational analysis of the shah's position among the constant allegations that he surrounded himself with Baha'is:

> Even if the Baha'is had been as numerous in the inner circles of the regime as was claimed, from a strictly secular point of view this should have been objectionable only if it could be proven that they were less qualified for the jobs they were doing than Muslim-identified Iranians, a contention for which there is no evidence. While Iran under the Shah was certainly not a meritocracy, one of the criteria by which those who served the regime were chosen was reliability, and given their precarious situation in society, Baha'is were trusted by the Shah. In fact, it could be argued that all those with a Baha'i connection were among the least corrupt members of the Shah's circle.[32]

Considering the prevailing prejudice against the Baha'is, the shah would have been risking much by appointing them to powerful posts. It is not impossible that the shah and perhaps even Hoveyda had imagined that in a country that was supposedly on the threshold of the "Gates of the Great Civilization," the issue of people's religious convictions was no longer relevant. The Islamic Revolution demonstrated how thin was the veneer of modernism with which the Pahlavi regime masked the nation's reality, and how different that veneer was from the truly modern reform of the mind which the Baha'i faith advocated, and which was constantly resisted by the clergy.

While the allegedly Baha'i ministers were serving in Hoveyda's cabinet, ordinary Baha'is were being persecuted and harassed. SAVAK, with Parviz Sabeti—also alleged to be a Baha'i because he had relatives who were members of the faith—at the head of its political operations, supported the Hojjatieh Society, whose mission was the elimination of the Baha'i faith, and initiated anti-Baha'i pogroms in an effort to divert the course of the revolution.

Even after the revolution and the shah's fall, almost forty years later the Baha'i community is still being falsely accused by the clergy in Iran of having collaborated with the shah's regime, and the Baha'i youth of today, who were not yet born during the shah's reign, are still paying for those trumped up charges by being deprived of higher education, employment, and the most basic human rights.

THE QUESTION OF NATIONAL LOYALTY

A vague apprehension that the Baha'is are unpatriotic and disloyal to Iran has persisted since the beginnings of the faith and has reinforced the more specific conspiracy theories and accusations of espionage. It is rooted in a misunderstanding of Baha'i teachings, including those that promote a universal love of all humanity, and in the concurrent rise of nationalism in Iran.

The emergence of nationalism in modern Iran was a product of historical circumstances: the humiliating defeats that Iran had suffered during two wars with Russia in the early nineteenth century; the insatiable meddling of the two great political powers, Britain and Russia, which reached a climax towards the end of the Qajar dynasty in the early twentieth century; the influence of cultural relationships with the Ottoman Empire, Egypt and India; and the spread of Western ideologies in Iran as a result of increased international travel.

This awakened a sense of national identity and linked the ideas of nationalism and modernity.[33] Poets and writers both echoed and fed nationalistic sentiment by glorifying Iran's past heroes and legendary kings who ruled over a vast empire in the ancient world. This movement affected even the Persian language, as Dr Mohamad Tavakoli-Targhi notes:

> The newly imagined Iran, constructed of textual traces and archaeological ruins, fashioned a new syntax for reconfiguring the past and refiguring national time, territory, writ, culture, literature, and

> politics. Language, the medium of communication and the locus of tradition and cultural memory, was restyled. Arabic words were purged, "authentic" Persian terms forged, and neologism and lexicography were constituted as endeavours for "reawakening Iranians" (*bidari-i-Iranian*). Iran-centered histories displaced dynastic and Islam-centered chronicles. To recover from a historical amnesia, pre-Islamic Iran was invented as a lost Utopia with Mah-Abad as a progenitor of humanity, Kayumars as the first universal king, Mazdak as a theoretician and practitioner of freedom and equality, Kaveh Ahangar as the originator of "national will" (*himmat-i-milli*), and Anushirvan as a paradigmatic just-constitutional-monarch.[34]

The linguistic purification of Persian intensified during the reign of Reza Shah Pahlavi, as the purging of Arabic influence on the language was linked to his efforts to modernize Iran and to minimize the power of the clergy. An organization named *Farhangestan-e Iran* (The Iranian Academy) was founded for the purpose of restoring or coining new Persian words and promoting their use. At the same time, Zoroastrianism was praised to the extent that it was rumored that the government was considering replacing Islam with Zoroastrianism as the official state religion. Anti-Arab and anti-Islamic sentiment surfaced in the writing of notable authors such as Sadeq Hedayat and Bozorg Alavi.

This nationalistic zeal and promotion of Iranian identity had emerged first in the mid-nineteenth century, reached a zenith at the Constitutional Revolution of 1906, and continued in full force during the Pahlavi regime. In such an environment, Baha'u'llah's exhortation to "glory not in love for your country, but in love for all mankind"[35] was mistakenly seen as evidence of the Baha'is' lack of patriotism.

Baha'u'llah's aim was to create a sustainable peace in the world and ensure the well-being and progress of all its peoples. The abuse of patriotism for centuries, and the fires of national prejudice that it kindles, have served as a pretext for the bloodthirsty to wage wars upon neighboring and distant countries. A second goal of Baha'u'llah's exhortation was for each country to be able to benefit from the learning—the scientific achievements as well as the cultural and technological accomplishments—of all other countries. The development of a culture in which all the peoples of the world are lovers of humanity, irrespective of nationality, language, or religion, would lead people to desire the well-being and prosperity of others, and to cooperate in all fields for the progress of the world community. This is no more unpatriotic than a humanitarian response to global warming, natural disasters, or a refugee crisis. Baha'u'llah's core message demands that individuals should be well-wishers of humanity and collaborate for the betterment of all.

The humanitarian universalism of Baha'u'llah's teaching is not new to Iranian culture. It resonates historically with several periods of enlightened governance and high civilization, and it echoes in the voices of the great Persian poets. Yet when repeated by Baha'is, this humanitarian and universal teaching is portrayed as disloyalty. Edward G. Browne, the famed British orientalist, might have been the first to cast doubt on the patriotism of Baha'u'llah's behest in his book, *The Persian Revolution of 1905–1909*: "an admirable sentiment, but not, perhaps, one which is likely to be of service to the Persians in this crisis of their history."[36]

Browne's comment came to be echoed by countless anti-Baha'i writers who have filled copious pages attesting to the apathy toward one's homeland implied in the belief that the entire world is a single homeland. Seyyed Muhammad Baqer Najafi dedicated a whole chapter in his book *The Baha'is*[37] to this subject. Najafi regards the Baha'i prohibition of holy war, as well as the non-combatant position towards other nations, as a sign of indifference and lack of affection of the Baha'is towards their country.

That the Baha'i faith does not support the concept of a holy war—that is to say, no war should be waged for the propagation of religion—is no sign of disloyalty. Defending one's homeland is the duty of every Baha'i. In his letters from prison in Akka, Baha'u'llah called upon the kings and emperors of Europe to strictly limit the size of their armies and thus lighten the burden of their expenditures. He counseled them to maintain only as much as was required to safeguard the security of their territories. Furthermore, professing love and affection towards another, whether that other be German or Burmese, indicates no lack of love of the Baha'is towards Iran and the Iranians. Those who divide the world into faithful and infidel, untouchable and clean, theist and pagan find it difficult to accept that all the peoples of the world are brothers and sisters.

Another objection raised by critics relates to the misconception that the Baha'i faith envisions a world controlled by a single government. Rather than advocating a world government with one specific ideology ruling over billions of people, the Baha'i writings envision a distant future world with united governments that aspire to harmony and unity while safeguarding the diversity that exists among different societies. Shoghi Effendi illustrates the relationship between such a unity in diversity and the love for one's homeland:

> Let there be no misgivings as to the animating purpose of the world-wide Law of Baha'u'llah. . . It can conflict with no legitimate allegiances, nor can it undermine essential loyalties. Its purpose is neither to stifle the flame of a sane and intelligent patriotism in men's hearts, nor to abolish the system of national autonomy so essential if the evils of excessive centralization are to be avoided. It does not ignore, nor does it attempt to suppress, the diversity of ethnical origins, of climate, of history, of language and tradition, of thought and habit, that differentiate the peoples and nations of the world. It calls for a wider loyalty, for a larger aspiration than any that has animated the human race. . . . The call of Baha'u'llah is primarily directed against all forms of provincialism, all insularities and prejudices. If long-cherished ideals and time-honored institutions, if certain social assumptions and religious formulae have ceased to promote the welfare of the generality of mankind, if they no longer minister to the needs of a continually evolving humanity, let them be swept away and relegated to the limbo of obsolescent and forgotten doctrines.[38]

When the Baha'i faith emerged during the second half of the nineteenth century, the concepts of "homeland" and "nation" in Iran were not viewed as they are today. The country was governed through a feudal tribal system, and the authority and jurisdiction of the central government hardly extended beyond the capital. In many of the Persian dialects and local languages of Iran, the word *vatan*, which now means homeland, then referred to one's home village or region, and did not imply the whole country. The Persian language that is now the nation's official language and an essential tie that binds the national identity of Iranians, was spoken only in a limited region. The distances between villages and towns, and the lack of modern modes of transport, meant that every region retained its dialect from antiquity, which was often incomprehensible to the people of neighboring towns. Very few people were literate and those who were, were students of religion who read Arabic before Persian; their publications, likewise, were often in Arabic and not Persian. Beyond the generally high illiteracy rates, half of the population, that is to say women, were almost entirely illiterate.

Concepts such as homeland, nation, country, and national unity only gradually developed into their present notions. From the middle of the nineteenth century, the Baha'i faith played an active role in reviving the Persian language and in creating interest in the land that is referred to as Iran. Yet, so far, this effort has been overlooked. The Bab, who was one of the founders of the religion, wrote his main book, the *Bayan*, in Persian, with a section in Arabic. This act not only made this religious text more accessible to the general public, it established the Persian language as the official language of his revelation. Unlike those who half a century later arose in antagonism against the Arabic tongue, the Bab's purpose was not linguistic purification, inasmuch as he also used Arabic in his writings, but rather the use of Persian as the language of the essential text of a new religion was a deliberate step towards forming an Iranian national identity. This is especially noteworthy when we bear in mind that this book was held in high reverence and sanctity, and was in wide circulation among the Bab's followers.

In their writings, Baha'u'llah and 'Abdul-Baha continually remind Iranians of the bygone glory of their nation, and strive to convince them that the people of Iran are not lacking intellect and talent, and as such are capable of manifesting the spirit required to restore their country to the heights of its past glory and civilization. In the *Tablet of the World* (*Lawh-e Dunya*), Baha'u'llah praises the people of Iran in exalted terms, expresses his astonishment at the level to which they have sunk during the nineteenth century and reminds them of the bygone glory and majesty of their country:

> O people of Persia! In former times ye have been the symbols of mercy and the embodiments of affection and kindliness. The regions of the world were illumined and embellished by the brightness of the light of your knowledge and by the blaze of your erudition. How is it that you have arisen to destroy yourselves and your friends with your own hands?. . . How strange that the people of Persia, who were unrivalled in sciences and arts, should have sunk to the lowest level of degradation among the kindred of the earth.[39]

Similarly, in *The Secret of Divine Civilization* and other works, 'Abdul-Baha calls attention to the glorious past of Iran, and points out that the Iranian nation has a high share of talents. He urges the Iranian people to wake up from the slumber of negligence and to mobilize their energies in the path of progress and the advancement of Iran. He portrays a clear image of an Iran that can be the aspiration of any individual. The authors of anti-Baha'i polemical literature have closed their eyes wholly to these facts in accusing the Baha'is of disloyalty to their homeland, and referring to them as stateless people.

THE NEW FAITH AS A MARK OF MODERNITY

The designations "Babi" and "Baha'i" became very rapidly linked with nonconformity and modernism, with a break from tradition and the passing of boundaries that no one had dared to overstep until then.

The term "Babi" evoked wonder and admiration in some, fear and apprehension in others, and sparked countless rumors. To Iran's Shi'i clergy, it triggered hostility and hatred; among intellectuals it stood for an enlightened identity, and was cause for pride. Shortly after the news of Bab's founding claims resounded throughout the country, traditional beliefs were freshly challenged by Tahereh's unprecedented action in casting aside her veil. Subsequently, any quest for renovation or modernization was associated with the term "Babi" or "Baha'i", and for quite some time Iranian intellectuals considered affiliation with that term as a mark of honor.

Negar Mottahedeh compares travelogues written by Europeans about their visits to Iran before the advent of the Bab, with those written after. Travelers who visited Iran before the Babi movement wrote that the Persians generally attributed the difference between veiled Iranian women and unveiled European women to the promiscuity of the Europeans. The narrative of the post-Babi travelogues presents a different view, that a woman who is unlike other women, and who has a mind and opinion of her own, is a Babi. Mottahedeh cites an example from the memoirs of Taj al-Saltaneh (1844–1936), the daughter of Naser al-Din Shah:

> Right up to my eighteenth year, I had held beliefs taught to me by my nanny that the heavens were pulled by a chain in an angel's hand, or that when God's wrath was incurred, the sound of thunder came . . . As I progressed in my studies day by day, my irreligiosity grew until I was a complete naturalist myself. Since these ideas were new to me, I was eager to impart them to my mother, my relatives, and my children. As I would begin to talk, however, my mother would curse at me, "You have turned Babi!" My relatives would invoke God's forgiveness and keep their distance, refusing to listen.[40]

The cultural history of the period of Iran's Constitutional Revolution illustrates the deep influence of Babi and Baha'i thinking on Iranian intellectual circles, from innovators such as Iran's first film-maker, Mirza Ebrahim Khan Akkas-Bashi (1874–1915) and the musician

Mirza 'Abdollah Farahani, who first collected and documented Iran's musical traditions at a time when the performance of music was forbidden by the clergy, to many authors of prose and poetry. The writings of the groundbreaking Azarbaijani poet known as Saber (1862–1911) were influential far beyond what might be expected of a soap-maker who lived simply and wrote in his Azari Turkish dialect. His satirical *Hop-hop Námeh* shows how the received wisdom of his time identified as a Babi anyone who indulged in such new-fangled behavior as reading newspapers, wearing boots, sending their children to school or socializing with school teachers, or even criticizing the clergy. In one verse he queries a servant and informer of the *mullah*:

> What's the news Mashhadi?
> May you be healthy—Haji Ahmad has bought a newspaper.
> What are you saying boy? Did you see him buy it?
> No, that's what people say.
> O God! Who is left from my community?
> If this is so, that blasted one is a fraud.
> He has turned his back to his religion and belief—has been led astray, and has become a Babi.[41]

The popular belief that any innovation or modernization was due to the influence of the Baha'is remained in force during the Pahlavi regime. One of the attacks that Ayatollah Khomeini directed at the shah was his inclusion of equality of the sexes in his "White Revolution." Khomeini explicitly regarded this act of the shah as a product of the teachings of 'Abdul-Baha, and threatened to dethrone him for it.[42]

The truth of the matter is that Baha'is have indeed played a large part in Iran's development as a modern society, and particularly under the Pahlavi shahs. Abbas Milani writes:

> During the Pahlavi era . . . Iran began to accept the rights of citizenship for Baha'is of the country. The relative safe harbor provided

by the Pahlavi kings unleashed an impressive burst of creative, industrial, commercial, and intellectual energies and innovations by members of the Baha'i community. In writing *Eminent Persians*—two volumes devoted to the lives of 150 of the country's innovators and industrialists—I was pleasantly surprised at how many of them were members of the Baha'i faith. Iran's biggest home appliance industry—more specifically the pioneering work of the Arj Group—the introduction of Pepsi Cola and television by Habib Sabet, the advent of child and family psychology by Dr [Mehri] Rasekh, who had been a student of no less a giant than Piaget—are all examples of the immense contribution of members of the Baha'i community to Iran's modern development. The *Shahyad* Arch and Square, now renamed incongruously *Azadi* or Freedom Square, was the work of a Baha'i architect[43]—a young man just out of college who surmounted incredible odds and obstacles to win the biggest architectural competition of his generation. Even after thirty years, the Islamic regime has not succeeded in supplanting this majestic structure, imbued with elements of Iran's hybrid and only partially Islamic culture, as the symbol of Tehran.

An impressively large number of Iranian writers, poets, scholars and filmmakers have come to recognize that as a nation, we owe the Baha'i's a word of apology, and a debt of gratitude. Apology for all they have suffered, and apology for all our silences; and gratitude that in spite of these inequities, they have invariably abided by the civility and peacefulness their faith professes, but they have never wavered in their love of a free, democratic Iran. From Encylopedia Iranica and the tireless work of Professor Yarshater to the brilliant scholarship of professors Banani and Moayyad, they have stood in the vanguard of the effort to show the world that there is an Iran different from the zealotry, bigotry, and brutality of its current rulers—an Iran of Neda Agha Sultans and Qurrat al-ʿAyn, the nineteenth-century early convert to Bab, a great poet and scholar and the first woman to lift her veil and give a public lecture in Iran.[44]

Many other names could be added to the list of Baha'is who have played a significant part in Iran's development, among them Hasan Fuadi Bushrui who was the founder of the science of linguistics in Iran. Fifteen of his papers on linguistics were published in the journal *Mehr* between the years 1934 and 1936, and his research introduced the recent scientific advances of European linguists to Iran.[45] Likewise, Dr Muhammad Baqer Hushyar (1905–58) made his mark in research, teaching, and writing about applied psychology in the field of education at a time when hardly anyone in Iran recognized psychology in its applied and experimental form. His untimely death was a great loss for Iranian culture. Others worthy of note include Dr 'Abdul-Karim Ayadi, one of the shah's personal physicians, who was entrusted with organizing the army's medical service; Shapur Rassekh, deputy-chairman of the Plan and Budget Organization and one of the first professors of sociology at Tehran University; Ali-Muhammad Khademi, general manager of Iran Air; and Habib Sabet, the successful industrialist who started Iran's first national television broadcast service and the first Pepsi-Cola factory, at a time when the wide distribution of a readily accessible uncontaminated drink was a significant development. Others who were Baha'i but later withdrew from the Baha'i community include Foad Rohani, advisor to Prime Minister Mossadeq during the nationalization of the oil company, who later held high posts at the National Iranian Oil Company and at OPEC.

FEREYDUN ADAMIYAT AND THE DISTORTION OF HISTORY

The hundreds of volumes of literature written to refute the Babi-Baha'i movement since its inception constitute a considerable library. Initially, the authors were mainly Shi'i clerics who opposed the movement on the basis of religion. When theological debate failed to weaken the spread of the faith, the arguments became more political in nature, with Baha'is presented as anti-government antagonists. The anti-Baha'i polemical literature published during the Islamic Republic relies on absurdly false accusations, and abusive and profane language, from authors who have no qualifications as historians or scholars, reducing the subject to trivialities.

But there are also scholars and intellectuals who echo the accusations that have become commonplace in Iranian literature, doing damage not only to the Baha'i community but also to Iranian scholarship and historiography, and to the nation's understanding of its own past. Dr Fereydun Adamiyat, who is highly regarded as a leading historian of contemporary Iran and of the Qajar period, serves as an example of how prejudice has led to the distortion and fabrication of historical events in respected academic publishing, although he presents himself as a secular intellectual without any special affiliation to Islam and his work appeared during the years prior to the Islamic Revolution.

His student, colleague, and defender, Homa Nateq, comments on the Iranian understanding of history, and our tendency to frame historical judgments in extreme dichotomy, which she sees as a vestige of religious thinking:

> Our criteria and yardstick in every field—irrespective of our aspirations and whereabouts, and despite of us being a believer in a religion or not—is in fact a religious one. Historical judgements are made in terms of either glorification or denouncement. Those judgements are either in the form of sheer exaltation or utter ejection. The characters in history are regarded either as redeemers and reflections of the Lord of the Age, or they are considered cursed and the incarnation of Satan itself.[46]

In Adamiyat's biographical studies of Amir Kabir and Sepahsalar, they are indeed portrayed as messianic redeemers, while the Babi and Baha'i movements are painted as satanic. Adamiyat's selective suppression of evidence available in the archives at his disposal that portrays any weakness or flaw of his heroes has been noted by Dr Abbas Amanat.[47]

In the first publication of his book *Amir Kabir and Iran*,[48] Adamiyat provides a description of the formation of the Babi movement under the heading of "The Insurrection of the Bab" (*Fetneh-ye Bab*) in which he attempts to connect the Babi faith to the activities of the British secret service. He asserts that the Bab's first believer, Mullah Husain Bushrui, developed an intimate friendship with the British intelligence officer Arthur Conolly who was visiting Mashhad in 1830 in the guise of a merchant. Adamiyat claims that Mullah Husain officially entered the British intelligence service and that Conolly sent him on a secret mission to Herat, and then to Kufa, with the purpose of spreading the news of the imminent advent of the Lord of the Age among the seminarians there. He adds that, a few years later, Mullah Husain went to Shiraz and persuaded Seyyed 'Ali Muhammad, the Bab, to claim the Babi advent, and he himself sought to spread that movement. As evidence, Adamiyat refers in the notes of his book to Arthur Conolly's diary, though without identifying any page number.

Conolly was a British officer who traveled through Central Asia under the punning pseudonym "Khan 'Ali." His objective was to protect British interests and to counter the rising threat of a Russian-backed rebellion in India. He traveled to Bukhara in 1830. On a later mission in Central Asia, in June 1842, he was executed together with a fellow British officer at the order of Nasrollah Khan, the governor of Bukhara, on charges of espionage. His diary and the memoirs of his journeys were published in two volumes in London in 1834.[49] At the time of Conolly's stay in Herat, Mullah Husain would have been fourteen or fifteen years of age. He had never been to Herat. After attending classes under Seyyed Kazem Rashti in Karbela, Mullah Husain returned to Persia in search of the Promised One, and embraced the faith of the Bab. His belief in the Bab did not bring influence or power—rather he lived a life of homelessness and endless travels, ending in his death in the Tabarsi Fort. There is not a single reference in Conolly's writings to Mullah Husain Bushrui, or to the Babi movement at all, as the book was published years prior to the advent of the

Bab. Conolly himself was executed in Bukhara two years before the start of the Babi movement.

Hasan Balyuzi, who was employed by the BBC Radio Persian Service, reports that his colleague Mujtaba Minuvi, himself a well-known Iranian scholar, challenged Adamiyat to locate his reference in a copy of Conolly's book that he presented. Adamiyat, realizing that the game was up, pleaded with Minuvi not to expose his fraud, and promised to delete this passage in subsequent editions, which he did.[50] He persisted, however, in his anti-Baha'i claims.

In *Resurrection and Renewal*, which deals with the history of the Babi movement in Iran, the historian Abbas Amanat examines the research presented by scholars and historians about the Babis, and regards Adamiyat's treatment of Babi history as "problematic." He writes:

> Though in his introduction the author promises to pursue an "analytical method free from bigotry" and claims that his "historical analysis" is "realistic" and "rational", he is by no means prepared to apply these much-vaunted values to his own work. Besides his obvious errors in historical fact[s], which demonstrate his insufficient knowledge and careless methodology, throughout his chapter on the Bab ("*Dastan-e Bab*") he uses highly polemical and abusive language in describing the beliefs and activities of the Babis. Referring to the Bab's ideas as a "sackful of straw" that has no bearing on "the world of knowledge and thought", calling the Babi fighters in Zanjan "miserable idiots" and other Babis "charlatans", "murderers", "executioners", and "villains", he indeed gives a disturbing picture of that so-called progressive school of modern Persian historiography of which he is a pioneer.[51]

Adamiyat repeats the same method in another work called *The Ideas of Mirza Aqa Khan-e Kermani* (*Andisheh hay-e Mirzi Aqa Khan-i Kermani*). He writes:

> Most of what has been said by the Sayyed-i Bab, and the entire works of Mirza Husain-Ali and 'Abbas Effendi, weigh heavily on

> mankind's stack of superstitions, and are utterly worthless in the world of minds and thoughts.[52]

Dr Abbas Milani responds to Adamiyat's comments by saying, "I assume that there is no need to explain that such repetitions of stereotype views, and the use of such a language is not befitting any serious and scholarly book."[53] Adamiyat damns the Baha'i faith as "worthless in the world of minds and thoughts," while failing to provide any critical engagement with Baha'i texts among which there are many that explain their views on education and how their religious teachings hold complementary attitudes towards scientific knowledge and reason. Ironically, when Adamiyat came across an early copy of 'Abdul-Baha's seminal treatise on the Baha'i faith and its role in the development of Persia, distributed anonymously by Baha'is under the title *The Secret of Divine Civilization*, he praised the work highly without being aware of the author's identity and quoted it at length in his own writing.[54]

His prejudice also singles out Baha'i scholars whose views differ from his for especially acrimonious attacks. In his account of the Reuter Concession he takes pains to attack Firuz Kazemzadeh's book, *Russia and Britain in Persia, 1864–1914: A Study in Imperialism*, published in the United States in 1968: "the author . . . is feeble in his evaluation of history and in his critique of evidences. He has no perception of history, and is unfamiliar with the techniques of diplomatic historiography. . . We will not even mention historical reasoning, for he is totally bereft of that. Furthermore, he has a bigoted animosity towards Iran and Iranians (the specific anti-Iranian animosity of the author has its roots in his belief in Bahaism)."[55]

What provoked this tirade? Here is the offending passage on the Reuter Concession from Kazemzadeh's book:

> Thus without any pressure having been exercised by foreign powers, without the slightest interference from the British legation, the King of Kings, the Shadow of God, gave away practically the entire resources of his impoverished and misgoverned nation to a

> greedy business manipulator of dubious reputation. For paltry sums which would not suffice even to maintain the Imperial Court, Naser al-Din Shah did not hesitate to sell the future of generations of his subjects. The pretty phrases about benefiting the country by bringing the fruits of European progress to Iran and the pretense at concern for the well-being of the people made the actions of the corrupt ruler and his equally corrupt ministers still more offensive by adding hypocrisy to treasonable greed.[56]

Adamiyat's admiration for the genuine accomplishments of Sepahsalar, Naser al-Din Shah's reformist prime minister, has blinded him to Sepahsalar's corruption in the matter of the Reuter Concession. Dr Kazemzadeh was a professor of history at Yale University. We can add that his book was later translated into Persian and met with great approval, but the harm done by the unsubstantiated claims and accusations of Adamiyat remains, and is damaging not only to the Baha'i community but also to Iranian scholarship and historiography more generally.

Chapter 5

The Shahrud Incident

In the aftermath of Reza Shah's abdication and the occupation of the country by the allied forces during World War II, the Baha'is were suddenly plunged back into brutal conditions similar to those they had faced during the Qajar period. Islamic councils in many towns generated anti-Baha'i propaganda. Newspapers such as *Parcham-e Islam* (*The Flag of Islam*) and *Niday-e Islam* (*The Call of Islam*) published attack pieces while the general ignorance about the Baha'i community among young Muslims created a fertile ground for the clergy to incite the populace against the Baha'is. People who had until then been seen as neighbors, friends, and relatives were suddenly labeled as ungodly infidels and untouchables.

The 1944 anti-Baha'i pogrom in Shahrud began with incidents of street harassment and verbal confrontation. The acts became increasingly violent, escalating into property damage, targeted assaults, and massacres which overtook entire towns. Though they appeared to erupt in chaotic fashion, many of the acts were carefully planned and had semi-official sanctions from local authorities. In particular, the new chief of police, Yavar Fatemi, played a key role as he would again a few years later in incidents in the towns of Babulsar and Kashan[1] when he held the same position there.

Much of our information on the incident comes from an eyewitness account entitled *Haqayeq-e Guftani* (*Truths that Must Be Told*), and published anonymously in 1945. Later investigations showed that the author was Naser Semino, a lieutenant of the Gendarmerie in

Shahrud and a follower of the secularist, Kasravi.[2] He was moved to document what he had seen after reading a false report on the events written by a local *mujtahid*, Shaykh ʻAbdollah Shahroudi, in a religious publication,[3] which shocked him both with its misrepresentation of events and its revelations concerning the self-serving motives of the authorities. "In this wonderland," Semino writes, "everyone, whether high or low, whether illiterate or learned, is merely concerned about protecting his own rank, and is only interested in safeguarding his own personal profit. In achieving this foul aspiration, he will not spare committing any felony, deceit, discrimination, and even oppression or murder."[4]

According to Semino, political rivalries were behind the deliberately planned disturbance. The elections for the fourteenth parliament had left disgruntled local contenders who failed to win. They hoped that civil disturbance might serve as an excuse to declare the vote invalid. Another round of elections would have to be held in Shahrud, and the desired results could then be ensured through electoral fraud. The easiest way to create a disturbance was to incite a mob against the local Baha'i community.

Shahrud is situated on the main highway that traverses northeastern Iran between the Great Salt Desert and the more fertile region facing the Caspian. At the time of the attack, fifteen Baha'i families lived in Shahrud and were known there as prominent leaders, businessmen, and shopkeepers who, as far as they knew, had maintained good relations with their fellow townsmen.[5] Shahrud is also a hub for smaller towns and villages in the region, such as Biyarjumand, Bastam, Sangesar, Anarak, and Miyamay, which also had Baha'i communities. For years, Baha'is from Miyamay and Sangesar had traveled to and from Shahrud to live and work for periods of time.

The *mujtahid* Shaykh ʻAbdollah Shahroudi led the *mullahs* of Shahrud and Miyamay in planning the attacks in such a way that Baha'is from the neighboring towns would be drawn in, spreading the conflict beyond Shahrud. They had financial support from landowners and others plotting to invalidate the elections.[6] Though he did not outwardly express hostility to the Baha'is, the chief of police Colonel Fatemi supported the plan, a fact which became obvious through his refusal to intervene once the violence started.[7]

The trouble began first in Miyamay. One night, a group of local men raided a house where a number of Baha'is from Sangesar were staying and stole six sheep, which were slaughtered with the clergy's blessing and the meat distributed to the town's residents. Some was said to have been barbecued and then served with vodka that very night.[8] On another night, they set fire to the door of the same house, formed a circle around it, and pelted it with stones, allegedly to protest that the Baha'is were proselytizing by distributing books in Miyamay.

A few of the Baha'is were injured. In a report taken by the Gendarmerie, the Baha'is said that they came from Sangesar to Miyamay every year to buy sheep. They had not had any trouble before, had always dealt peaceably with everyone, and had never given any books to anybody. The report confirms that none of the plaintiffs had any Baha'i literature in their possession. The Baha'is from Sangesar received no response to their complaint to the authorities and a few days later they were forcibly driven from Miyamay.[9]

Similarly, in Shahrud *mullahs* began to deliver hateful speeches against the Baha'is in public to provoke the populace into turning against them. Their words had no effect upon the inhabitants for a while, as relations between the Baha'is and the rest of the population had always been very amiable.

The Local Assembly of the Baha'is of Shahrud was aware of the dangerous consequences of the clergy's provocation. The Assembly repeatedly approached the mayor of Shahrud and other authorities, asking for the harassment to be stopped. Each time they were assured that the Baha'is were in no danger.[10]

The situation escalated by the day. The gate of the Baha'i Center in Shahrud was set on fire one night, and the locks on Baha'i shops were covered with excrement. The Assembly appealed to the governor requesting that an inspector be dispatched from the capital to investigate the case. This request was never heeded. Sensing danger, a few of the Baha'is left the town. Others who remained closed down their shops and stayed home. Semino describes the mood from the viewpoint of the Baha'is:

> The hostile treatment shown lately by the Shi'is is not to be disregarded. There is more to it than meets the eye. Their mannerisms, their gaze, their walk and the way they talk all seem unusual. This bizarre behavior spells a painful disaster to the Baha'is.[11]

Groups of up to twenty people were led to obstruct the alleyways and provoke Baha'is by insulting their faith. Children were taught to chant an obscene song that insulted one of the central figures of the faith. The Baha'is seldom appeared in the streets and those who did go out would not react. "They exerted their utmost not to give the slightest reason to the enemy, nor to provoke an implementation of its terrifying plan."[12]

The Local Assembly of the Baha'is of Shahrud consulted urgently and at length, and asked for guidance from the National Assembly of the Baha'is in Tehran. They finally decided to gather groups of families in individual homes. The National Assembly advised the congregants of Shahrud to pray, and wrote to the prime minister, the minister of internal affairs, and members of parliament for help. They received no response.[13]

A dangerous mood swept over the city as the mob prepared for violence. The local authorities, seemingly undisturbed by the imminent disaster on their hands, carried on exchanging letters, from time to time asking for guidelines from the capital to evade responsibility. They finally released this public statement:

> As a result of our efficient actions, the capital has issued explicit orders for all Baha'is to leave Shahrud as quickly as possible. As instructed, we notified them all, and further informed them of the dire consequences of not complying with this order. Seeing that they have not left, whatever happens is now their own problem![14]

Habib Namdar, a sergeant serving at the time in the Gendarmerie in Shahrud, wrote a memoir that adds another point of view. The Gendarmerie was separate from the municipal police of each town, being a centrally governed security force that functioned as a highway patrol and a police force in rural and tribal areas. Namdar writes that his commander, who was also a friend, showed him a letter he had received from Colonel Fatemi, the chief of police in Shahrud. Fatemi was asking for a number of gendarmes to be sent to assist the police force, due to the extraordinary situation in the town and the inability of the police force to maintain law and order. In Namdar's opinion, the real purpose of the letter was to absolve the police of any responsibility in the upcoming events. His commander was aware of the clergy's efforts to turn people against the Baha'is, and also knew that Fatemi was collaborating with the clergy. He proposed sending Namdar himself, with ten other gendarmes, to the Shahrud police headquarters. Namdar continues:

> The head of the local police knew me well, and was fully aware that I was a Baha'i. When he saw me, and the military police commander's letter stating that they were dispatching the most competent officer together with ten other gendarmes, he went pale in the face. He remained quiet. He could not disagree with my appointment to this mission. . . Finally, together with my group, I went to town and took charge. We worked in a manner that our men would reprimand even the slightest omission by any of the police officers. This situation continued for ten days and all possibilities of irregular conduct by the thugs were thwarted. . . Consequently, the fanatic hooligans informed the instigators that as long as Namdar remained the head of the military police, they would be unable to carry out any of their plans. On the following night, one of the religious leaders announced in the mosque that they must force the Gendarmerie commander to recall Namdar and send another officer instead.
>
> The head of the squad called me. . .on the following day. . . He told me to take a seat. He then opened his desk drawer, showed me a sum of money, and said: Look, this is the three thousand *tumans*

> that they have paid me to replace you with another officer; so that they can carry out their plans undisturbed. Now, if you Baha'is pay me an equal sum, I will send back their money and keep you in your post... I do like your lot, but I much prefer money.
>
> I asked him to give me a day to consult about it... After thorough consultations, the local assembly did not deem it advisable to pay any money to this man... As such the commander replaced me with another officer.[15]

On August 8, a number of Baha'is set out for their shops in the bazaar. One arrived to find the lock to the entrance had been smeared with excrement. The shopkeeper spoke up against this act, which led to an altercation with nearby shopkeepers:

> Within a few minutes the entire Bazar was closed down, and an uproar ensued. The few Baha'is immediately tried to leave the Bazar and take refuge in the police headquarters. The shopkeepers and the joining mob blocked all the exits... There were shouts, followed by attacks and assaults. The violence that developed and the strokes of clubs and rods resulted in two broken skulls; one, of a Shi'i shopkeeper named Muhammad Husain 'Amudi Qannad, and the other, of one of the Baha'is of Sangesar named Yusef Subhani[16]... The wounded fled to the police headquarters. They entered, closed the gates and took refuge there.[17]

The distance between the police station and the site of the incident in the bazaar is barely a hundred meters, yet not a single police officer intervened. When the Baha'is arrived at the station, the officers assaulted them, breaking the shoulder blade of one—Qubad, who was the accountant of the Shahrud railway.[18] The mob swarmed the police station's gate and threw stones at the building, demanding that the Baha'is be handed over to them. The chief of police, Fatemi, surrounded by officers and constables for protection, emerged on the second floor balcony and addressed the crowd: "How can I hand over these Baha'is to you, so that you cut them to pieces? I will personally execute them tomorrow. Go your ways; behave." The police chief's lukewarm efforts at handling the situation, and his pledge to execute the Baha'is, apparently emboldened the mob. They continued their rampage at the homes and shops of other known Baha'is.[19]

A crowd set off towards the Shabdari quarter. They came upon Aqa Muhammad-e Jazbani, the head of the Shahrud post office. He was lame in one leg but known for his polite manners and well liked among the town's inhabitants.[20] When the mob saw him, they shouted as if in joy and, "like a pack of devouring wolves that had found a single lamb lagging behind the flock. . . each one rushed to be first to rip him apart."[21] Before the crowd could reach him, one of Jazbani's Muslim friends offered to carry him to safety.[22] Jazbani refused. It was as if he could not believe that the same people who the day before had greeted him courteously in the street would now be intent on taking his life. The mob set on him with knives and clubs and he fell to the ground unconscious. Leaving him for dead, the crowd went on to ransack Baha'i shops. Two Muslim passers-by carried Jazbani to a nearby doctor's surgery, where his head and neck wounds were treated. Some of the mob heard what had happened and stormed the doctor's office. They flung Jazbani from the second floor onto the street. He died within moments but still they slashed at him with knives and then stoned him.[23] Later that afternoon, the police sent out four men to carry him to the municipal hospital. It was reported that they intentionally dropped the stretcher several times to ensure that no life was left in the mutilated body.[24]

Another group that had sacked and set fire to Khudai's shop now turned to the store belonging to Aqazadeh. They looted his property, poured kerosene on the building and set it aflame. They continued to the stores of Muhajerzadeh, Tabatabai, and Athari, looting and burning their merchandise, and then turned to the homes of Naderi and his neighbor Ruhbani.[25] The latter had left town for Tehran with his wife and two children a few days earlier.[26]

Naderi was the head of the Tobacco Company in Shahrud. Namdar describes him as "a wonderful young man, creative, and faithful" who "enjoyed a special popularity among the people of the town."[27] He "treated all people—clients, and visitors, even villagers and peasants—with the utmost kindness, modesty and compassion. He behaved towards the governor and the peasant alike, treated the Shi'i and the Baha'i in the same manner, and made no distinction between the inhabitants of Shahrud and those of the village of Anarak. He applied the same work regulations to all, with no difference whatsoever."[28]

A few days prior to the incident, the governor of Shahrud wrote him an official letter asking him to leave the town. Finally, "as a result of the governor's letter and due to the persistence of friends and the pleas of his wife, he decided to temporarily hand over his official responsibilities at work to one of his employees." He decided to hide at home, rather than leave without his wife and children. Upon arriving at Naderi's home, which was across the street from the police station, the crowd were shouting religious chants. They broke down the door and swarmed in, searching the rooms. Not finding anyone, they started looting. They carried off whatever they could and burnt the rest. At this time, the crowd that had killed Muhammad Jazbani joined the mob in Naderi's house. One of them shouted out loud when he "caught sight of a man, pale faced, perturbed, and anxious, standing in the corner" of the kitchen.[29] They dragged Naderi to the courtyard, kicking and beating him with clubs and daggers. He held up a copy of the Quran in his hands and said "I adjure you by this Quran to have mercy on me, my wife and our children." No one took any notice. One man "raised his axe and lowered it with such force upon the head of that young man that it penetrated the skull half way, cutting it open, and shattered his brain in such manner that pieces of brain were splattered on the walls of the cellar stairway and the steps."[30] Others, unmoved by the cries of his terrified wife and children, attacked his body with knives, cleavers, and clubs. "That afternoon a non-Baha'i [acquaintance] managed with great difficulty to enter the house. He found Naderi's body lying with his hands folded, his face and head drenched in blood; the eyes were partly open and looking upwards; of the skull, only the forehead was left; the spinal column was torn away, and only the shoulders were still in place."[31]

Semino writes of four different groups that murdered and then looted their victims' homes, each "under the guidance of leaders and according to prior plans." After killing Naderi, looting his house and setting it on fire, the mob moved on to the homes of other Baha'is. On the way they came across a young Baha'i, Hedayatullah ʿA'zamian. They assaulted him with daggers, spades, and axes, and left him for dead. He was taken to a hospital in Tehran and survived.[32]

The mob next attacked the homes of Tebyani, Aqazadeh, Jazbani and Khudai. Jazbani had been killed a few hours earlier and the others had left for Tehran. Finding the homes deserted, the crowd looted and then set fire to them. They then stormed the house of Hasan Muhajerzadeh, an elderly man of seventy years. He had gathered with a few other Baha'is at Namdar's home for safety. When he returned to his own house later that day, against the advice of his companions, he found the situation more dire than he had imagined. A mob was in the course of looting the house in Shabdari Street. As he ran towards the house to rescue his wife and children, a second crowd descended, killing him instantly. They proceeded to beat his wife and children—even though the clergy's provocation had excluded the killing of women and children as forbidden by Islam.[33]

After killing Muhajerzadeh, they tied his feet together with a rope, hoisted his body to the rooftop, and threw it down into the courtyard. They raised the body up and threw it down again and again, saying that he was a Baha'i angel, and so he must fly.[34]

The last place that was swarmed by attackers that day was the home of Habibollah Namdar, the Baha'i Gendarmerie officer who had been detained at headquarters so that he could not prevent the attacks on the Baha'is. Namdar's house was situated just outside town, near the headquarters of the Soviet occupation force.

A number of fearful Baha'is had gathered in his house. After killing Naderi, a crowd set out towards Namdar's home, and started to curse and throw stones at the door and windows. The door to his house was secure and did not break, but the mob would not give up and kept flinging rocks and stones at it. The Baha'is inside went up to the roof and tried to disperse the crowd by throwing bricks at them. One of them took Namdar's gun up to the roof and tried to scare off the crowd. The congestion and noise caught the attention of the guard on duty at the Soviet headquarters. His commander immediately dispatched a number of Jeeps and an ambulance towards Namdar's home. As soon as the crowd saw the Soviet Jeeps, they fled. The Russians entered Namdar's home and treated a child who had been injured. Meanwhile, the municipal police chief made no effort to intervene. He ordered his policemen to return to the station, and sent the gendarmes to their own headquarters.[35]

At the same time, other groups sought the other Baha'is, and found a few in alleyways and corners. They beat them unconscious. Their faces were so covered with blood and dust that it was impossible to identify them.[36]

By the evening of August 9, the town of Shahrud was in chaos. Following the emergence of the Soviet armed forces in town, the attorney general, the chief of police, and other officials who until then had kept out of sight suddenly appeared. Each one now looked busy, rushing about and giving orders. They finally decided that groups of gendarmerie guards should patrol the streets to restore law and order. A pall of black smoke from the burnt houses rose over the city, and some people were still busy searching the wreckage for things of value left to ransack.

The Baha'i men, women, and children gathered in a clear state of distress. They searched for missing family members, and those who could not be found were assumed dead. Rows of corpses lay in the infirmary while legal formalities were carried out and burial permits were issued. The Baha'is asked the municipal police for permission to come at a quiet time in the evening for a final viewing and to perform their own burial rites. Their request was denied. There was a palpable sense of indignity in the surviving Baha'is encounter with the bureaucracy of death, after a massacre had just been committed against their community. The corpses were piled into a dirty carriage, taken to the outskirts of town and flung into a mass grave.[37]

The following day, all the remaining Baha'is of Shahrud, young and old, were loaded onto a truck. They were not allowed to take any items from their homes. They were taken to the railway station and sent to Tehran in two cargo wagons like prisoners of war. The pillage started afresh as looters went back to their houses and shops to take anything that was left—"even the brooms and the shovels."[38]

Speaking on behalf of the agonized Baha'is who lost their lives and livelihood in such a manner, Semino asks:

> O Muslims! Is this the meaning of being a Muslim? O followers of the Prophet! Are these the teachings of your religion? O believers in the Quran! Is this the example set by the Quran? How come the murder of us Baha'is was not an obligation until now? Why is it that the properties of the Baha'is are lawful to you, but our men and youth are untouchable and unlawful. . . Are you not ashamed of having teamed up with hundreds of thugs, gangsters, and murderers at the order of a group of parasite-type betraying *mullahs*; and of having assaulted a few defenseless and unprotected families, killing plundering, and pillaging them?[39]

He goes on to recount that those responsible for the crimes raised the considerable sum of one hundred thousand *tumans* and sent the money, along with "a number of men representing the *ulama*, *mullahs*, chiefs, Bazar shopkeepers, and looters," to Tehran. There they met with Gholam Reza Fouladvand, a high-ranking member of the Ministry of Justice. Arrangements and promises were made verbally and in writing, and Fouladvand was appointed as the inspector for the case.

In collaboration with the clergy and other influential individuals, Fouladvand prepared a 344-page report that banned any prosecution of those who were involved in the crimes and acquitted them of all charges.[40]

The report blames the victims for inciting the attackers in a claim devoid of credibility. Fouladvand notes that the Baha'is "have recently been carrying out their activities openly and boldly. Even on the eve of the third of Sha'aban. . .Valiollah Subhani Sangisari, a resident of Shahrud, publicly scorned Islam in Tehran Avenue."[41] The third of Sha'aban is a religious holiday in celebration of the birth of Imam Husain, and fell just two weeks before the rioting began, when tensions in the town had reached a peak. Semino describes the scene:

> At least a hundred of the inhabitants of Shahrud were gathered in front of the smallest of shops. Some were seated, some standing; having tea, sweets, smoking cigarettes or the hookah; and listening to the gramophone or to rented radio sets. The streets were decorated and illuminated on the eve and on the day of that celebration, as well as on the following two nights and days. At the emphatic advice of their elders, the Baha'is were nowhere to be seen outside their homes during this time. They would only come out if really necessary; and even then, only in daylight and by avoiding the quiet alleyways and paths.
>
> In all fairness, let us be reasonable. We are talking about a town on the verge of being ignited, waiting for a single spark; especially at an eve so conducive to a riot break-out; at a time when even the Baha'is who have stayed at home feel unsafe; and above all in the middle of a street where at least a hundred Shi'is are gathered before the smallest of its shops. Can it be even conceived that under such conditions, a single Baha'i would even dare to openly ridicule the sacred beliefs and teachings of Islam?[42]

Similarly, Fouladvand deflects blame for the actions that sparked the riot on August 8, claiming that it began with a child cursing the Baha'is in the bazaar, with no mention of the excrement smeared on the lock.[43] Fouladvand's report is quoted at length in the article by the *mujtahid*, Shaykh 'Abdollah Shahroudi, that drove Semino to tell the story as he had witnessed it in order to correct the historical record.

As a reward for his services, Fouladvand was elected as the member of parliament for Shahrud for the fifteenth and sixteenth terms. The daily journal *Mehr-e Iran* ran two articles on August 14, 1944, one by its editor-in-chief Hashimi Ha'eri, and one by D. Amini, both condemning the Shahrud incident.

Chapter 6

Eighty-One Stab Wounds: The Murder of Dr Berjis in Kashan

In February 1950, a prominent and well-loved Baha'i physician was stabbed to death in broad daylight in the city of Kashan, targeted for his faith in a pre-meditated attack.[1] The coroner later counted eighty-one stab wounds on the body of Dr Suleyman Berjis. Some months later a criminal court convened in Tehran to try four men who had confessed to taking part in Berjis' murder. All four were acquitted.[2] Ruhollah Mehrabkhani, who was a member of the local Baha'i Assembly of Kashan, witnessed the whole episode and wrote a commentary at the time.

Reza Shah's abdication in 1941 and the occupation of Iran by Allied troops gave political parties and religious minorities an opportunity to expand their activities. The Baha'is, along with secular followers of Kasravi, members of the Communist Tudeh Party, and various Islamic groups, had begun openly advancing their views throughout Iran. Hundreds of Baha'is left Tehran and other major urban centers to settle in more remote areas where they could share information about their faith with others. These activities rekindled the opposition of the Shi'i clergy, who began in their sermons to incite the populace to commit acts of violence against the Baha'is. In Kashan, an otherwise peaceful town on the edge of the desert, organizations such as the Devotees of Islam (*Saziman-i Fada'iyan-i-Islam*), the

Dr Suleyman Berjis

Islamic Propaganda Society (*Anjuman-e Tablighat-e Islami*), and the Organization of Islamic Activists (*Hay'at-e Du 'at-e Islami*) were formed with the express goal of curtailing the influence and expansion of the Baha'i faith, and eliminating the Baha'i community.[3]

The cleric Turbati, who was known for incendiary sermons condemning the Baha'is, was sent from the city of Qom to Kashan for the purpose of provoking violence. Mehrabkhani calls him "a stirrer of sedition, a foul-mouthed *mullah*. . . who on several occasions fueled the fire of religious fanaticism in Kashan and Aran, fanned the flames of strife, and after being assured of the success of his endeavors, would flee from the midst of it."[4]

Turbati agitated against the Baha'is in numerous sermons which were broadcast through loudspeakers all over Kashan. He called them immoral and corrupt, and declared that shedding their blood was lawful. The local Assembly of Kashan, chaired by Dr Berjis, wrote a letter to the town's police chief, Colonel Fatemi (who was previously the police chief in Shahrud during the anti-Baha'i rioting there) and explained the dire consequences that such preaching would have on the Baha'i community. Ruhollah Mehrabkhani was assigned to deliver the letter in person and draw Fatemi's attention to the critical responsibility that he held. Fatemi's reply was familiar: "Rest assured that nothing will happen." An hour later, a police intelligence officer by the name of 'Ali Naraqi informed a Baha'i shopkeeper that it was useless for Baha'is to complain to the police, as they could not prevent people from practicing their religion.[5]

The National Spiritual Assembly of the Baha'is of Iran wrote a letter to General Zahedi, head of the national Gendarmerie, in which they noted numerous cases of collaboration between Colonel Fatemi, 'Ali Naraqi, and Islamic activists.[6] 'Ali Naraqi had been encouraging Turbati in his opposition to the Baha'is, and had promised him the support of the local police.[7]

Turbati's activities continued and other *mullahs* followed in his footsteps. By inciting members of the Islamic Propaganda Society (*Anjuman-e Tablighat-e Islami*) he was able to form a splinter group—the Organization of Islamic Activists (*Hay'at-e Du'at-e Islami*) that directed activities against "the wayward and the heathens."[8] In a quiet town like Kashan, this was a big affair. People anticipated violence, and rumors circulated that Dr Berjis would be targeted.

Suleyman Berjis was born in 1898 into a family of a long line of doctors who had converted to the Baha'i faith from Judaism. His father was a highly skilled physician who was honored by the governor of Zanjan for treating him successfully.[9] Berjis completed his primary education in Kashan in the *Vahdat-e Bashar* Baha'i School, and set off for Tehran at the age of 19, where he completed his education in the Dar al-Funun, Iran's first institute of higher learning.[10] He studied and served at both the government hospital in Tehran and the Baha'i *Sehhat* Hospital. He then returned to Kashan where he assisted in his father's practice and gained a reputation as a skilled physician.[11] He was employed by the health department in Kashan, and ran his own medical practice in the afternoons. Well-known for his generosity, he not only treated the poor free of charge but provided financial support for many patients, and found ways to do so that were discreet and respectful of their dignity. He made house calls, however far, when needed.[12]

Dr Berjis was active in the Baha'i community and for several years was elected to the local Assembly of Kashan, where he served as chairman. On numerous occasions he represented Kashan at the national Baha'i convention held annually in Tehran. He was profoundly knowledgeable about the Quran and Islamic tradition,[13] which, like the Old and New Testaments, were considered integral to the Baha'i faith and essential to effectively defending the faith in religious discussions with their fellow countrymen.[14]

Harassment of the Baha'i community in the villages surrounding Kashan at that time took the form of vandalism and destruction of Baha'i-owned crop storage, homes, and fields. The trees of their orchards were being hacked and damaged under cover of night. Cattle disappeared. Every few days, terrorized Baha'is arrived from the villages to take refuge in Kashan.[15]

Dr Berjis was harassed in ways that targeted his profession. There were no cars in Kashan at that time and he made his house calls on horseback, though people would throw stones and jeer, saying that a Babi should not ride a horse. His horse was eventually killed in the stable at his home, and when he bought another horse that one too was killed, and so he traveled to his patients on foot.[16] The clergy then destroyed his practice by banning various strata of society from using his services. Very few went to him other than those who could not afford to pay, and yet he continued.[17]

Eventually, a *mullah* named Khalesizadeh, who preached openly that attacks on the Baha'is were meritorious in God's view, exhorted his congregation: "Drag Dr Berjis, who is the head of the Babis, out of his surgery! Kill him, as he is an infidel, he is ungodly, and a filthy Babi."[18] Khalesizadeh was influential. He was the son of an ayatollah, the founder of religious schools, and much involved in politics. He had gathered many young followers in activities that combined religion and politics.[19]

Rumors that his murder was being planned seemed to call for caution, but Dr Berjis laughed them off, saying, "Don't worry, nothing will happen; one has to be worthy of martyrdom."

As the perpetrators' later confessions made clear, Dr Berjis' murder was carefully planned. Turbati chose the men who would perform the deed and convinced them with assurances that the police would support the plan, which involved luring Dr Berjis to the home of a certain Shaykh Baqir where members of the Organization of Islamic Activists (*Hay'at-e Du'at-e Islami*) would force him to recant. If he refused, they would kill him and throw the body in a pit they had already dug in front of the house.[20]

On the morning of February 3, 1950, two men appeared at Dr Berjis' surgery, pleading in tears for the doctor to come and attend to an old woman whose health was in a critical state. Dr Berjis apologized to the other patients waiting, and accompanied the two young men. It was snowing and they claimed their destination was in a desolate part of town. They stopped in front of a home where a religious mourning ceremony was being held. Rasulzadeh and a few others came out and asked Berjis to join the ceremony. Sensing danger, he turned back.[21]

They surrounded him and attacked with fists, stones and knives,[22] flung him inside the open door of a neighboring house, and viciously stabbed him. The owner of that house tried unsuccessfully to intervene, and then ran to the rooftop and called for help. They then threw Berjis down from a window three meters above street level, and fell upon him again. Rasulzadeh drew a knife, sat on the inanimate body, and cut open his throat and both his wrists. After that, they all cut up the body, leaving with their hands and faces covered in blood.[23] Rasulzadeh sat on the sidewalk for a moment and cleaned the blood off his hands with the snow on the ground.[24] (Years later, Ahmad Imami, who was one of the main perpetrators, would brag of his role and claimed that he, not Rasulzadeh, had been the one to cut open the jugular vein, and that he should take credit for the murder.[25])

The killers "left the scene of the crime, shouting *Allahu-Akbar* [God is great],[26] and collected a crowd who followed them as they passed through the bazaar, announcing in every alley, 'We killed a Baha'i, we killed a murderer!'"[27] Many shopkeepers closed their stores and followed the mob to the police station.[28] In Mehrabkhani's view, the aim was to "have a few hundred people present themselves as the killers," diluting the blame. But at the police station, the crowd held back.[29] The original eight men confessed to the officer on duty that "they had fulfilled their religious duty, and had done away with the leader of the wayward Baha'i sect in Kashan." Astonished and apprehensive, the policemen stared at the killers who still held knives and had blood splattered all over themselves. After a while, Colonel Fatemi sent several of his men to the office of the justice department, and another group of officers to the scene of the crime, where a few thousand people had gathered and were making access difficult.[30]

At that time, the town's judge, Muhammad Taqi Damghani, had gone hunting in the plains near Kashan. Two officers came to notify him of the Berjis killing. Forty-five years later, he wrote his memories of the scene:

> It was a pleasant and mild Friday... It was around noon. I noticed from far that two policemen were approaching, and they were trying to catch my attention by waving their arms and shouting... Judge! Dr Berjis has been killed. There is no interrogator or attorney general in town, and the head of the justice department said that in their absence, you are the only competent judge for this investigation.
>
> Q Who killed him? Have any of the killers been arrested?
>
> A Yes, Judge. They are members of the Devotees of Islam (*Fada'iyan-e Islam*). They are four men; they have introduced themselves and are waiting at the police station for you to come and start the investigation. The body of Dr Berjis is also still at the scene of the murder. The forensic doctor is also waiting your instructions to issue the burial permission.
>
> We arrived at the police station half an hour later. The leader of the murderers was a man named Rasuli [Rasulzadeh] who had a shop in the bazaar selling yarn for weaving carpets. He had a pointed chin with a henna-tinged beard. Together with his three

> accomplices—three young men whose faces barely had a shade of a soft beard—they were sitting quietly and very composed in the office of the chief of police, and were mumbling some verses. . . Clearly and with no hesitation whatsoever, they confessed to having committed the murder. Each and every one claimed that he had not inflicted the first blow, but rather, all four meted it together with chants of *Allahu-Akbar*. It was clear that they were making all efforts to confuse the case. They had obviously been trained. . . I asked them why they killed Dr Berjis. They replied in unison that he was a heretic, and that he was trying to mislead and misguide the Muslims. I said that he was a philanthropist, a humanitarian person, a competent physician, and a refuge for the needy. They said that he did all that in order to mislead the Muslims; that he was trying to plant the seeds of discord within the Muslim communities; that he was teaching the Baha'i faith to people; and that according to the religious decree issued by the *greatest of the ulama of the time*, they felt that it was their religious duty to carry out the death sentence of this man, and that they had fulfilled their religious duty. However, they would not mention the name of whoever issued the death sentence. . . The plain confession of the accused, the examination of the body, the report of the forensic doctor, and the blood tinged knives left no doubt whatsoever. . . I issued the order for the arrest of all four men.[31]

A few hundred people gathered in front of the police station, demanding the release of the perpetrators. This confrontation continued late into the evening. Eventually, the police dispersed the mob.[32] The medical examiner was finally dispatched to the scene of the crime. His report states that Berjis was killed as a result of eighty-one stab wounds.

Members of the Baha'i community now gathered anxiously at Dr Berjis' home, waiting to see how the situation would develop. History told them that the murder of one Baha'i in a town often led to further attacks on the community—more murders and looting.[33] The body was still at the scene of the murder, and the growing crowd chanting religious slogans prevented anyone from approaching to remove it. Police officers asked the Baha'i community to retrieve the corpse, which was an impossible task given the circumstances.

Finally, at ten o'clock that night, after the crowd had largely dispersed and several more policemen and gendarmes arrived to provide protection, a number of Baha'i men carried the body reverently to the Baha'i cemetery outside the town. The next morning, after the doctor's immediate family had arrived from Tehran, the body was interred. While Dr Berjis' brother was speaking, asking those present to pray for the perpetrators and not seek retribution, the news arrived that a mob had shut down the bazaar and were moving to attack the police station, demanding that the murderers who were held there be freed. Colonel Fatemi, the chief of police, said he was unable to stop the crowd. The attorney general reprimanded him and threatened to send in the gendarmes. Finally, the gendarmes intervened, and after a few shots were fired, the crowd dispersed and the Baha'is gradually went home from the cemetery.[34]

Tensions in the city remained high for a few days, with Shiʿi activists forcing people to close shops and offices to protest against the fact that the attackers were still jailed, and additional police and gendarmes arrived to bolster security at the Kashan police headquarters. An article in the national *Ettelaʿat* described the state of affairs briefly, reporting the arrest of eight men in relation to the murder,[35] and the *Keyhan* newspaper of February 6 followed up with the terse statement: "News was received today that the town is back to normal and total security has been established. All shops are open and the traders and merchants are back at work."[36]

For the Baha'i community, the fact that the two major newspapers in the capital, *Ettela'at* and *Keyhan,* gave so little attention to the horrific murder and the ensuing unrest in Kashan came as no surprise. *Ettela'at* did not mention that Dr Berjis was a Baha'i, although it did mention that the assassins were members of the Islamic Propaganda Society *(Tablighat-e Islami),* and that the event had taken on a religious aspect. *Keyhan* did not hide the fact that the victim was the chairman of the Assembly of the Baha'is of Kashan, but made no reference to the murder having been incited by religious animosity, treating it as an ordinary crime. The political journals, whether leftist or nationalist, ignored the incident. Everyone was busy campaigning for the parliamentary elections and it would not have been wise to offend religious voters. Fear of the *Fada'iyan-e Islam* may also have played a part.[37]

Two weekly journals published a number of articles on the incident: the progressive *Mellat-e Iran*, and *Naysan*, the publication of the Jewish community in Iran, both denounced the murder as being contrary to the spirit of Islam and human rights. The progressive publications *Ferdowsi* magazine and *Atash* newspaper, both ran articles eulogizing Dr Berjis and attributing his murder to religious fanaticism. *Ferdowsi* noted that there was a plan to kill all nine members of the Local Assembly of the Baha'is of Kashan. At the same time, the Union of Physicians of Iran also wrote a letter to the shah requesting that the murder be punished as soon as possible, so that similar incidents could be prevented.[38]

The Baha'i community was prohibited from publishing periodicals, but sent many letters to the offices of the shah, the prime minister, the justice minister, the chief of police, and to the newspapers, requesting that justice be carried out.[39] Representatives of the Baha'i community met with Prime Minister Saʿid, and the head of the National Police Force, General Zahedi, to make the same request and ask that something be done to prevent similar incidents in future.[40]

* * *

The case was prepared for trial very quickly. Four additional men who were accused of collaborating in the murder were arrested. One of them, Reza Gulsurkhi (who later became an ayatollah and one of the leading teachers in the Qom School of Islamic Studies) testified that he, together with seven others who killed Dr Berjis and had left the scene chanting "There is no God but Allah," were provoked by the preacher Turbati.[41] In the absence of a criminal court in Kashan, these eight defendants were sent to Tehran.[42]

Having failed to liberate the killers by closing the bazaar, chanting verses, and creating a commotion in town, the clergy tried another course of action. In Golpaygan, a town 150 kilometers from Kashan, the Friday prayer leader led a group of men threatening a sit-in in protest against the arrest of the perpetrators in Kashan. The governor of Golpaygan stopped them at the telegraph office where they had sent cables asking the Grand Ayatollahs in Qom and Tehran to intercede for the prisoners, and reassured them that the authorities would take care of matters. The governor himself sent a telegram reporting the incident to the interior minister. It is presumably the minister who wrote the words now found at the bottom of the telegram sent originally on February 16, 1950: "Action should be taken based on precedence. The murderers must be severely punished. Islam does not permit brutality and murder, and sit-ins would serve no use."

The government was apparently unaware of its weak position relative to the clergy involved in the incident and had no intentions of interfering in the affairs of the Ministry of Justice. A few days later, the shah's office sent a memorandum informing Prime Minister Saʿid that Muhammad Faiz, a high-ranking religious leader in Qom, was requesting "assistance" for the Muslim killers, and directing him to convey the appropriate message. We have an incomplete draft of a communication, presumably from the prime minister, that seems to be his effort to put the shah's order into effect, though it is not clear whether the letter was sent:

> Prime Minister
> It is hereby informed: The telegram dated 3 February 1950 [14/11/1328 SH] regarding the murder of Dr Berjis has been brought to the attention of his Imperial Majesty the Shah. Your honorable self no doubt agrees that if the shedding of blood were to become a free act where each person could defile his hands at will with the blood of the other, the system of law and order would

> fall apart, and this is neither desired by the reformists, nor is it in the best interests of the country and the people. As investigation of a murder is approved and confirmed by the religious law, it has been necessary that the order be issued for the case to be legally followed up. Once the case becomes clear, you will of course be informed. May the days of grace continue!

A trail of further communications between the prime minister and the interior minister suggest that letters and telegrams had poured in to the Interior Ministry from various towns, requesting the liberation of the murderers. The prime minister continued to insist on enforcing the rule of law and punishing the killers. Meanwhile, gendarmes were sent to augment the local police force in Kashan and calm was restored.

On April 3, 1950, Prime Minister Saʿid resigned and was replaced by ʿAli Mansur. There was an immediate and complete change in the government's handling of the affair. It was as if the new cabinet were brought in to rescue the murderers. Two days after the new cabinet was formed, in a confidential letter addressed to the Ministry of Internal Affairs, Prime Minister Mansur wrote:

> The letters received by the government offices in the name of the Assemblies of the Baha'is have no official value, and they are not even worthy of reply. All demonstrations and instigations created by these elements in the capital or other towns must be seriously stopped and the instigators must be legally prosecuted. The necessary instructions in this regard shall be issued to the governors and the governor-generals.[43]

Naser Muhajer notes that there had been no Baha'i demonstrations whatsoever. The Baha'i community had never openly protested its oppression, always limiting its actions to written letters of appeal to the authorities.[44]

Thirty-five years later, the *Keyhan* newspaper—then owned by Ayatollah ʿAli Khamenei, the leader of the Islamic Republic—disclosed how efforts to influence the judiciary had been orchestrated:

> The nation's Shiʿi clergy entered the arena in order to prevent the execution of a number of young Muslim men who had carried out this act [murder] as a completion of a divine and religious duty. Late Ayatollah Boroujerdi, late Ayatollah Kashani, and. . .were all mobilized to prevent the execution of their brethren. Groups were sent from the theological centers in Qom to the provinces throughout the country in order to inform the local clergy in other provinces of the situation; following which the flood of cables and telegrams were sent from all corners of the country. . . to announce solidarity with and support of the group.[45]

Seven months after the crime, on August 28, 1950, the trial was held in the high criminal court of Tehran. The atmosphere was tense. The public gallery was filled with turbaned spectators who supported the murderers with chants of blessing, or cries of *Allahu-Akbar*, as well as bazaar merchants, supporters of Ayatollah Kashani and Mosaddeq, and others who were demonstrating against the oil agreements.[46] The country was in a precarious situation as negotiations with Britain for control of Iranian oil were continuing, and General ʿAli Razmara, newly installed as prime minister, was conscious of the need to retain the support of religious leaders.

Twelve attorneys were appointed to defend the accused, including prominent lawyers of the judiciary such as Arsalan Khalʿatbari, known as a liberal nationalist, and Sadeq Sarmad, a poet, journalist, and a director of the Bar Association. The appointment of these two lawyers to the defense can be seen as "a comprehensive and calculated provision by the tide of the clerics and politicians. . . who were geared up to acquit the criminals of the charges of the murder, and to conceal the facts."[47] The family of the victim had only one lawyer, a Muslim by the name of Razi. Because of threats that he received, he was only able to attend two court sessions.[48]

Press coverage of the trial was surprisingly muted. Muhajer writes:

> From. . . 27 August/5 *Shahrivar* when the court started its investigation, up until Wednesday 13 September there was not a single,

> I repeat, a single word in the newspapers about the court case and what was said and done. The policy of *Keyhan*, up to the day of the announcement of the verdict, was to observe total silence. But once every few days, *Ettela 'at* would mention a few words about the court case.[49]

What *Ettela 'at* published made no mention of the accusations or the substance of the defense, but focused on courtroom procedure—which lawyers were present, who spoke and in which order, and similar. Finally, on September 12, *Ettela 'at* published the following:

> Today, after five hours of consultation (from 11:00 to 16:00 hours), and due to the absence of any case evidence, the eight men accused of the murder of Dr Berjis in Kashan were acquitted of charges of murder by the Criminal Court number 2.

Keyhan also broke its sixteen-day-long silence by publishing a similar announcement.

The jury delivered four votes in favor of acquittal and one in opposition.[50] Damghani writes in his memoirs:

> Although it was said that Razmara had personally asked the Justice Minister for the acquittal of the accused from charges in order to quieten the public, I must say that this acquittal was a dishonor and scandal for the Judiciary in Iran. The Criminal Court of Tehran, consisting of five notable and high-ranking judges. . . acquitted of murder charges those who had clearly confessed to having committed the crime, and who had written and personally signed their confessions in total freedom and liberty.[51]

The criminals, now hailed as heroes, left the courthouse in Tehran with people chanting blessings on them, throwing sweets, and sacrificing animals in their path. On their return to Kashan, they were greeted by a crowd of supporters who came thirty kilometers out from the city to welcome them with the sacrifice of hundreds of cows and sheep. Until his death in 1988, Rasulzadeh was held in the highest regard by the citizens of Kashan and by the Islamic Republic.[52] *Keyhan* commemorated his passing with an obituary that is extraordinary for its blatant lies:

> The political life of Rasulzadeh started in 1941/1320. In 1950/1328 following the terror that led to the murder of a Zionist member, it entered a new phase. In the company of seven of his friends, he undertook the killing of the leader of the Zionists of Kashan and the surrounding areas. That man was a well-known Zionist disguised as a doctor (although he had never studied medicine). He had violated the lives and honor of many Muslims, and had openly and publicly burnt a copy of the Quran. The son of the murdered Zionist, who himself was one of the renowned Zionists in the country and the personal physician of the Shah stepped in dominantly and manipulated the case in such wise that eight months after the detention of Haj Rasulzadeh and his friends, the court issued their death sentence. The nation's clergy then entered the scene... and finally, after a very difficult period Haj Rasulzadeh and his friends were released from prison and received a hero's welcome in Tehran... With the activities of the *Fada'iyan-e Islam* during 1953/1332, the martyr Navvab Safavi... appointed him as his representative and the leader of the *Fada'iyan-e Islam* in Kashan. . . In 1962/1341 when the demand-for-Islam and the battle-with-infidelity led by Imam Khomeini was called for from the centre for Shiʿi jurisprudence (in Qom), he [Rasulzadeh] was among the first to wholeheartedly reply to the call of the Imam, and from that very start, he displayed his active presence in all arenas... After the victory of the Islamic Revolution... he always advised people to never neglect following the Imam, even be it for an instant. He has been in the forefront of the revolutionary activities.

It is worth noting that none of Dr Berjis' sons were ever physicians to the shah, and no mention of Zionism or the burning of a Quran exists in any of the contemporary records.

Muhajer notes that the shameless acquittal of eight Shiʿi fanatics who had openly admitted their participation in the murder caused no protest:

> No sound of disapproval came from the liberals and intellectuals; neither did the media and newspapers mention anything. The development-seeking or progressive political reformists did not react in any way, nor even the Baha'i community itself that always refrained from any public protest. . . It was only the *Jahan-i Ma* (*Our World*) newspaper that demonstrated a fitting reaction to this shameful action of the nation's judiciary system by referring to it as an obvious indication of ethnic and religious prejudice, and a violation of the civil rights of the minorities.[53]

Damghani relates the incident in Kashan to the growing strength of the Islamic movement through its opposition to the Baha'i faith and ultimately to the establishment of the Islamic Republic.[54] Muhajer concurs, drawing a line from Kashan to the assassination of Prime Minister Razmara by a member of the *Fada'iyan-i Islam* in March 1951, and the similar acquittal of his murderer. Dr Mohamad Tavakoli-Targhi also sees the anti-Baha'i movement as instrumental in the development of political Islam and the Islamic Revolution:

> The anti-Baha'i movement that was blended with the *Tablighat-e Islami* (Islamic Propaganda) movement since the 1940s/1320s played an important role in changing "Islamic beliefs" into "political struggles." Instead of examining the teachings and beliefs of the Baha'i Faith, the Islamic activists emphasised that the Baha'i Faith is a "political movement" created by the colonial governments for the weakening of Islam. . . As such, the meetings of the anti-Baha'i associations, societies and parties became suitable places for attracting people towards organizations such as the People's

Mujahedeen of Iran (*Mujahedin-e Khalq*), the Unified Nation (*Ummat e-Vahedeh*), the Islamic Nations' Party (*Hizb-e Mellat-e Islami*), and the Islamic Coalition Party (*Hey'at-e Mo'talefeh*). With the merging of the anti-Baha'i, anti-Zionist, anti-Colonialist, and anti-Imperialist movements, the struggle to purge Iran from its Baha'i citizens was transformed into a struggle to overthrow the Pahlavi regime.[55]

Chapter 7

True Crime: The Incident at Abarqu

The brutal attacks that targeted Baha'is with impunity for over a century made them easy scapegoats for crimes of which they were entirely innocent. On January 3, 1950, a woman and her five children were bludgeoned to death in their home in Abarqu, a town in central Iran 150 kilometers from Yazd, in the aftermath of a failed romance. To protect the name of a well-connected family, and with the collusion of a number of corrupt officials in the security forces and the judiciary, innocent men were framed for murder. What began as a crime of passion was conjoined with religious and political opportunism to maximize the harm done.

At the time, the press capitalized on the Abarqu incident to feed the public appetite for sensational true crime stories, and by implicating the Baha'is, however falsely, echoed the propaganda that linked Baha'is to degenerate and sordid criminal acts. Six decades later, following the renewed persecution of Baha'is since the revolution, the newspapers of the Islamic Republic once again revived interest in the incident. A number of articles rehashing it were published in *Keyhan* in February 2006. In 2009, the Islamic Republic's television network (IRIB TV3) broadcast a program called *The Invisible Infiltration* (*Nufuz-e Namar'i*) as part of the series *The Secrets of Obscurity* (*Asrar-e Tariki*), retelling the story with the same false allegations and featuring gruesome photographs of the victims' bodies to arouse public sentiment against the Baha'is.

A full account of the events in Abarqu and the trial that followed was recorded at the time by Muhammad Taqi Afnan, a Baha'i from Yazd, in a manuscript entitled *The Innocent Ones* (*Bigunahan*). The following draws upon his account, together with additional information that has recently been made available.

The landowning Umidsalar family were among the wealthiest and most powerful in the Abadeh and Abarqu region at the time of these events. Muhammad Reza Khan Umidsalar enjoyed exceptional authority as an elected official who served in parliament for several terms. He was influential in appointing local government officials, and his father-in-law was Abadeh's Friday prayer leader. He boasted that the Qajar king, Ahmad Shah, and his entourage, including the officer who would later become Reza Shah, had stopped at his father's home in Abadeh for lunch, and he had the honor of extending hospitality to the royal family on two other occasions: in 1927, when Reza Shah and the young crown prince had stopped in Abadeh, and in the spring of 1944, when Muhammad Reza Shah and his first wife Fawzieh passed through town.

His sister, Maryam Salari, was married to her paternal cousin, Muhammad Hasan Khan-i Salari, and would inadvertently play a key role in the murders at Abarqu. When Maryam's husband died, his brother—Isfandyar Khan-e Salari—who was already married with children, set his sights on the beautiful and wealthy widow of his late brother. Despite his perseverance, she rejected him and started a relationship with a tall, handsome preacher by the name of Seyyed Muhammad Qayyumi who performed Shiʿi mourning ceremonies with a captivating voice. It was Maryam's maid Sughra who had introduced the couple and it was at her home that the secret lovers met nightly.

When rumors of the love affair reached the Salari family, they threatened Qayyumi repeatedly. He informed police officials of the threats, and that if any harm came to the couple, the Salaris would be to blame. The couple then secretly traveled to a small hamlet some four leagues from Abadeh where they registered their marriage.

After news of the wedding became public, Sughra and her five children—ages six to fifteen—were found dead in their home on the evening of January 3, 1950. There was no evidence of a break-in or forced entry, suggesting that the killer (or killers) were known to the victims. A blood-stained shovel and hammer found in the courtyard suggested that the killers had not come armed—or with the intent to kill—but used what was to hand. It was surmised that the mother had been killed first in the course of an argument that turned violent, and then her children, having witnessed the crime, were also murdered.

The head of the local gendarmerie in Abarqu led the preliminary investigation into the grisly case. Three men who had been at Sughra's house late on the night of the crime—including her son-in-law—were arrested. Isfandyar Khan-e Salari's enmity toward Sughra for her role in the union of Qayyumi and Maryam was common knowledge and everyone assumed that he had instigated the murder. He had been seen leaving town in a perturbed state the morning after.[1]

A report on the investigation was submitted to the courthouse in Yazd. The governor of Yazd, Baniadam, ordered the arrest of the suspects and informed the capital of the murder and the motive. The news was reported in the press in Tehran as well as locally.

The public prosecutor and the chief of the gendarmerie in Yazd set out for Abarqu. They were intercepted en route by the Salaris and made a detour to Mehriz to seek the advice of Khakpur Faraghi, the warrant-officer and head of the gendarmerie in Mehriz. He was a trusted confidant of Isfandyar Salari, and was already aware of the situation. They determined that, in order to distance the Salari family from the crime, they would have to free the perpetrators and arrest others who could be charged with the murder instead.

They proceeded to Abarqu, dismissed the gendarmerie officer who had led the investigation, and appointed warrant-officer Khakpur in his place. Khakpur immediately released the three prisoners, and removed the existing interrogation documents and finger-print records. He then arrested one of Sughra's neighbors, Muhammad Shiravani, his seventeen-year-old son, and another man, charging the three men with murder based on the claim that Sughra owed money to Shiravani, and had used abusive language towards him when he demanded repayment.

The public prosecutor returned to Yazd three days later and by then the story had changed. He claimed that the murder was the result of a religious dispute, and revealed that Sughra's neighbor Shiravani was a Baha'i. The information about Sughra's debt was removed from the case file. The new charge was that Shiravani killed Sughra because she insulted the Baha'i faith. The only problem was that Shiravani was not a Baha'i, nor had he ever been, and during his interrogation he vehemently insisted that he was a Muslim.

While many people in Abarqu knew that Shiravani was not a Baha'i, no one, including the newspapers, dared to question the allegations. As such, the story of a woman's grisly murder at the hands of Baha'is in a heated religious skirmish began to take hold of the public. The Salaris reconciled with Qayyumi, their new in-law, who testified that whenever he had denounced the Baha'is in his sermons, Sughra used to raise her voice in the mosque and curse the Baha'is.

Curiously, there was not a single Baha'i living in Abarqu at the time of the murder. A few years earlier, three Baha'is had been brutally killed there, after which the remaining Baha'is fled. While interrogating Muhammad Nekui, one of the three "suspects," officer Khakpur discovered that he had a Baha'i brother named Ahmad who lived in the village of Dah-bid, some 240 kilometers away. Khakpur concluded that Nekui stole furniture from the home where the murders took place, transported it to his brother in Dah-bid and then returned to Abarqu the same evening. No one questioned how such a trip would have been possible at a time when motorized vehicles were not used in the area.

An order was sent to Dah-bid for the arrest of Ahmad Nekui. Some time earlier, he had moved away from that village to Shiraz, even further from Abarqu. When the police tracked him down in the city, the people in the caravansary, or inn, where he worked, as well as other Muslims, testified that he had been in Shiraz on the night of the murder. Given the number of witnesses, the public prosecutor of Shiraz was reluctant to arrest him.

Isfandyar Salari set off for Shiraz to convince the authorities to arrest Ahmad Nekui, without success. He then hastened back to Yazd, secured an arrest warrant from the prosecutor there, and returned to Shiraz. This time Nekui was arrested. Salari personally accompanied him to Abarqu and delivered him to the gendarmerie, whereupon all three detainees were transferred to the prison in Yazd.

Khakpur had tortured Shiravani, but he refused to confess to being a Baha'i. His teenaged son confessed to what was demanded after being hung from the ceiling, lashed, branded, and forced into the snow in the middle of winter. He agreed that three Baha'is from Isfandabad had come to Abarqu during the night and, together with his father, had murdered Sughra and her children. The three were arrested in Isfandabad on murder charges and sent to the prison in Yazd. When a number of Muslim witnesses testified that all three were in Bavanat, a village 150 kilometers from Abarqu, on the night of the murder, the prosecutor had no choice but to release them.

However, Baniadam, the governor of Yazd who was a fair-minded man, knew the truth of the case, so Isfandyar and his contacts in Yazd and Tehran arranged to have him removed from office. He was replaced by the head of the magistrate's court in Yazd, who was a trusted accomplice of Isfandyar. All obstacles were thus removed. It was necessary to make up for the failed framing of the three Baha'is from Isfandabad, so the chairman of the local Baha'i Assembly of Isfandabad, a man named Haj Mirza Hasan Shamsi, was accused of the murder and sent to jail in Yazd after refusing to pay a bribe to Khakpur.[2]

Gradually, more Baha'is were drawn into the case. Allegations were circulated in Yazd through the mosques and local newspapers resulting in the arrest of eight of the nine members of the local Assembly of the Baha'is of Yazd on charges of colluding in the murder of Sughra. The fact that Dr Manshadi, the ninth member of the Assembly who was present at all its meetings, was not arrested shows how baseless the charges were. He was most likely spared because, as a very highly regarded physician in the city, linking him to such sordid, far-fetched accusations would not be credible and would have cast doubt on the other arrests.

But a warrant was issued for the arrest of yet another Baha'i, a trustworthy merchant in poor health by the name of Jalal Binesh. He was charged with having written a letter to Hasan Shamsi informing the latter of the receipt of some tobacco from Abarqu, which the interrogator in Yazd determined was a secretly coded message informing the recipient of the murder.

At that time a young man died in Yazd, and rumors were spread that he was murdered by the Baha'is. His corpse was placed in a coffin and carried through the city by a group of pallbearers chanting anti-Baha'i slogans. Plans for attacking Baha'i homes and a possible massacre became the talk of the town. A number of Baha'is were beaten, nearly to death, and their belongings were stolen. The government finally declared a curfew in Yazd. The violence and unrest spread to the nearby town of Taft and the city of Kerman, 350 kilometers southeast of Yazd, where several Baha'is were murdered. Ardakan and Amirabad also saw further unrest and some 300 Baha'is were expelled from the two towns. A prominent Baha'i in Allahabad was attacked and hospitalized for several months with severe injuries. None of these crimes were prosecuted. The Baha'is appealed to Prime Minister Razmara and to other authorities, but to no avail. Razmara personally issued orders that the appeals of the Baha'is be left unanswered, as he feared being branded as a Baha'i himself.

The public prosecutor in Yazd finally issued his indictment, charging the three individuals arrested in Abarqu, the eight members of the Local Assembly of Yazd as well as Hasan Shamsi, the chairman of the Local Assembly of Isfandabad, and three other individuals from that town (names yet unknown to the prosecutor) with the murder of Sughra.

The accused were transferred from Yazd to Kerman for the trial. However, the court in Kerman declined to accept the case: it was too obviously a frame-up. Two months later, on February 26, 1951, the case was transferred to Tehran and the prisoners sent to the capital. It was rumored that Prime Minister Razmara had given orders for the accused to be killed in a fake accident on the way to Tehran and thus relieve the authorities of the problem. It so happened that Razmara was then assassinated by a member of *Fada'iyan-e Islam*, and the bus transporting the prisoners arrived safely in Tehran. There, too, the judiciary saw the case as fabricated, and some—though not all—of its obvious flaws were pointed out.

In Tehran, the case was then turned over to another prosecutor, Asadollah Zamaniyan, who traveled to Yazd to reopen the investigation. He raided the homes of the Baha'is and the office of the city's Local Assembly, confiscating a large number of letters and documents utterly unrelated to the case, which he sent to Tehran. He then traveled to Isfandabad and interrogated the three Baha'is there who had previously been cleared of charges. All three worked in the production of wood charcoal and were illiterate. The prosecutor tricked them into signing a confession to the murder. Consequently, the number of Baha'is charged with the murder rose to 14, alongside the four Muslims who were also accused.

The plan to involve the Baha'is in the Abarqu incident had initially been instigated by Isfandyar Salari to save his own neck. Greater powers were now taking advantage of the opportunity he had created. Absolved of any charges for Sughra's murder, Salari went his own way.

As the date for the trial grew closer, the clergy, led by Ayatollah Behbehani, began actively inciting anti-Baha'i sentiments among the populace, and intimidating the judges and the judicial system. Numerous announcements in threatening tones were made throughout the capital. It was stated that in the absence of a guilty verdict and the execution of all of the accused, the people would carry out such a sentence. A sum of some seventy thousand tumans was raised to employ attorneys to build a case against particular plaintiffs. Members of

Fada'iyan-e Islam, as well as other fanatical individuals, spent days and nights in meetings preparing for the trial, with the intent to intimidate the authorities and coerce them into ignoring the flaws of the case.

Ten attorneys were assigned to defend the relatives of the victim. Haji 'Ali Akbar Taha, a lawyer who later became president of the Bar Association, told Ahmad Naseri, one of the defense attorneys, that as long as the funds were forthcoming, two things were bound to happen: either a Baha'i would be slain every year and bounties would be collected for the murderers and pocketed by the authorities; or a Baha'i would be accused of murder and money would be collected in support of the plaintiffs.

The trial started on May 7, 1952, at the High Criminal Court in Tehran in the presence of five judges. The Baha'is' defense team consisted of three Baha'i lawyers, Azizollah Navidi, Kazem Kazemzadeh and Ahmad Naseri, as well as a number of Muslim lawyers. The courtroom sessions were attended daily by a large number of clerics and fanatically angry merchants from the bazaar. They were not there to follow the case, but rather to disrupt the court, intimidate the defense, and influence the verdict.

The assistant prosecutor, Khalil Sabri, happened to be a Sunni who, to dispel any doubts that might arise from his own affiliation with a religious minority, made seditiously provocative statements and extreme claims that the Baha'is had been murdering people for the past fifty years. In his closing remarks, he requested the court to issue the most severe penalties to prevent the public from taking the matter into their own hands.[3] Following this provocation, unprecedented in any Iranian court, four of the defense attorneys submitted their resignation to the judges. They pointed out that the assistant prosecutor's speech had been so seditious and was such a procedural violation that it had incited the spectators and that the attorneys felt their lives were in danger. The chief judge reinstated the attorneys as public defenders, and assured them that he would not allow the spectators to demonstrate further.

Apart from the daunting atmosphere inside the courtroom, large crowds of *mullahs*, theology students, and bazaar merchants gathered around the courthouse every day, shouting slogans and distributing anti-Baha'i pamphlets. One advertised the event:

> How were Sughra and her five innocent children murdered? Why were they killed? Who are the murderers? You are invited to attend the Criminal Court daily from 9am to witness the trial. What are the state authorities and the respected court officials going to decide in face of this catastrophe? Will you deliver the guilty and the murderers to the gallows; or will you turn over the judgment to the public? Disconsolate and heartbroken, we are awaiting the final day of the trial for the verdict to be issued.

The prosecution attacked and insulted the Baha'i faith, portraying it as deeply superstitious. In the defense attorneys' numerous objections to the defamation, the judge sided with the prosecution. Attorney and member of parliament 'Amidi Nuri represented the private plaintiffs. He was also the editor of the *Dad* newspaper that had originally reported the murder in the context of the scandal that surrounded Maryam Salari, and his statements in court seemed designed to back-track from what had been printed. Referring to the sensationalist forgery attributed to the Russian Prince Dolgorukov,[4] Nuri called the Baha'is traitors and disloyal to their homeland.[5] It appeared that the entire Baha'i community was on trial.

Seyyed Mahdi Razavi, one of the attorneys for Sughra's only surviving daughter, stated: "During the trial of the murderers of the *Mahdur al-Dam* Baha'is [i.e. whose blood can be shed with impunity], such as in the Shahrud case or the murder of Dr Berjis in Kashan, we created a great commotion in court. The judges were intimidated and coerced in absolving the accused of all charges." With these words, he explicitly conveyed to the judges and the spectators what needed to be done.

Another attorney, Adib Razavi Yazdi, remarked that prior to the Constitutional Revolution, killing Baha'is who dared to make themselves known was a binding obligation for Muslims. Hundreds of Baha'is had been killed in Yazd under *fatwa*s issued by the *ulama*.

Since the enactment of civil laws, the clergy were no longer permitted to issue death warrants. Thus the Baha'is needed to be condemned by similar civil methods before they could be exterminated.

Yet another attorney suggested that the Baha'is be handed over to the various guilds for slaughter, recalling the bloody age of the Babis at the time of Naser al-Din Shah. One of the attorneys hired by Ayatollah Behbehani even claimed that the Baha'is had killed Naser al-Din Shah's prime minister, Amir Kabir.[6] Another lawyer declared that the Baha'is killed Sughra and her children because fifty years ago the Muslims in Abarqu had murdered two Baha'is. Continuing with a tirade of insults against the beliefs of the accused, he added other false and misleading statements that he attributed to Comte de Gobineau, Edward Browne, and the playwright Bernard Shaw. Meanwhile, agents of *Fada'iyan-e Islam* who had crammed into the public area of the courtroom kept proclaiming *Allahu-Akbar* in support of these statements. The plaintiffs' attorneys were able to make their case freely, while the defense attorneys were interrupted time and time again. As soon as the defense attorneys responded to the opposition's claims or tried to present the Baha'i views that might rectify some misunderstanding, the judge would overrule their comments as having no bearing on the case. The hostile atmosphere had so intimidated the defense attorneys and the accused that they had no hope of survival. They simply awaited the conclusion of their case.

Bahram Choubineh has written an account of the trial that honors the courage of those non-Baha'i lawyers who defended the Baha'is during that critical time:

> The most courageous and skilled attorney that the Baha'is had was a man named 'Abdollah Razi. He was a pious Muslim who believed that the Baha'is would never disrupt the general order of the Iranian society. He upheld the view that they were tax payers, and as such they were entitled to their rights. He also believed that their dignity and their beliefs must be safeguarded against any harassment. He had represented the Baha'is in court on several

> occasions, and had always wholeheartedly exerted himself in carrying out his duties. In the Abarqu case he agreed to defend the Baha'is, believing fully in their innocence. He was an experienced and skilled lawyer. Other than his verbal defense, he submitted a written copy of his defense so to prevent any possible future allegations against him by the court. 'Abdollah Razi had fully discerned the polluted and foul atmosphere of the court, and he was well aware of the ruthlessness of the *Fada'iyan-e Islam* organization. He placed a copy of the Quran on his head, approached the bench and voiced loudly and clearly that he was a Muslim and that he felt it his duty to defend a group of innocent people. At times he would support his statements with verses from the Quran or Islamic history to ingratiate the judge and the *Fada'iyan-e-Islam* group; and yet, he would proceed to audaciously call the whole case a fabrication aimed at convicting a group of innocent people.[7]

Twenty-one days later, on May 27, 1952, the court heard the brief and simple final statements of the accused, and the trial ended. While the judges retired for consultation, a large crowd, mainly young theology students, gathered as spectators. They waited for a couple of hours and then dispersed, as it was not known when the verdict would be announced. At 3pm, the crowd started to gather again. Strong security measures had been in place throughout the trial but were intensified that day. Police officers patrolled the public areas, the corridors, terraces, and the main hall.

The court read its verdict after 7.30 that evening. Sughra's Muslim neighbor, Muhammad Shiravani, and the three Baha'is from Isfandabad were sentenced to death. Abbas 'Ali Purmahdi and Mirza Hasan Shamsi were given ten years' hard labor. The members of the Local Assembly of Yazd were sentenced to three years' hard labor. The two Nekui brothers were acquitted.

The Baha'is appealed the verdict, whereupon their case went to the Court of Appeals. There the judge confided to the defense attorneys that the verdicts were unjust and must be set aside. Subsequently, under pressure from the clergy and the bazaar merchants, he only managed to reduce the death sentence of the three Baha'is to ten years' imprisonment. Shiravani, who was falsely accused both of being a Baha'i and of the murder, was executed in Yazd. To the end he insisted that he was innocent and that Isfandyar Salari was the murderer. Until his last moment, he was also adamant about his belief in and affiliation to Islam.

The members of the local Assembly of Yazd, who had no involvement in the murder at all, were finally released in September 1953. Two of their members had died in prison: Jalal Binesh prior to the start of the trial, after suffering for eleven months under deplorable conditions, and Mirza Hasan Shamsi after his appendix was removed in an improper and unhygienic operation. The Baha'is of Isfandabad served their sentence and were released in 1960.

This summary excludes numerous Baha'is who were attacked and beaten—and some killed, in various towns and villages as a result of the case. It suffices to end with the closing remarks of Bahram Choubineh's commentary:

> Now that we have reached the end of this survey, you and I are left with no choice but to honor the memory of Sughra and her blameless and ill-fated children, and to pay tribute to those innocent Muslims and Baha'is who fell prey to this ghastly crime, and who were made victims of religious prejudice.

Chapter 8

The Events of 1955: Hojjat al-Islam Falsafi, the Ramadan Broadcasts, and the Military Occupation of the Baha'i Center

In 1955, an anti-Baha'i pogrom was launched during the fasting month of Ramadan, when religious fervor runs high. It was at first sanctioned by the shah's government. As a reward for supporting the shah in the coup against Prime Minister Musaddeq and in hunting down members of the Communist Tudeh Party, the Shi'i clergy had insisted on a presence in every aspect of the nation's social, cultural, and political life. But a series of coercive and overreaching political maneuvers on their part threatened the country's stability and left the shah's government no choice but to take a hard stand. In so doing, the regime provoked deep opposition among the clergy, which would last until the shah was ousted in the revolution.

The emergence and spread of Shi'i organizations that carried out violent acts in the name of religion was one factor that prepared the grounds for the violence of 1955. A number of influential political and intellectual figures in Iran had been recently assassinated. The religious reformist Ahmad Kasravi, who had been a seminary student before abandoning Shi'ism and creating a new religion he called

Pakdini, was murdered by the *Fada'iyan-e Islam* in 1946 for his public anti-clerical statements. The *Fada'iyan-e Islam* also falsely accused one of the shah's ministers—'Abd al-Husain Hazhir—of being a Baha'i before assassinating him[1] in 1949 in the Sepahsalar Mosque during a religious observance. In 1951, the prime minister, General Razmara, was shot and killed by a devotee during his participation in a memorial service.[2]

Razmara, who was renowned for his courage and for being an efficient officer, had made an effort to ally himself with the clergy by cracking down on the Baha'is during his term as prime minister (June 1950 to March 1951). Jazayeri, the minister of education under Razmara, dismissed all the Baha'is employed by the Ministry of Education. He explained his decision as a response to Ayatollah Boroujerdi's message to the shah stating that "at the order of Shoghi Effendi, the Baha'is are actively displaying their belief, and this is leading to discontent and complaints among the Muslims."[3] Ayatollah Boroujerdi's protest was based on the fact that the Baha'is had begun to be open about their beliefs, and to identify their faith as "Baha'i" on employment forms. It was during this period that the Baha'i Dr Berjis was murdered in Kashan, and Razmara's justice minister swayed the courts to absolve the murderers of all charges.[4]

During Musaddeq's term as prime minister (1951–53), his role in the establishment of a secular democracy revitalized the spirit of nationalism in the country. His appointment drew crowds in the street, supporting his proposal to nationalize the country's oil industry. His supporters consisted of a broad coalition of nationalists, socialists, liberal-democratic citizens, and bazaar merchants who increasingly began to drown out the special interests of the Shi'i clerics. Musaddeq himself was highly motivated to keep the country from falling into religious strife, which put him at odds with the clergy who fought to reverse their dwindling influence by suppressing religious minorities.

Muhammad Taqi Falsafi, who would play a key role in the pogroms of 1955 and the military occupation of the National Baha'i

Center, wrote of an early meeting between himself and Musaddeq during the prime minister's first year in office:

> I told him, "You are the head of the Islamic government of Iran, and the Baha'is are active in towns and are causing problems for the Muslims. Letters of complaint about this are continuously pouring in for the attention of Ayatollah Borujerdi. He considers it necessary that you take some action in this regard." When I finished my statement, Dr Mosaddegh burst into a loud and sarcastic guffaw, and said: "Mr Falsafi, in my view, there is no difference between Muslims and Baha'is. They all belong to the same nation, and are all Iranians." This reply astonished me. If he had asked me for the difference between the Baha'is and the Muslims, I would have explained it to him; but after his mocking and disdainful laugh, there was no room for explanation or for further comments. So, I remained quiet, and when I was in the presence of Ayatollah Borujerdi, I reported the conversation. He too listened with the utmost perplexity and astonishment.[5]

In Musaddeq's years in office the influence of the leftist movement grew while the clergy severed their relations with the prime minister and aligned themselves more closely with the royal court. When Musaddeq's refusal to compromise in the negotiations with the US and Britain over the nationalization of the oil industry, the CIA led a coup d'état against Musaddeq on August 19, 1953. The agitation of leading ayatollahs and their support for the coup were instrumental in its success. Following Musaddeq's trial, many opposition groups were suppressed, including the Communist Tudeh Party, which culminated in the exposure of the Tudeh party's network that had infiltrated the army, and the targeting of political "enemies" for mass imprisonments and killings. Throughout this turbulent period, the Baha'is faced a routine and long-established level of harassment, persecution, and discrimination in towns and villages throughout the country.

When the shah's position had stabilized after the coup d'état, and during the prime ministership of General Zahedi, the clergy once again raised the Baha'i question. Possibly in compensation for their support during the coup, they demanded that the shah provide a final solution to exterminate the Baha'is. In many cities, the fire of anti-Baha'i sentiment that has always smoldered under the ashes in Iranian society suddenly burst into flame, incited in large part by the efforts of the populist preacher Muhammad Taqi Falsafi. For the length of the fasting month of Ramadan (beginning April 23, 1955), his noon sermons attacking the Baha'is were broadcast on national radio for an hour every day. In an interview with the *Ettehad-e Melli* newspaper on May 8, 1955, as well as in his later memoirs, he relates that Ayatollah Boroujerdi suggested the topic for the Ramadan sermons: "Now that the situation of the oil industry is resolved, and the problem with the Tudeh Party is also settled, we must make plans about the Baha'is and stand up against them." Boroujerdi also encouraged him to meet with the shah, who gave his approval.[6]

Falsafi's sermons started by criticizing the government for a few days before broaching the subject of the Baha'is, and then he gradually escalated his attacks. Many of his accusations were entirely invented—for example, that the Baha'is were planning a coup for the following year. In others he claimed to be voicing the opinion of Ayatollah Boroujerdi. Another individual named Shokuhideh was broadcasting similar anti-Baha'i propaganda over the Air Force Radio, a local military radio station in Tehran. He portrayed the Baha'is as posing a greater threat to the country than that of the Communist Tudeh Party.

The Baha'is were devastated. They recognized the nationally broadcast sermons as part of a scheme by the clergy to make anti-Baha'i campaigns part of official government policy, as they had been in the Qajar period. Rumors were also circulating among progressive Iranians. Some blamed a British plot to damage Iran's international image through the persecution of religious minorities, and thus discourage foreign companies, and especially Americans, from investing in Iran. Another story interpreted the anti-Baha'i campaign as an American-inspired distraction to undermine opposition to Iran's joining the CENTO regional military alliance between Turkey,

Iran, and Pakistan, or to Iran's unfavorable negotiations with the newly established Oil Consortium (NIOC).[7]

An issue related to the shah himself, unknown to the public at that time, came to light later on. During the shah and Queen Soraya's last trip to America, a photograph of Soraya in a low-cut bathing suit and another photo of the shah at a frivolous party were published in an American magazine. A copy of this magazine fell into the hands of Boroujerdi, who threatened the shah that unless he complied with the clergy's wishes regarding the Baha'is, he would lose his throne. It was following this threat that the shah gave free rein to the clergy to oppose the Baha'is.

When Falsafi's sermons started, anti-Baha'i violence was sparked across the country. The cities of Rasht, Abadeh, Isfahan, Ahvaz, Urumiyyeh, Shiraz, and Karaj were all affected, as well as the villages of Takur, Hesar, and Mahfuruzak, which are significant in the history of the Baha'i faith. Baha'i homes and shops were looted and burnt down, their crops and livestock destroyed. Baha'is and their children were beaten; Baha'i girls were abducted and forced to marry Muslims. Men, women, and children took refuge in ditches, aqueducts, or hid in caves. Amir Asadollah 'Alam, the interior minister, wrote in his memoirs:

> Falsafi managed to fool both the Shah and the military authorities and start a campaign against the Baha'is that dragged the country to the edge of disaster. It was Ramadan. [Falsafi's] noon sermons were broadcast throughout the nation via radio and caused violence and terror in many locations. People killed a few Baha'is here and there. Falsafi justified these acts by saying that they increased the Shah's prestige. I had no choice but to order him, in my own rash way, to refrain from giving further speeches until order was reestablished.[8]

Falsafi bluntly refused to comply with "'Alam's order to end the sermons, but conceded in advising his audience not to exceed legally recognized limits." The call to restraint was ignored by those, whether clergy or opportunists, who saw advantage in attacking the Baha'is. In contrast, many intellectuals expressed their abhorrence at the violence and trumped-up propaganda. The *Khandaniha* magazine quoted the newspaper *Sahar*:

> Mr Falsafi started to discuss the subject of the Baha'is on Tuesday . . . This matter soon led to the question why such an issue should erupt at a time when the nation is on the verge of reform; when the authorities have initiated a widespread fight against corruption; and at a time when national solidarity needs to be strengthened more than ever. Regret and surprise gave way to severe concern when on Friday Mr Falsafi directed his attacks towards a highly regarded and reputable individual who is close to the Shah, and religious propaganda and interference in the monarch's private affairs became the subject of public debate. It was surprising that these statements, made by an unofficial source, were fully aired over the radio, and clearly stirred an atmosphere of general frenzy in Tehran as well as in other cities and towns.[9]

A full account of the hundreds of heartrending incidents that occurred as a result of the Ramadan sermons would be painful and also risk desensitizing the reader. Two incidents are presented here as illustrative of many more, each of which caused untold suffering. The lives that were torn apart and the homes that were uprooted cannot be compensated. The deep emotional wounds will not be healed within a lifetime, and all because the religious leaders dictated what people should believe. While these actions were supported and authorized both by religious leaders and the government, and were started under the pretext of religion, in reality they appeased the vicious nature of the mob. They ended with tributes to the perpetrators, and with no retribution. Now to the first incident. . .

Hurmuzak is a small hamlet near Yazd, with a pleasant climate. Its inhabitants were Baha'is and most were related to each other. Next to Hurmuzak is another village called Sakhvid, where the residents were not Baha'is, but were related to the inhabitants of Hurmuzak. A police station was located three kilometers from Hurmuzak.

After the incitement of Falsafi's radio sermons, the villagers' relationships with their Baha'i neighbors turned cold. Harassment began with preventing the Baha'is from using the public baths, cutting down their fruit trees, and injuring or killing their animals. The Baha'is' appealed to the police, but to no avail. Among the people behind these actions were Mullah Ali, a resident of Bagh-Bid who regularly went to Sakhvid to preach, the village chief, Mirza 'Ali Akbar Tavakoli, and one Muhammad Jalali Sakhvidi. The warrant officer in charge of the police station, Corporal Jamili, further provoked the conflict with the aim of taking bribes from both sides.

Finally, an innocent family of seven Baha'is was brutally murdered. Fereydun Hormozaki, an elderly man of seventy, usually hosted Baha'i meetings at his home, and as such the Baha'is referred to his house as the *Haziratul-Quds*, or Baha'i center. Following the government's order for the occupation of the Baha'i centers throughout the country, Corporal Jamili assigned a constable to occupy Fereydun's home. He immediately took over all the rooms, and ordered Fereydun and his wife to confine themselves to the balcony.

Their son filed a complaint with the authorities in Tehran and sent numerous letters of protest. As a result, in July 1955, several police officers interrogated Fereydun and several other Baha'is in Hurmuzak for hours, humiliating, insulting, and also threatening them. At the end of the interrogation, a clerk from the police station sent an officer to Sakhvid, telling people "to come and slaughter these damned Baha'is."

Two days later, the police chief ordered all his men to go to Sakhvid, including the officer who now lived in Fereydun's home. A few hours later, a Muslim woman by the name of Khavar, who had Baha'i relatives in Hurmuzak, emerged in the village square in Shakhvid, wailing in lament that the Baha'is were destroying Islam. A crowd gathered around her. They armed themselves with rods, shafts, and clubs, mounted horses and donkeys, and marched off towards Hurmuzak led by Khavar and her son Reza. Drums and cymbals accompanied them, as if they were performing the traditional passion plays commemorating the death of Imam Husain. The police had already reached Sakhvid, but made no attempt to prevent the looming violence.

When the crowd reached Hurmuzak, one of Fereydun's nephews, Hedayatollah, who heard the uproar, came out of his house to see what was going on. On seeing him, Reza struck a violent blow to his neck with the sharp edge of a shovel. Injured, Hedayatollah fled to Fereydun's home, followed by the crowd. They stormed the house and broke down the door. Fereydun's wife, a sixty-year-old woman, came down the stairs to see what was going on. The crowd attacked and killed her with a massive mace.

Some went upstairs and dragged down Fereydun, who had two broken legs in plaster. They killed him with the same weapon, then attacked and killed his brother-in-law. Fereydun's seventy-year-old brother rushed out of his neighboring home to see what was happening. They killed him with knives and clubs. In the meantime, another group looted the house. The mob swarmed the upper floor, ransacking the wardrobes, and found a young boy whose mother had hidden him there. They threw him out the window, and the crowd in the street below split his head open with a rock. In another wardrobe, they found his brother, the boy who had first been injured in the neck. They beat him, covered him with a blanket soaked in kerosene, and set him alight.

They set fire to the house and even to the beehives. They seized two mules that had not managed to escape and slit open their bellies with knives. The crowd set off for Sakhvid in a celebratory mood. On the way, they ran into another of Fereydun's nephews, who was returning from the fields, oblivious to what had happened. They attacked and killed him too.

After the mob left, the few remaining family members who had hidden in a furnace and a well came out to survey the bloody scene. Fereydun's niece, Manzar Amiri, who had already lost two of her brothers, found some sign of life in Hedayatollah, who had been burnt in the kerosene-soaked blanket. At that moment, two policemen arrived. Manzar begged them to help save her brother. They promised to go and bring help, but they never returned. It was not until the next afternoon that the police chief and his men finally arrived in Hurmuzak to inspect the results of what they had helped to provoke.[10]

Another example is the events that occurred in Hesar, a mountainous area forty kilometers north of Turbat-e-Haydariyyeh in northeastern Iran.[11] From the early days of the Babi and Baha'i movements, many people in that area embraced the religion and were persecuted for it. The broadcasts during the month of Ramadan in 1955 fanned the flames of old conflicts, and the village *mullah* goaded the people into harassing the Baha'is. The attacks gradually intensified.

On January 19, 1956, five Baha'is were seized. Mule saddles were tied to their backs, ropes were fastened around their necks, and they were paraded around the streets while the villagers kicked them. The next day, people raided the home of 'Ata'ollah Azimi, fired shots, and then set fire to the house. That day, they also looted the home of an elderly woman named Mah-Pari Qaffari. Other Baha'i homes were entered under the pretext of inspection, and robbed.

On January 21, organized mobs raided the homes of the five men who had been paraded through the village, and arrested them. Fifteen more Baha'i men were seized from their homes. The crowd tied ropes around their necks, and insulted and beat them while they led them to the mosque. There they tried to force them to recant and to curse what they held sacred. The following day, gangs attacked Baha'i women in the streets and the bazaar. Forty-six women were seized and tortured horribly before being taken to the mosque to recant their faith. Some had bells tied around them and were dragged through town with the hostile crowd jeering at them. Several prominent citizens arranged for guards to keep watch around Hisar and the roads to Mashhad so the Baha'is could not escape from the village and appeal for justice. They were warned that if they complained, they would forfeit their properties, their honor, and their lives.

The lack of any response from the gendarmes increased the mobs' boldness. On the night of February 4, a man named Hasan Eshaqi went to the home of 'Ata'ollah Azimi and threatened and insulted his wife Zinat. He placed a knife to her throat, threatened to kill her, and then raped her. The following day, the distressed woman complained to the provisional police station and to officer Naseri. No action was taken. Similar events continued throughout February and March of that year. Eventually, several Baha'is managed to leave the village one night and reached Mashhad and Kashmar on side-roads to ask for help from the authorities. No action was taken and the harassment continued. Finally, news of the situation reached the governor-general and gendarmerie chief for the province, and the persecution in Hesar subsided on government orders.

In Tehran, the government decided on a military occupation of the National Baha'i Center, ostensibly to reduce tensions that had been sparked by the Ramadan broadcasts but in fact to collaborate further with the clergy. The Baha'i Center was not a place of worship, but simply a building used for administrative affairs of the community. Located on Hafez Avenue in northern Tehran, it consisted of a large building surrounded by a vast garden of over seven acres, filled with trees and flowers—hence its name *Haziratul-Quds*, or "paradise." Adjacent to the center was another plot of land with volleyball, basketball, and tennis courts. The building itself contained a number of meeting halls and a library of several thousand volumes. The largest of the halls, under the building's dome, accommodated several hundred people. The dome was designed in the Safavid style and exquisitely decorated on both the exterior and the interior, which was painted with peacocks fanning their tails over the expansion of the arc. Decorative plasterwork by master craftsmen covered the entire building, which was considered an outstanding example of Iranian architecture.

Every afternoon, members of the *Fada'iyan-e Islam* together with youths from the bazaar gathered in front of the entrance shouting invocations to the Prophet and Imams, and chanting the call to prayer. At times they would harass people who entered the garden surrounding the building. Some evenings they cut off the electricity, disrupting meetings that were being held. The military governor of Tehran, General Teymur Bakhtiar, gave the order for the occupation on

May 7, 1955, which concluded with a request to the populace to keep order and refrain from arbitrary incitement.

After the occupation of the center, hundreds of people from all strata of society would enter the building to perform their daily prayers. Various organizations and groups sent letters of congratulation and appreciation to the shah, and the streets and shops were lit up in celebration. Ayatollah Behbehani and other religious authorities sent cables expressing their gratitude to the shah and congratulations to each other.[12]

Ayatollah Boroujerdi also wrote an open letter of thanks to Falsafi, published in the newspaper *Ettela'at*:

> I would like to respectfully say that the valuable services that you have rendered in the past few days to the sacred Religion of Islam, nay rather, to the Supreme of all Religions; and to the Holy Quran, nay rather, to the Supreme of all holy and heavenly Books; as well as to the freedom of the nation, towards the safeguarding of the monarchy, the government, the army, as well as all the population of Iran and the entire Muslim world... has been a source of great joy for this humble one as well as for all the Muslims, and even has brought joy to His Holiness the Lord of the Age Himself – may our souls be a sacrifice for Him.[13]

Boroujerdi goes on to describe the activities of the Baha'is as political endeavors, and suggests that Baha'is should therefore be dismissed from government offices.

Following the occupation of the center in Tehran, the clergy attempted to pass certain bills in the parliament to make circumstances as difficult as possible for the Baha'is. Both public and closed sessions of the parliament debated these bills. The content of the debates consisted mainly of accusations leveled against the Baha'is, and the members' attempts to excel each other in recounting their anti-Baha'i activities. Other members of parliament were silent and watched in wonder. On 10 May 1955, the member for Qazvin, Seyyed Ahmad Safai—the only member of parliament who was a clergyman—presented a bill that was supported by Ayatollah Boroujerdi. It contained four clauses:

> Clause 1: The corrupt community of the Babis and their affiliations, whether Azalis or Baha'is, are regarded as a threat to the national security and must be pronounced illegal.
> Clause 2: From now on, membership in this community, any display of its beliefs, or any association with it, in whatever possible manner, will be considered an offence punishable by two to ten years of solitary confinement, as well as the deprivation of all civil rights.
> Clause 3: All properties pertaining to the gathering centers or the associated organizations of this community, or any properties that the income obtained thereof is spent on the activities of this community, will be turned over to the Ministry of Culture to be utilized for the founding of [Islamic] educational institutions, and the dissemination of religious studies and doctrines of worship.
> Clause 4: Any members of this community currently employed in government organizations or any of their associated offices, will be dismissed from this date onwards and may not be re-employed under any circumstances.

While parliament debated Safai's bill, telegrams were pouring in from clergy all over the country, stating that they considered the bill's approval to be the duty of members of parliament to Islam.

The proposed bill was, however, strongly opposed by 'Alam, the interior minister. It contained points that were in conflict with the constitution as well as international treaties that Iran was bound by. International organizations were also exerting increasing pressure on Iran regarding its treatment of the Baha'is. Although Safai's bill was rejected in the end, members of parliament made constant assurances in their speeches that sufficient laws existed for combating the Baha'is, that the government would take the required measures, and that there was no need for new legislation. Dr Parviz Natel-Khanlari, a university professor and well-known literary scholar who at the time served as 'Alam's deputy minister, stated in an interview with *Ettela'at*:

> Putting a stop to the activities of this sect is nothing new, inasmuch as, consistent with the regulations of the country, such a sect is not recognized in Iran. In 1950/1329 SH, the Prime Minister (General 'Ali Razmara) issued an order to the Interior Minister (Mohsen Nasr), instructing him to advise the governors and the governor-generals that state officials are not permitted to mention the name of the Baha'i sect in their correspondence, for such a sect is not officially recognized in Iran.[14]

The speaker of the parliament, Sardar Fakher Hekmat, was also not eager to approve the bill. He kept insisting that the Baha'i issue was a matter for the administration and not the parliament.

Meanwhile, the disturbances were intensifying in towns and villages across the country. In Shiraz, several raids were made on the house where the Bab was born, and much damage was inflicted. Finally, to restore order, the government used the armed forces to seize the Baha'i centers in all towns. The centers in Isfahan and Ahvaz were occupied at midnight on May 15, 1955. *Keyhan* reported: "The *Haziratul-Quds* of Isfahan covered an area of seven thousand square meters, and a large edifice to seat five thousand people was under construction. After the occupation of the *Haziratul-Quds* in Ahvaz people raised a banner on top of the building with the words 'Victory comes from God and the conquest is nigh.'"[15] Baha'i centers in Shiraz, Bandar-Pahlavi, and other towns were also occupied by the armed forces.

The Baha'i community strongly protested in writing to the shah's court, the parliament, the governor-generals, and other authorities. They pointed out that Falsafi's accusations were all unfounded, and they requested that the government take action to prevent the unfortunate events that he had instigated. No reply was ever given to any of these letters. Similar letters were sent to the newspapers, and were never published. The numerous reports received in the capital from all over the country about the pillage, arson, and harassment of the Baha'is were not covered by the press, nor were they mentioned in parliament.

Very few found the courage or the strength to swim against the current. The governor-general of Fars, Major Himmat, was one of those who stood up against the anti-Baha'i rioters and troublemakers. As a result, he was accused of being a Baha'i and dismissed from his post.[16]

The injured and distressed Baha'is who had lost their livelihood in towns and villages all over the country headed to the capital in hopes of finding refuge there. They were sheltered in the homes of other Baha'is, and treated at the Baha'i-run Misaghieh Hospital and other health centers.

Provincial and city governors reported the unrest to the capital, where the government feared the disturbances could lead to a revolt and political uprising. On May 17, Interior Minister ʻAlam proposed a bill to parliament that would authorize the provincial and city governors to suppress all anti-religious action. Because the bill did not explicitly specify the Baha'is, several deputies objected. Finally, Dr Shahkar, a member of parliament, proposed an amendment that would incorporate the four-article bill previously put forward by Safai. He presented the following addition to the bill that ʻAlam had proposed:

> The formation of sects which, under the guise of religion, spread disorder, and which have adopted the name of Baha'ism in order to implement political objectives is proscribed, inasmuch as their existence is illegal and the cause of the dissolution of order and security; and since they contradict the true religion of Islam.[17]

This clause did not survive in the government's final bill, though it would reappear later, along with many other more onerous regulations, under the Islamic Republic. In the parliament's session of

May 18, 1955, while reporting the occupation of the Baha'i centers in other towns, 'Alam, the interior minister, stated:

> The government authorities will most vigorously prevent any disruptive or corrupt activities. Local authorities have been ordered to take measures to dissolve the organizations causing religious and secular sedition, and those that are a disruption to the national security.

His orders to local authorities were clear:

> You should severely suppress any action that is taken under the pretext of fighting misleading sects [i.e. Baha'is] or that incites the people against the security of the country. This applies to those who commit any act that may inflict even the slightest damage to public security and national order. . . in which cases measures are to be taken according to the provisions of the criminal code.[18]

One of the reporters hands a pickaxe to General Batmanqelij to photograph him demolishing the dome of the Baha'i Center in Tehran.

Throughout this time, the authorities debated what should be done with the confiscated buildings. They first considered purchasing them from the Baha'i community. Aside from the fact that this would have been rejected by the Baha'i community, such an act would in itself be an acknowledgement of the Baha'i community as a legal entity. Others suggested that the buildings be converted into mosques, but this would mean mosques being built on seized property. Finally it was decided to demolish the center in Tehran.

During the last days of Ramadan a crowd composed of: General Batmanqelij, the chief of army staff; General Bakhtiar, the military commander of Tehran; the preacher Falsafi; and a number of reporters and journalists inspected the demolition of the building. It was during this visit that General Batmanqelij used a pickaxe to inflict several blows on the dome. The journal *Taraqqi* reported:

> A large crowd had gathered around the *Haziratul-Quds*. As the general public was not permitted entry, people were climbing over each other to see what was happening inside the building... Some fifty laborers and workmen were busy demolishing the pillars around the dome with sledgehammers and pickaxes, but the building was so solid that it could not be destroyed... The tearing down of the bricks, the columns, the demolishing of the foundation and structure of an edifice fortified with metal beams, needed welding equipment... it was decided that same Sunday to ask the military engineering guild for its large cranes. . . An hour after the commencement of the demolition work, a few men arrived with a green flag, and with the permission of Mr Hariri, the commanding officer for the soldiers in that area, they raised the green banner on the top of the edifice. The words on the flag read: "The Hand of God is above all hands."[19]

Following the complete demolition of the dome, the building was left without a roof for some time. A tin roof later replaced the dome to prevent rain and snow entering the building. Subsequently, the offices of General Bakhtiar and the military government of Tehran were

Hojjat al-Islam Falsafi participating in the demolition of the dome of the *Haziratul-Quds*.

moved to the *Haziratul-Quds*. The Baha'i properties that were confiscated by the authorities in other towns were either closed down or similarly used by the local authorities.

The orders from the Interior Ministry led to a decrease in the most visible of anti-Baha'i activities. Another factor that influenced the reduction in the attacks was the international Baha'i community's action in coordinating communications from all areas of the world where Baha'is resided: Thousands of cables were sent to the shah, the administration, and the parliament. These cables voiced the international Baha'i community's protests and decried the actions of the Iranian government as a violation of human rights and contrary to the Charter of the United Nations. Meanwhile, Baha'is in different countries contacted their own governments, requesting them to raise objections in international assemblies against the actions of the Iranian government towards a religious minority. The events in Iran were reflected in the world media, and the news, often accompanied by a photo of General Batmanqelij taking a pickaxe to the dome, brought the persecution of the Baha'is to the world's attention.

Until that time, the name "Baha'i" had been relatively unknown outside Iran. This exposure, however, was a challenge for the Iranian government. With the new revenue available after the nationalization of the oil company, the shah planned to undertake a series of fundamental development projects. He did not want foreign countries to perceive Iran as aggressive and religiously intolerant. The country was in dire need of Western investment and technical knowledge, which would not be forthcoming unless he could provide a secure environment. For this reason the shah's government did not entirely fulfill the clergy's demands concerning the Baha'is, but tried to cover up the situation as much as possible.

Ayatollah Boroujerdi was disappointed with the outcome of the anti-Baha'i campaign, and his relationship with the government and the shah's court began to deteriorate. His requests were ignored and he became suspicious and disheartened.[20] A schism that arose among the clergy in Qom at this time, with a group led by Ayatollah Sadr challenging Boroujerdi, also contributed to the Baha'i issue fading from prominence for reasons that had nothing to do with the Baha'is themselves.

Two years later, the groundwork was prepared for the restoration of all the Baha'i centers that had been closed. With the ending of military rule in Tehran and the establishment of the Organization of Intelligence and National Security (SAVAK), the office of the military government that was situated in the former Baha'i Center shut down, and only a few soldiers remained on the premises. Finally, on November 3, 1957, the center was quietly returned to the Baha'is on the condition that no meetings be held there. The Baha'i community respected that commitment, and the *Haziratul-Quds* of Tehran was never again used for public gatherings.

After the Islamic Revolution, the center was once again taken over by the government. Hojjat al-Islam Falsafi was honored for his services to Islam and his memoirs were published. The years following the revolution witnessed the posthumous publication of Asadollah 'Alam's diaries. He wrote about Falsafi:

> I went to some traditional lamentation meetings on a few evenings. In one of those Muhammad Taqi Falsafi was preaching from the pulpit. This clergy has a prolonged record. To start with, he is a very skillful preacher; secondly, he has a very good memory; third, when speaking, he has a truly mesmeric and appealing voice. But, he is the most corrupt of men. He is a filthy person. Despite his apparent devotion to Islam, he is among the most decadent of people. He smokes opium; he drinks, but outwardly he seems very decent. . . When I was Prime Minister, he became the leader of the clergy and the feudalists against the reform plans of the Shah, until the riots of 5 June [1963]/16 Khurdad happened. . . I then arrested and imprisoned him. While in prison, he only asked me for vodka and opium. I sent them to him.[21]

PART TWO

The Islamic Republic in Confrontation with the Baha'i Faith

The revolutionary ideals of freedom and justice that led the Iranian people to overthrow the shah in 1979 were in stark contrast to the reality that ensued with the Islamic Republic's repression of the Baha'is and other progressive groups. It was a repression that bore no resemblance to freedom and justice, and that began its violence in the first hours of the victory of the revolution. Millions of people who had been shouting slogans in demonstrations in the streets would remain silent in the face of the inordinate cruelty of the regime towards a religious minority. None of the political groups, including the Communist Tudeh Party, which allied itself with Khomeini during the first few years of the revolution, ever raised a single objection to the crackdown on the Baha'is.

Eliz Sanasarian, a professor of political science at the University of Southern California who has specialized in the sociology of non-Muslim communities in Iran, identifies several factors that characterized the reality of life for Iran's religious minorities: their numbers are not large, and unlike some of Iran's ethnic minorities, they make no claim to a distinct portion of Iran's territory, nor are they regarded as outsiders, they identify as Iranians and are affected by changes in national ideology, education, and economic well-being. Having experienced severe persecution in the past, they were obedient subjects of the modern centralized government during the Pahlavi era, always aware of the menacing alternative. Such factors naturally led to upward social mobility and improved social conditions for the Baha'i community, as well as other non-Muslim minorities, during the Pahlavi era.[1] The Islamic Republic targeted the Baha'is for persecution by identifying them as the elite of the shah's regime, and this label was applied even to Baha'i factory employees and farmers. The fact that the shah's personal physician had been a Baha'i became an excuse for harassing and massacring innocent individuals who had never so much as heard that physician's name. As Sanasarian notes:

> The Baha'is represented everything that it was sanctioned (by the state, the Ulama, the Muslim community, and the secular, even Western-educated) to hate – namely, apostasy, association with the West and Israel, pro-monarchism, and an elite club bent on self-promotion and propaganda. . . In contrast to other non-Muslim minorities, the Baha'is have been spread throughout the country in villages, small towns, and various cities, fueling the paranoia of the prejudiced.[2]

The persecution of the Baha'is was made to seem natural following a century and a half of negative propaganda from the clergy. Baha'i children were regarded as unclean and as outsiders even by their playmates, who were only reflecting the outlook of their families. Fanatical teachers who harassed Baha'i students as a supposed religious duty also served as role models for their non-Baha'i students.

From the earliest days of their faith, the Babis and Baha'is had been subject to attacks by the clergy and the state, which resembled other historical clashes between established religious authorities and innovative or reformist movements. After Iran's revolution and the establishment of the Islamic Republic, these attacks not only took on a new intensity and a greater reach, they also assumed a different structure.

The Baha'is were accused of having ties to foreign powers such as Russia, Britain, Zionism and Israel—illogical allegations that came in the guise of facts. The accusation claiming the Baha'i faith to be a creation of, and supported by, foreign powers has no evidence to support it. In the logic of the Islamic Republic, any measures taken by foreign governments during recent years in defense of the human rights of the Baha'is only fuel this fallacy. But progressive concerns for human rights are not limited to the Baha'is, and they do not represent the support of foreign powers for the Baha'is.

At a time when the Islamic Republic intends to eradicate all signs of the Baha'i faith in Iran and distort its history, it becomes necessary to identify the patterns of persecution adopted by the regime as a step towards a full description of these crimes in the future.

Chapter 9

Baha'i Persecution during the Last Days of the Shah's Regime

Demonstrations against the shah began in the fall of 1977 and grew steadily, with opposition coming together as an ad hoc alliance of Shi'i clergy, secular progressives, and leftist factions, including the Communist Tudeh Party and various Islamic leftist groups, each with their own motives and priorities. Ayatollah Khomeini provided charismatic leadership from a distance—first from Iraq, where he had lived in exile since the 1960s, and in the final months from France, where his access to the international press contributed to the increasing speed of events. The shah's responses to the growing demonstrations were conciliatory, if not vacillating. After escalating violence in November 1978, the shah imposed a temporary government under General Azhari, but the military response was, for the most part, restrained. The beginning of the Shi'i mourning period of Moharram fueled tensions further, until several millions were partaking in demonstrations. The shah appointed one of the more moderate opposition leaders, Shapour Bakhtiar, as prime minister, and left the country in January 1979, pending a referendum planned for the spring on whether the nation would continue as a monarchy or republic.

During the final weeks and hours of the shah's regime, amid the chaos and instability of a revolution in full flow, the Iranian Baha'i community was subject to a new wave of persecution. This time, the attacks did not originate with the clergy, but with SAVAK, the shah's secret police, who were supported by the army in some areas, as part of the regime's last efforts to hold onto power.

Historically, there has been a pattern that attacks on Iran's Baha'i community escalate during periods of turbulent change in the country. During the Qajar period, in the aftermath of the assassination of Naser al-Din Shah, Baha'is were attacked in many towns and villages under the pretext that the assassin was a Babi. The extent and intensity of the assaults were such that the prime minister saw fit to send telegrams nationwide assuring the populace that the assassin was not a Babi. A similar wave of persecution swept over the Baha'i community during the Constitutional Revolution of 1906. The pretext varied with the political viewpoint of the attacker, either accusing the Baha'is of supporting the revolution or of being against it. Likewise, in the transition from the Qajar to the Pahlavi dynasty, widespread killings of Baha'is took place in Tehran and other cities. The American vice-consul, Major Imbrie, was murdered by a mob that gathered when someone accused the foreigner taking photographs of a local religious endowment, *Saqqa-khaneh,* of being a Baha'i. Martial law halted the violence in Tehran, but it continued in other towns and villages throughout the country.

This pattern of increased aggression during periods of instability was repeated at the end of Muhammad Reza Pahlavi's rule. In the final months, just before the Islamic Revolution claimed victory, those in control of the nation's security forces planned to thwart the movement by diverting public attention towards a religious uprising that targeted the Baha'is. Up to that point, the rhetoric of Ayatollah Khomeini's efforts to mobilize the revolution emphasized social justice and had not alienated secular and progressive allies. SAVAK calculated that by inciting a wave of religious persecution against the Baha'is, and by linking that persecution to the Shi'i sentiments that were feeding the revolution, they could cause the movement to be perceived by secular intellectuals as extremist and religious. The intent was to dissuade the more progressive demographic from joining the revolution, and buy time for the shah's regime to seek a solution to its desperate situation. Given the longstanding enmity toward the Baha'i community, it would be easy enough to bribe a few local clergy to stir up attacks.

These attacks, which continued for a year in some areas, took the form of beatings, raids on Baha'i homes, and setting fire to their houses and harvests. Incidents were reported in over fifty towns and cities across the country, but we will focus on two examples in the province of Fars.

The village of Sa'diyeh, on the outskirts of Shiraz where the tomb of the poet Sa'di is located, had developed into a modern suburb where Muslims and Baha'is, often from the same families, lived side by side. In the winter of 1978, mobs of men and youths rallied in the streets in the evenings, shouting insults at the Baha'is and threatening to tear down their homes. During the Muslim holy month of Muharram, when religious sentiment runs high, a *mullah* by the name of Zebarjadi delivered provocative sermons in the Jami' Mosque, inciting the public to demolish the Baha'i cemetery. A mob raided the cemetery, uprooted trees, broke open graves, pulled out corpses that had been buried just days earlier, and set them on fire. They then burnt down the cemetery's hall.

Around 6pm on December 13, an angry mob entered a dead-end alley where a few Baha'i families lived. They gathered in front of the house of Sefatollah Fahandezh, an army officer and the chairman of the Local Baha'i Assembly, hurled insults and yelled that they had come to abduct his daughter. Armed military guards present in the street took no action to disperse the crowd. Fahandezh went to the rooftop with his children and brothers and pleaded with the people to disperse. A few men started to climb the walls of the house, and Fahandezh fired a shotgun into the air in warning. Shots were fired from the crowd as well, and several people were injured or killed. The medical coroner of the Sa'diyeh hospital later reported that those killed had been shot by G3 guns, a model used only by the military guards. None of the fatal shots were fired by Fahandezh's shotgun.[1]

At 5am the following morning a large gang broke into the house and looted the premises as well as the homes and shops of many other

Baha'is. Sefatollah Fahandezh was killed in that raid. After each looting, a new gang would raid the house to ransack whatever remained. All doors, windows, water and electricity meters—even power sockets—were stripped. Finally, the buildings were set on fire. The raids continued for a few days: a total of 700 shops were looted, 171 houses were burnt down, and 131 more homes were plundered and demolished. To intensify the frenzy of the mob, forty corpses wrapped in shrouds were taken from the morgue in Shiraz and lined up in front of the Sa'diyeh hospital, with the claim that they were killed by the Baha'is.

The lootings and arson were fully supported by the army. Eyewitnesses testified that army trucks transported youths to the Pepsi-Cola factory that was said to be owned by a Baha'i, and encouraged them to vandalize the building and set it on fire. As the violence continued, military guards watched on and made no effort to intervene or make arrests. A police officer who was observing the events from a nearby tea house was asked to intervene; he replied that it was not yet time.

Through the intervention of the governor of Fars province, who appealed to Ayatollah Mahallati and other clergy of Shiraz, the incident was confined to the Sa'diyeh neighborhood and did not spread to the city of Shiraz, as no doubt its instigators had hoped.[2] The clergy had recognized that the mob action was incited by SAVAK with the ultimate intention of driving a wedge between the secular and religious wings of the revolution. They responded by declaring attacks on the homes and livelihoods of the Baha'is as unlawful.

In Shiraz, the Ayatollahs Mahallati and Dastgheyb made efforts to quiet the situation. Mahallati's son was dispatched to Sa'diyeh to urge calm. In a series of statements released in December and January, Ayatollah Mahallati denied that Muslims had any malicious intentions towards the Baha'is of Sa'diyeh, and that it was solely the "authorities" whose negligence and provocation had led to the attacks. He urged Muslims to refrain from giving any excuse to opportunists, and to abstain from any assault on the lives or belongings of the religious minorities. Any such action, he declared, was "harmful for the Islamic movement and forbidden under the present circumstances." (Obviously, circumstances could change and the ban was not a matter of principle.) At the same time circulars were being distributed throughout Shiraz encouraging people to kill the Baha'is and pillage their homes, and calling into question Ayatollah Mahallati's religious authority for his statements urging non-violence against the Baha'is.

Iraj Mehrzad, the member of parliament for Shiraz, accused the government of General Azhari, then interim prime minister, and SAVAK of being responsible for the events in Shiraz, and gave a detailed account of the acts of demolition and arson that he had witnessed, though the broadcast of his statements was suppressed. Interviews with Ayatollah Khomeini, in which he cautioned people against the looting and demolition of homes on the grounds that they were harmful to the Islamic movement, were widely circulated among the general public. During anti-regime demonstrations where hundreds of thousands of protestors rallied in the streets of Tehran, new banners were added to the previous slogans, reading: "*Baha'i brother, we are not against you*", and "*Baha'i, an equal, a brother*".

The plan of SAVAK and the army to divert the course of the revolution was not ultimately successful, but any hope that a more enlightened attitude toward the Baha'is was surfacing would be eclipsed by events of the next decades as the Islamic Republic hardened its position.

In the meantime, hundreds of Baha'i families had lost their livelihoods. Many were given shelter at the Baha'i Center in Shiraz and others took refuge in other Baha'is' homes. Once the outcome of revolution was no longer in doubt, the situation changed completely. The Revolutionary Guards and local mobs, led by the clergy, once again attacked the Baha'is. Revolutionary Guards occupied the Baha'i Center in Shiraz, and those who had taken refuge there were forced out. Some returned to their demolished houses, a few were given refuge in Muslim and Armenian homes, and others left town. Hundreds of homeless Baha'i families found themselves displaced throughout the country and facing hardships that would become normal and entrenched for decades.[3]

A second account of the anti-Baha'i violence during the early period of the revolution is taken from a report published by the Baha'i community on events in the mountainous region of Fars inhabited by the Boyer-Ahmad tribe.[4]

The tribe consists of eleven clans; most of those members of the tribe who follow the Baha'i faith belong to the Sadat-e Mahmudi clan. On January 12, 1979, a few hundred non-Baha'i members of the Sadat-e Mahmudi clan raided the hamlet of Guruzeh, where eight families dwelt, six of whom were Baha'is. They hurled insults, fired shots, and threw stones at them, burnt the fences around their houses, and wrecked the village mill. The Baha'i families escaped into the mountains in the confusion of the sudden attack and returned to their homes the next morning.

The attacks continued for six nights and escalated on the final night when the mill was burnt to the ground, homes were looted and destroyed, cattle stolen, the fields damaged, and orchards uprooted. The attackers then started shooting and one Baha'i was injured. The Baha'is took refuge in the village of Darreh-Shur, where forty out of the forty-eight households were Baha'i. The inhabitants of Darreh-Shur were also attacked, and the mob was so frenetic that two Muslim families were caught up in the violence and had to flee into the mountains with the Baha'is. Their belongings were later returned to them, whereas the Baha'is were forced to leave the ruins of their homes, their cattle, and their fields to the looters. The nightly raids and the daily threats and insults continued for two months and spread to eight more neighboring villages.

Here was a tribe whose people had lived in harmony for generations, who suddenly found their social ties and customs shattered. The revolution unleashed both religious frenzy and opportunistic greed, and granted license not only to those who looked to the promise of rewards in the hereafter, but also to their neighbors' healthy cattle and fruitful lands. The tribal culture of the Boyer-Ahmad places a high value on courage and loyalty, including the defense of family and clan. The fact that the Baha'is of the tribe did not retaliate under attack shows the extent of their belief in a commitment to non-violence.

The situation of the Baha'is both here and in the rest the country grew worse with the victory of the revolution and Khomeini's return to Iran. After two months of armed attacks, the Baha'i families of Guruzeh and Darreh-Shur fled, leaving everything behind, and sought refuge in the village of Kata, which consisted of seventy-eight households where all but ten were Baha'i. Each Baha'i family of the village received and cared for a number of the refugees. As the numbers grew in Kata, they too were attacked and the raids grew in violence. Orchards were destroyed, the village mill was set on fire, and nightly raids and gunshots terrorized the inhabitants. On five occasions, a number of *mullahs* came to Kata and warned the Baha'is to recant their faith and embrace Islam if they wanted to save their lives and properties.

A few weeks after the general referendum in which the people of Iran voted for an Islamic Republic, the persecution entered a new stage. The arrival of Habib Bahadur, a well-known tribal leader, brought some hope. He convinced the Baha'is to gather a large sum of money to pay off the assailants, and thus settle the conflict, only to pocket the money himself. The next day, May 4, 1979, his own gunmen joined the attackers, and fierce gunfire broke out. Several Baha'is were injured and a woman was killed. Finally, the Baha'is met and decided to send a delegation to the attackers. They asked for time to gather their wives and daughters who had dispersed outside the village, before making a collective decision whether to recant their faith, abandon their village, or face death. They were given a five-day grace period. In that time, they sent a messenger to Isfahan to consult with the Local Assembly there, who advised them to come to the city immediately.

They made the journey on hazardous mountain roads in heavy rain. With little means of transport, they carried as many of their belongings as they could manage. The first convoy of exhausted refugees from the Boyer-Ahmad tribe arrived at the Isfahan Baha'i Center in the evening of May 7, 1979. Preparations had been made for their arrival, and blankets, food and other provisions awaited them. One person had died en route as a result of injuries from being severely beaten. Several were injured or sick. Three women gave birth prematurely soon after their arrival. The Baha'i Center could not accommodate their large numbers, so the men were transferred to a desert campsite at Mihyar near Isfahan where tents were set up. The women and children, as well as the old and the infirm, remained in the Baha'i Center. A group of local Baha'is took care of the refugees' needs and cooked for them.

Soon armed men from the local Komiteh, or "revolutionary committee," arrived at the Baha'i Center. They roughly arrested the members of the group taking care of the refugees, and commanded the tribal group to vacate the premises within twenty-four hours and to leave the city within seventy-two hours. Two hours later, another group of gunmen arrived. They assaulted the Baha'is with their rifle butts, threatened and insulted them, and evicted them from the Baha'i Center, counter to all assurances given by the government.

The sick and injured were taken into the homes of individual Baha'i families, and the others joined the men in the camp, where numbers now reached 1,200. As soon as the basics of food and shelter were organized, a school program was begun in the campsite, along with adult classes. Doctors among the refugees set up a simple dispensary.[5]

The Baha'i community tells stories of remarkable acts of courage during this time. Two weeks after the desert camp was set up, a number of Revolutionary Guards abruptly entered the grounds, accompanied by a clergyman who used a loudspeaker to denigrate the Baha'i community, the faith, and its founders. The Baha'is spoke up and countered the accusations. Finally, one of the gunmen asked who the teacher was in this camp. One of the crowd led a young child forward and said, "This is one of our teachers." He then took the loudspeaker and held it for the child who calmly chanted a prayer as the crowd listened in silence. The young child's courage and devotion had an impact on the soldiers. After a momentary silence, one of them gently said that they had come to the camp merely to see if the Baha'is needed anything. After that, they left the campsite and led the clergyman away.

The Mehyar campsite functioned for nearly three months until mid-July 1979. At that point, the influential *mullah* of the region who had instigated the anti-Baha'i persecution was disgraced by the revolutionary authorities and removed for reasons totally unrelated to the Baha'is. The Baha'is were then able to return to their burnt down homes in their villages, but they continued to be subject to harassment and attacks during the course of the revolution, and at times were imprisoned and tortured. Finally, they gradually decided to leave Iran. Hundreds of Baha'i families of the Boyer-Ahmad tribe are living today in Nashville, Tennessee, in the United States. While robbed of their traditional tribal lives, they have safeguarded their beliefs and cherish the hope of returning some day to their homeland.

Chapter 10

The Baha'is—the First Victims of Oppression in the Islamic Republic

With the shah having left Iran in a chaotic state, Prime Minister Bakhtiar invited Ayatollah Khomeini to return from exile. Bakhtiar envisioned a coalition government with the Ayatollah playing an advisory role from Qom—the Shi'i equivalent of the Vatican. But the fervor of the welcome from several million Iranians who greeted Ayatollah Khomeini on his arrival in Tehran on February 1, 1979, put the country on another course. Within days, Khomeini had denounced Bakhtiar for his links to the shah and established the basis of an Islamic government, appointing Mehdi Bazargan as interim prime minister.

In its first months, the vast majority of Iranians hailed the revolution's triumph as the fulfillment of a long-awaited hope for a government based on social justice. Even during Bakhtiar's brief transition, political prisoners had been freed, press censorship lifted, and the shah's secret police disbanded. Iran's Baha'i community viewed the rapid stream of events with a mixture of fear and hope. Many, especially the young, were caught up in the prevailing optimism, believing that conditions would improve following the revolution, and that religious tolerance and democracy would unite all the peoples of Iran under a common banner. Ayatollah Khomeini did not rush into giving his government a religious hue, even asking some of the clergy appointed to high posts to dress in ordinary attire. Although his anti-Baha'i sentiments and the accusations in his earlier writings and sermons linking Baha'is with Zionist espionage were well-known, the new transparency promised by the breakdown of old institutions led many Baha'is to believe that once the revolutionary authorities gained access to the previous regime's documents they would see that past accusations against the Baha'is had been groundless. Likewise, although Prime Minister Bazargan was known to his students at the School of Engineering for his anti-Baha'i sentiments, many Baha'is were hopeful that with his new responsibility to the nation as a whole, reason would prevail. The elders of the Baha'i community had experience enough to be distrustful, however, and did not hide their misgivings. Events during the transition and beyond would confirm their fears.

An interview that Khomeini granted to Professor James Cockcroft of Rutgers University prior to his return to Iran from Paris foretold the loss of the Baha'is' meager rights as Iranian citizens. In reply to the question whether the Islamic government would grant religious and political freedom to the Baha'is, Khomeini stated, "They are a political faction; they are harmful. They will not be accepted," and further denied they would be allowed to practice their religion.[1] This brief statement laid out in essence what would become the Islamic regime's policy towards the Baha'is. Soon after Khomeini's return to Iran, the Islamic Republic's spokesman in the United States reassured American Jews that religious minorities would retain full political, cultural, and religious rights in Iran. However, he emphasized that Baha'is would not receive the same rights as they were a political group and not religious.[2] Likewise, Prime Minister Bazargan, in one of his speeches, emphatically stated that Iranians of all ethnicities and religions would have equal civil rights in the new regime. The Baha'is, however, being identified as a political group, were not included.[3]

THE CONSTITUTION OF THE ISLAMIC REPUBLIC AND DENIAL OF CIVIL RIGHTS TO BAHA'IS

During the summer and autumn of 1979—a time marked by executions of officials from the shah's regime, fighting among various revolutionary factions, and the capture of the American hostages in the US Embassy—a special Assembly of Experts met to deliberate on the new constitution of the Islamic Republic of Iran.

The original draft proposed by Bazargan's provisional government, which was closely modeled on the secular 1906 constitution, was extensively revised by Ayatollah Montazeri, the chair of the Assembly, and by the vice-chairman, Ayatollah Beheshti. Their draft enshrined in law the Shi'i concept of *velayat-e faqih*, or the Guardianship of the Jurist, which entrusts to an Islamic jurist custody of the nation in the role of the Supreme Leader. It secured the dominance of the clergy and enforced strict Islamic law throughout the administration, especially in the educational and judicial systems. Women's rights that had been won over a century of struggle were disregarded, severe restrictions were imposed on religious minorities, and the Baha'is were denied any civil or human rights.

The provisions of the new constitution were of great concern to religious and ethnic minorities in Iran; their fate depended on them. Eliz Sanasarian offers a detailed account of the debates that played out among the seventy-three members of the Assembly, of whom fifty were clerics belonging to the Islamic Republic Party.[4] Barred from direct representation, the Baha'is approached the deputies of the officially recognized religious minorities—Zoroastrians, Armenian and Assyrian Christians, and Jews—who were included in the Assembly and asked them to speak on their behalf.

Ayatollah Beheshti, who controlled the proceedings, honored the rights of the non-Muslim deputies and allowed them to freely voice their opinions. He intervened frequently to head off criticism of the minority religions from the Muslim delegates, except in the case of the Baha'is. Any criticism of the Baha'is was permissible.

Debate arose over diverse articles relating to minority religions. The Sunni deputy from Baluchistan argued against the designation of the official state religion as Twelver Shi'i, and proposed that Iran should be declared an Islamic state without reference to Shi'i or Sunni. He noted that the Sunni minority was given less standing than the non-Muslim minorities. His concern foretold the discrimination and repression that Iranian Sunnis would face under the Islamic Republic, and the tensions between the Sunni minority, particularly in Baluchistan, and the central government.

Article 13 was debated at length. It identified Zoroastrian, Jewish, and Christian Iranians as the only recognized religious minorities, "who, within the limits of the law, are free to perform their religious rites and ceremonies, and to act according to their own canon in matters of personal affairs and religious education."[5]

In a long speech, the Armenian deputy appealed for the "recognition of the rights of all ethnic and religious communities" as well as "other religious denominations." The question of recognizing "other religions" was repeated by several of the minority deputies and has been interpreted as an indirect reference to the rights of the Baha'is. The majority of the Assembly did not yield to this view, and no mention of "other religions" was included in the constitution in its final form. Sanasarian believes that the exclusion of the Baha'is from all rights was definitely intended by those who prevailed.

Rustam Shahzadi, the delegate and head priest of the Zoroastrian community, set himself apart through his inclusive defense of all minorities equally. Framing this with a patriotic stance based on the Zoroastrian faith's unique historical and cultural connection with the land and its people, he protested against discriminatory practices such as the dismissal of non-Muslim teachers from schools and attacks by religious extremists on religious minorities' holy places. He made the case for interfaith understanding and for clerics to become better informed about religions other than their own.

The Jewish deputy, Danishrad, was in the most precarious position. A climate of fear and insecurity prevailed in the Jewish community and many were leaving the country. Meanwhile, in Israel there was public talk of probable military action against Iran if Jews there were harmed.[6] Danishrad directed all of his energy to convincing the assembly that he and his people were loyal citizens of Iran and avid anti-Israelis. He went so far as to call the constitution of the Islamic Republic "the most progressive constitution" in all Islamic and Christian nations.

The other religious minority deputies did not concur. Rustam Shahzadi boldly and frequently pointed out shortcomings in the constitution. The religious minorities, he said, were being treated as enemies who had just recently put down their arms and taken refuge under the protection of Islam. He noted that minorities were denied the presidency, the prime-ministership, ambassadorships, ministerial posts, and top-level military positions, and that the freedom to practice their religion was recognized only "within the limits of the law"—in other words, under Islamic regulations which remained undefined.

Sanasarian summarizes the situation for the Baha'is:

> Anti-Baha'ism was obvious throughout the proceedings. This was most apparent in haggling over every word and expression of certain articles to assure the exclusion of the Baha'is. For instance, Article 26 of the constitution addresses the right to form political parties, societies, and professional associations whether they be Islamic or belong to one of the recognized religious minorities. In the ensuing debates the original version referred to "official religious minorities." The speaker of the committee that had worked on the wording of the article explained that the expression was selected on purpose in order to ensure that the Baha'is would not be included. In another discussion over the issue of freedom of the press, a deputy commented that, if the press was allowed to operate freely, "the stray Baha'i sect" through their publications would "seduce" the people.[7]

Language designed to exclude the Baha'is appears even in an article that quotes the Quran on Islamic justice and equity towards non-Muslims:

> Article 14: In accordance with the sacred verse; "God does not forbid you to deal kindly and justly with those who have not fought against you because of your religion and who have not expelled you from your homes" [60:8], the government of the Islamic Republic

> of Iran and all Muslims are duty-bound to treat non-Muslims in conformity with ethical norms and the principles of Islamic justice and equity, and to respect their human rights. This principle applies to all who refrain from engaging in conspiracy or activity against Islam and the Islamic Republic of Iran.

The final sentence was crafted for the purpose of excluding the Baha'is from the rights granted to other non-Muslims. Given that conspiring or acting against Islam and the Islamic Republic of Iran is in itself a crime, even if committed by Muslims, the clause serves only to underline the Baha'is' status as outsiders, and a constant threat.[8] Artavaz Malikiyan explains the Quranic reference further:

> The language of Article 14 indicates that the framers of the constitution viewed religious minorities as equal to slaves or prisoners of war, and not as individuals with rights equal to those of Muslims. Ayatollah Mesbah Yazdi noted that granting minorities full citizenship rights implied the possibility of a Jewish or Zoroastrian president. "Such claims are even worse than cow-worshipping," he said.[9]

The constitution that was finally adopted by the Islamic Republic of Iran denies the followers of the Baha'i faith any civil rights or legal protection. It forbids Baha'is from holding government positions as well as non-governmental posts. It bars Baha'i students from entering universities and institutions of higher education. While marriage registrations are valid for members of the recognized religious minorities, and of course for Muslims, Baha'i marriages are not recognized, creating significant problems for families when it comes to obtaining birth certificates, applying for joint passports, and similar circumstances that require interaction with the law. The constitution treats Baha'is as aliens who have no right to live in Iran, and contains provisions through which any violence, atrocity, or violation of rights is legal if done in the name of Shi'i Islam and in its defense.

Chapter 11

The Persecution of Baha'is under Bazargan and the Revolutionary Council

The new constitution was approved in December 1979, just a month after Bazargan's provisional government collapsed following the takeover of the American Embassy in Tehran and the ensuing hostage crisis. Bazargan's efforts to release the captured American Embassy personnel were opposed by hardline Shi'i clerics. Unable to secure the hostages' release, Bazargan and his cabinet resigned on November 6, 1979, and a revolutionary council temporarily assumed the powers of government for the next ten months.

Even before the establishment of the interim government, harassment and persecution of the Baha'is began with the formation of the Komitehs. These autonomous committees, locally organized in mosques, schools, and workplaces, sprang up all across the country, with some 1,500 in Tehran alone. Armed and free from any legal restrictions, they consisted mainly of religious youth, including members of the Hojjatieh and other Islamic organizations, as well as opportunists. Some Komitehs dominated by Hojjatieh agents were dedicated entirely to harassing Baha'is, and went as far as creating private prisons and torture chambers for the purpose.

By raiding the Baha'i centers in Tehran and other cities, members of the anti-Baha'i Komitehs were able to seize documents and the Baha'i community's membership lists. Likewise, in attacks on Baha'i homes, documents, photographs and books were confiscated. There is evidence that the telephone lines of those serving in Baha'i institutions were tapped, and their activities and movements monitored. The Hojjatieh had begun seizing Baha'i community records under SAVAK's protection during the closing months of the shah's regime,[1] and numerous documents that had been collected by SAVAK subsequently found their way into the hands of the revolutionaries. This wealth of information identified the Baha'i faithful and the leadership, their businesses, properties, organizations, and the sites that held special historical and spiritual significance for the community. In short, it identified targets.

The result was a series of attacks on members of the faith across fifty locations in Iran that led to the killing of dozens of innocent people, the burning of homes, and the destruction or confiscation of property, historic sites, businesses and farms. The speed and intensity of these events were extraordinary. It was as if the attackers feared that the events of the 1953 coup d'état would be repeated—when after having fled the country the shah once again returned—and the opportunity to eliminate the Baha'i community while the country was in turmoil might soon be lost. The critical first few years of the revolution were dominated by the hostage crisis and conflicts between the moderates and religious extremists, all of which overshadowed the ongoing persecution of the Baha'is. Anti-Baha'i groups such as the Hojjatieh, some Komitehs, and some government agencies took full advantage of the opportunity.

DISAPPEARANCES AND EXECUTIONS OF BAHA'I LEADERS, 1979–80

The Baha'i religion has no priesthood, as worship is considered a personal and private relationship with God, but it does have a democratically elected leadership that deals with community governance, social services, education, and similar matters. The Baha'i Local Assemblies are bodies of nine members elected annually by secret ballot in every city and village to administer the affairs of the Baha'i community of that locality. Every country has a National Assembly, also elected annually, that oversees the affairs of the Baha'i community for the country as a whole and appoints committees to assist in various service areas. These National Assemblies in turn periodically elect a world governing body, called the Universal House of Justice.

A direct outcome of the seizure of records was the systematic attempt to eliminate the leadership of the Baha'i community. The executions began in 1979 and continued through 1986, and were intended to paralyze the whole community. Until 1986, half of the Baha'is who were executed in the regime's prisons, by firing squad or by hanging, were members of the Assemblies. Among them were members of three terms of the National Assembly of Iran as well as nearly all members of the Local Assemblies of the major cities.

Almost all of the accounts of executions that have reached us include the demand that the prisoner recant the Baha'i faith and return to Islam, made under threat of death and sometimes under torture. The authenticity of any such conversion would of course be doubtful, but recantations were extremely rare, even under such circumstances. The persistent refusals of Baha'is to deny their faith seem to have been an especial provocation to those opposed to them.

ABDUCTION OF MEMBERS OF THE NATIONAL ASSEMBLY OF THE BAHA'IS OF IRAN, 1979–80

On November 11, 1979, Dr 'Ali-Murad Davudi, who was at the time the secretary of the National Assembly of the Baha'is of Iran, and a professor of philosophy at Tehran University, was abducted while walking in Laleh Park. Various efforts to find him bore no result. On January 3, 1980, Ruhi Roushani, secretary of the Local Assembly of Tehran, was abducted on his way home from the Baha'i National Center. He was never found. Three days prior to this, a group of armed men had raided the Baha'i National Center and seized all the documents, files, and typewriters.

In March 1980, a few months after the abduction of Dr 'Ali-Murad Davudi and Ruhi Roushani, guards went to the residences of two

Dr 'Ali-Murad Davudi, Muhammad Muvahhed and Ruhi Roushani.

members of the National Assembly, Dr Husain Naji and Yusef Qadimi. Neither were at home, but their wives were arrested. Dr Naji sent telegrams to Ayatollah Khomeini and other officials, describing several invasions of his home by armed men and the arrest of his wife.[2] He was informed that no official warrant for his arrest had ever been issued.[3] This response compounded the community's anxiety as it showed the authorities' refusal to take responsibility for the arrests.

On August 21, 1980, all nine members of the National Assembly, along with two members of the auxiliary board, were kidnapped by Revolutionary Guardsmen during a regular session of the Assembly at a private home. Their host was also abducted. The missing individuals were 'Abd al-Husain Taslimi, Hushang Mahmudi, Ebrahim Rahmani, Dr Husain Naji, Manuher Qa'em-Maqami, 'Ata'ollah Muqarrebi, Yusef Qadimi, Mrs Bahiyyeh Naderi, Dr Kambiz Sadeqzadeh Milani, Yusef Abbasiyan, and Heshmatollah Rouhani.

Their families pursued the case relentlessly only to face an extraordinary level of deception and psychological manipulation. They met with Attorney General Ayatollah Quddusi, Head of the Iranian Judiciary Ayatollah Muhammad Beheshti, and Speaker of Parliament Akbar Hashimi Rafsanjani.[4] In a meeting on September 2, 1980, Rafsanjani informed the spouses of the abducted individuals that they had been arrested for their involvement in the planned Nozheh military coup that had been thwarted earlier that summer. The allegations were denied by the Baha'is and Rafsanjani promised to investigate. A week later he confirmed the arrests were legitimate and denied access to the prisoners until their interrogation was complete.[5] He assured the family members that they would be released if found not guilty.

On October 6, Revolutionary Guards went to the prisoners' homes and said reports of their detention had been mistaken and that they had in fact been taken by private plane to Israel. Three days later Rafsanjani informed one of the spouses that the government had not arrested any members of the National Assembly, and asked if she knew where they were. At a later meeting, he told three of the spouses of the abducted Assembly members that the head of the Komiteh who had made the arrests had himself been arrested and confessed that he had plotted with the Baha'i National Assembly to help them escape from a secret airport by private plane to Israel. When the wives refuted these claims, Rafsanjani replied, "Well, husbands do not tell everything to their wives." In several subsequent meetings the authorities so thoroughly denied any knowledge of the arrests and disappearance of Assembly members that their story began to seem convincing to at least one of the spouses. The Baha'i community came to suspect that an independent group such as the Hojjatieh Society was behind these extrajudicial disappearances, which would explain the authorities' lack of information.[6]

Immediately after the disappearances, the National Assembly was reconstituted with a new membership drawn from the next tier of nominees in the previous secret ballot, a method that allowed for continuity of leadership even when circumstances prevented another election. When these Assembly members were also eventually arrested and executed, the actions were officially acknowledged by the government and the pretense of denial was dropped. The community could only assume that the first members of the National Assembly had met a similar fate.[7]

One of the earliest executions that only came to light much later was that of Muhammad Muvahhed, who was abducted in Tehran on

May 25, 1979. Muvahhed came from a Shi'i clerical family in Shiraz. He had received a religious education as a seminary student and was assumed to be destined to become a high-ranking member of the clergy in Shiraz. In the course of his studies, he had come across a Baha'i book that led him to embrace the faith. His family was shocked but could not dissuade him. He consequently left Shiraz for Tehran and during the shah's time was pursued and harassed by the members of the Hojjatieh Society. During the revolution he was arrested and interrogated on multiple occasions. After one sudden disappearance, the efforts of his wife and of Baha'i organizations to trace him in the regime's prisons were to no avail. Years later, information about his death appeared on a non-Baha'i website titled *AsemAn-e Abi* (Blue Sky). According to the account published there, Ayatollah Khalkhali had asked Muvahhed, while he was in prison during the first months of the revolution, to recant his faith and to return to Islam. When he refused, the Ayatollah placed a pillow over his face and shot him in the head.[8]

ARRESTS AND EXECUTIONS OF THE LOCAL ASSEMBLY OF TABRIZ

Five members of the Local Assembly of Tabriz were arrested in May 1980. After five months in prison, two of them, Dr Faramarz Samandari, professor at Tabriz University and a well-known physician, and Yadollah Astani, a respected local businessman, were executed by firing squad at midnight on July 13, 1980. The two men had been charged with conspiring against the government, spying for Israel, plotting against Islam, and participating in Baha'i conferences in London and New Delhi.[9]

The executions were apparently precipitated by a visit to the region by Ayatollah Khalkhali, Iran's infamous "hanging judge." The head of the Iranian judiciary, Ayatollah Ardebili, presided over a hearing where no witnesses were present, the defendants were not permitted access to counsel, and the proceedings were not made public.[10] Tehran Radio broadcast the news of the executions. It was an

Members of the National Assembly of Iran who were abducted during the first months after the revolution (August 1980), and disappeared. Seated from left to right: Ebrahim Rahmani, 'Ata'ollah Muqarrebi, Bahiyyeh Naderi, Hushang Mahmudi. Standing from left to right: 'Abd al-Husain Taslimi, Dr Kambiz Sadeqzadeh Milani, Dr Husain Naji, Yusef Qadimi, Manuher Qa'em-Maqami.

ominous shock to the Baha'i community, the first time that such executions were carried out in a government prison and covered by public media.

ARRESTS AND EXECUTIONS OF THE LOCAL ASSEMBLY OF YAZD

The city of Yazd had a long record of harassment and persecution of its Baha'i community, beginning with the massacre of 1903 that was covered in Chapter 2. Anti-Baha'i attacks in Yazd increased during the last years of the shah's reign, largely at the prompting of Ayatollah Sadduqi, the Friday prayer leader who closely supported the Devotees of Islam and the Hojjatieh. With the start of the revolution, the crackdown on the Baha'is intensified further. A Komiteh led by a man named Kashmiri looted Baha'i properties in such audacious fashion that they would extort protection money from the homeowners before raiding the house.

The arrest of the members of the Local Assembly of Yazd, and of some of the Baha'is of nearby villages, started in the summer of 1980. The raids took place at midnight, and all books, correspondence, and photographs were confiscated. Fifteen Baha'is were detained at the prosecutor's offices in Yazd. This was the first time since the revolution that the authorities acknowledged arresting Baha'is. The Baha'i National Assembly dispatched two Baha'i attorneys to Yazd, Messrs Yadollah Lutfi and Masha'allah Rahmani, to assist. Both were arrested and imprisoned.[11]

Initially, the Baha'i prisoners shared the same cells as other prisoners, political and criminal. But after the Baha'i prisoners had established friendships with other inmates, they were moved to small cells in the basement. These cells had no outlet for fresh air, and the prisoners were allowed to go out into the courtyard just twice a month.

On September 2, 1980, the fifteen Baha'is were brought to trial in Yazd. The trial was conducted without a judge, but in the presence of the head of the Revolutionary Courts, the prosecuting attorney, and the interrogator. The proceedings were taped for broadcast on local radio and television. The indictment consisted of the familiar allegations: misleading Muslims, supporting Zionism, and spying for the United States and Israel.[12]

Nurollah Akhtar-Khavari, a prisoner who was secretary of the Yazd Assembly, read the defense responding to each of the allegations that he had prepared the previous night with the help of the attorney Lutfi, now a fellow prisoner. The trial proceeded in the manner of a kangaroo court, with Lutfi presenting rational defenses to false accusations. The prosecutor read out letters that SAVAK officers had prepared, claiming that the Baha'is in Yazd were planning to form a government in Iran and were compiling a list of Baha'i military officers for that purpose. None of the accused were mentioned by name in any of the reports presented. A farmer, who rarely had reason to even visit Yazd, was accused of international espionage. The prosecutor even charged that the Baha'i faith allowed incestuous marriages. In response to the defense that there was no evidence of any such marriages, he claimed that Iranian Baha'is were currently "exempt" from practicing them.

The court was adjourned before the accused could be questioned. Before it could be reconvened, at 1am on September 8, 1980, the prosecutor entered the prison with a few soldiers, and called out the names of seven prisoners: 'Azizollah Zabihiyan (age 56), Fereydun Faridani (age 58), 'Abdul-Vahhab Kazimi Manshadi (age 85), Nurollah Akhtar-Khavari (age 61), Jalal Mustaqim (age 52), 'Ali Mutahhari (age 44), and Mahmud Hasanzadeh (age 41).

He instructed them to pack their bags immediately to be transferred to the capital. They said their goodbyes to the other prisoners and left. A few hours later, one of the guards who had accompanied them returned, threw down Kazimi's hat from the small opening on top of the basement cell, and said that the minibus that was transferring the prisoners had had an accident. He then threw down some sweets and, referring to the son of Baha'u'llah, said, "Abbas Effendi ('Abdul-Baha) is weeping tonight." He closed the porthole and left. The other prisoners were released a few weeks later.

Keyhan published news of the executions on September 9, 1980, repeating the vague accusations of espionage and "hundreds of other reasons available in the file." The verdict was described as validation for the "blood of the thousands of martyrs" who had given their lives "to water the tree of the revolution."

The judicial authorities did not anticipate the negative reaction among the population of Yazd that the news coverage of this trial, both locally and nationally, would cause. The Baha'i prisoners were familiar and respected farmers, shopkeepers, and office clerks. Letters of protest poured into the court. From that time on, the proceedings of Baha'i trials were no longer publicized.

Chapter 12

The Presidencies of Banisadr and Raja'i

Abol-Hasan Banisadr was elected as president of the Islamic Republic on February 4, 1981, two weeks after the release of the American hostages. Winning the presidential election by a substantial majority, Banisadr in theory had the political capital to counterbalance the extremist hardliners who were immediately at odds with him over his choice of prime minister. Not only did the hardliners get the prime minister they wanted, however, they also won a majority of seats in the parliamentary mid-term elections. On top of that, the war with Iraq, which had started four months earlier, further complicated matters.

Whatever conflicts Banisadr, who was also a member of the revolutionary council, had with the hardline clerics, and especially with his prime minister Raja'i, they did not appear to disagree regarding anti-Baha'i activities. Soon after the victory of the revolution, and before his election as president, in a series of talks at Tehran University, Banisadr had rationalized the persecution of the Baha'is.

Representatives of the Baha'i community appealed to him with their concerns over the arrests and executions, as well as the destruction of Baha'i holy places that began at this time, but he refused to meet with them to hear their protests. His own newspaper, *Inqelab-e Islami*, published a denunciation of the Baha'i community by Ayatollah Sadduqi of Yazd, which claimed that the Baha'is were plotting against the revolution in every city in Iran, and called on people to hunt down any Baha'is known to them and turn them over to the Revolutionary Courts.[1] The French newspaper, *Le Monde*, that was then covering the news of the massacres and the persecution of the Baha'is, noted that the effect of the publication of the Ayatollah's sermon in so prestigious a newspaper would be catastrophic for the Iranian Baha'i community.[2]

In a press interview, and in reply to appeals from Western journalists to halt the executions of members of the National Assembly, Banisadr was surprisingly frank: "My opponents are only waiting for a *faux pas* in order to mow me down; what worse *faux pas* can I commit than to intervene on behalf of the Baha'is?"[3]

The last months of Banisadr's brief presidency were especially turbulent. The increasing opposition of the Islamic Republic Party, led by Ayatollah Muhammad Beheshti, and its outspoken criticism in the party's newspaper, together with Ayatollah Khomeini's discontent, all resulted in Banisadr's impeachment and removal from office in June 1981. This was considered a great victory for hardliner clerics like Beheshti.

A month later, Muhammad-Ali Raja'i was elected president. A committed anti-Baha'i activist who had played a leadership role in the Hojjatieh Society while he was a part-time primary school teacher before the revolution, Raja'i was appointed minister of education during the interim government, and then served as Banisadr's hardline prime minster before becoming president.

The first step Raja'i had taken as minister of education was to discharge all Baha'i teachers from the educational system, cancel their retirement pensions, and demand that they repay the government all salaries they had previously received. As prime minister and then president, Raja'i would have free rein in persecuting the Baha'is. During this period, referred to as the "third Islamic revolution," Ayatollah Beheshti led the clergy in implementing a plan to create a purely Islamic society purified of all other elements.[4] The most severe attacks on the Baha'i community were inflicted during these years.

Beheshti's triumph did not last long. Together with over seventy members of the Islamic parliament and his colleagues in the ruling party, Beheshti was killed by a bombing at the party's central office.

Raja'i, who was also attending the meeting, had stepped outside the building only a few moments before the explosion. Less than three months later he was killed in a second explosion at his office, along with Prime Minister Bahonar.

The bombings were initially blamed on Israel. A government source told the *Christian Science Monitor* that they had acted through Baha'i agents in the capital.[5] Later the bombings were officially attributed to the militant Islamic leftist group, the *Mujahedin-e Khalq*, though they never claimed responsibility. The possibility of these acts being the result of internal power struggles also exists.

In any case, these events did not succeed in shaking the foundations of the Islamic government. On the contrary, a period of terror, repression, and massacres began, initially targeting the *Mujahedin-e Khalq*, which advocated the violent overthrow of the government. Large numbers of the organization's members, mainly youth and teenagers, were arrested and brutally killed in the government's prisons. As this was taking place, the crackdown on Baha'is also gained momentum.

Up until 1981, Baha'is were executed under the pretext of espionage. Subsequently, simply "being a Baha'i" was a crime punishable by death. Ayatollah Sadduqi categorized the Baha'is as *mahdur al-damm*—people whose blood may be shed with impunity and with no legal process. Ayatollah Tabrizi, the attorney general, stated explicitly: "The Qur'an recognizes only the People of the Book, that is to say Muslims, Jews, Christians and, by special dispensation, Zoroastrians, as religious communities. Others are heretics. Heretics must be eliminated."[6]

The consequences of such public statements were predictable. In the village of Nuk, near Birjand, Muhammad Husain Masumi and his wife Shekkar Nesa were drenched in kerosene and set on fire. The attackers watched them burn to death. Baha'i girls were kidnapped and forced to marry Muslims; Baha'i cemeteries were destroyed, graves broken open and the newly buried bodies dragged out and jubilantly burnt on garbage heaps. During a memorial meeting held for the fallen soldiers of the Iran-Iraq war, Ayatollah Jannaati, the head of the Council of Guards said: "Humanity, other than the Muslims, are the same as the animals that graze on earth and spread corruption."[7] After Jannaati's declaration that non-Muslims were sub-human, in some areas Baha'is were bridled like donkeys, led through the streets, chained in stables and fed on grass. The aim of all this was ostensibly to force Baha'is to recant their faith and embrace Islam.

After a Baha'i was executed, their family was compelled to pay the price of the bullets that killed them before the body was returned or the burial place was revealed. During the war with Iraq, Baha'i prisoners, like others who were condemned to death, had much of their blood drained out for medical use before they were executed. All this was taking place against the background of daily life in which Baha'is had become social outcasts, regarded as *najes*, infidels, and counter-revolutionaries. They were dismissed from their jobs and widespread action was taken to suppress the Baha'i community economically.

The arrests and executions of Baha'i Assembly members continued, but torture now became a normal part of the effort to force recantations of their faith. The goal, which was never realized, was to broadcast such recantations on public media.

Chapter 13

Arrests and Executions of the Baha'i Assemblies, 1981–85

After the disappearance of all the members of the National Assembly in August 1980 (see Chapter 11), a reconstituted (second) National Assembly administered the affairs of the Baha'i community of Iran during one of the most critical periods in its history.[1] From their very first meeting, the members knew that their actions were being monitored and their phones tapped, that they could be arrested at any time, and that they would likely be killed. In spite of this, they were still able to raise their voices courageously in protest against the persecution of the Baha'is. Their protests took the form of visits to civil and religious authorities and letters to members of parliament and newspapers. They acted with caution to be able to continue functioning, meeting only in small groups of three or four and regularly changing their meeting places. The chairman and secretary of the Assembly moved frequently, staying in different locations.

Given the concurrent attacks on the Local Assemblies and the execution of members of other Baha'i institutions, the National Assembly remained the final refuge for the Baha'is of Iran. The secretary of the Assembly received calls, messages, and letters daily from all over the country concerning the persecution of the Baha'is, and had to convey that information to the rest of the community. The lack of a permanent and suitable base and the constant movement of the officers made matters even more difficult.

The second National Assembly of Iran and the Local Assembly of Tehran. All the individuals in this photograph, except one, were executed by firing squad or by hanging. Seated from left to right: Manuher Qa'em-Maqami, Husain Naji, 'Abd al-Husain Taslimi, Hushang Mahmudi, Zhinus Mahmudi, Giti Vahid (Qadimi) (she was absent from the meeting due to surgery, and was therefore not arrested), Bahiyyeh Naderi. Standing from left to right: 'Ata'ollah Muqarrebi, Kambiz Sadeqzadeh Milani, Ebrahim Rahmani, Yusef Qadimi, Buzurg Alaviyan, Kurush Tala'i, Qudratollah Rouhani, Jalal 'Azizi, Heshmatollah Rouhani, Khosrou Muhandesi, Mahmud Majzub and Kamran Samimi.

During one critical situation, the Assembly decided that it was necessary to hold a plenary session. Eight members of the Assembly who attended the meeting on December 13, 1981, were arrested. The ninth member, Giti Vahid (Qadimi) was scheduled for an operation on the following day and could not be present. The arrested members were: Kamran Samimi, Zhinus Mahmudi (Ne'mat), Mahmud Majzub, Jalal 'Azizi, Mehdi Amin-Amin, Sirus Roushani, 'Ezzatollah Furuhi, and Qudratollah Rouhani. Farideh Samimi, wife of Kamran Samimi, was arrested too, but was released some time later. She provided the Human Rights Document Center with an account of the arrest and interrogations:

> Zhinus and another Assembly member were saying goodbye and leaving. But a few minutes later, they returned, accompanied by three Revolutionary Guards with guns. It seemed that several other Revolutionary Guards were surrounding the house, we could hear them outside. When the Revolutionary Guards came, they immediately told everyone to stand with his or her face to the wall without making any noise. So we all obeyed and they searched our bodies... They knew everything: that I wasn't a member of the Assembly, that I was Kamran's wife, detail by detail, they knew everything... They did not show us a warrant. Mr Mehdi Amin-Amin who was a lawyer (there were three lawyers altogether on the Assembly) asked them if they had a paper for our arrest, but the Revolutionary Guards didn't need any warrants. Whatever they said would go. . . They then carefully searched the house. They did not find anything. They each had a list of the things that we were not allowed to have. They searched the members of the Assembly one by one, and took away the items that were on the list. They then told us to get ready. They blindfolded us while asking questions at the same time. They put us in a van and told us that they were taking us away, but did not say where. After some time the driver stopped. Kamran whispered in my ear that we were being taken to the Kakh-e Javanan (Youth Palace). Apparently he managed to peek from the side of the blindfold. There was a greenhouse behind the Kakh-e Javanan that had been turned into a prison with small cells.[2]

Zhinus Mahmudi and Farideh Samimi were placed in the same cell, separate from the others. Their interrogations were also conducted separately. Mrs Samimi continues:

> Our first interrogation was unlike any of the others. They took Zhinus to another room and then four people came to where I was. Out of the four, three were clergy. The fourth was one of the Revolutionary Guards who had arrested us... One of them was a member of parliament and the other was a representative of some

> sort. . . They entered the prison, only this one time I was not blindfolded for interrogation. They started to ask me questions. They said if I told them a single lie they would know and they would send me to Evin. They would ask questions that they already knew the answers to; I knew this because when I would make a mistake they would correct me.
>
> During the daily interrogations they would take off my blindfold and position me so that I was facing the wall and couldn't see who my interrogator was, but I know that it was a man. I don't know if he was a Revolutionary Guard, I never saw him, but I doubt it because the person asking the questions seemed to have more knowledge than an ordinary Revolutionary Guard would. During these interrogations, they always asked us for names of other Baha'is. . . During the interrogation I realized that the interrogator knew the names of all our friends, family, and their addresses. If I would make a mistake due to the nervous atmosphere of the interrogation, he would correct me and warn me not to give false information.
>
> There were two other Baha'is in a different cell, a man and a woman. God knows what they did to one of them, because she recanted her faith. The authorities asked questions and she answered and finally recanted. And so they brought us sweets and offered them to us to eat, telling us that those two have recanted from our wayward sect and have come to Islam. It was never clear to us what happened that made them recant. The other person was in the same situation and was made to recant. Whether it was a sham performance or not, it was not clear.[3]

After being held for nearly a week, Mrs Samimi was released, her husband having convinced the interrogators that she had no access to useful information. Even after she was released, Revolutionary Guards continued to pressure her to help them identify other Baha'is:

> Several times a week, they'd come and take me to the Revolutionary Guards' headquarters to ask me questions about Kamran's friends.

> They'd also take me to the rooftop and ask me to show them the houses of the Baha'is. . . They'd tell me to give them the names of Kamran's friends and I gave the names of those who had been executed. They would respond by saying that the people I had named had all been executed. I'd say, "Those are the ones I know."[4]

A week prior to the executions, the prisoners were transferred to Evin prison. On December 27, 1981, the eight members of the second National Assembly of Iran were executed without trial. (Footage has surfaced of a sham trial that was apparently staged for the film.) There is doubt as to whether some of them died under torture or were shot, but there was evidence suggesting they had been tortured. Their corpses were dumped in a pit in the cemetery in the middle of the night and covered with soil. The executions were not announced publicly; the families of the deceased were not even informed. The news reached them indirectly through an acquaintance of a *mullah* at the prison. Accounts of torture that reached the Baha'i community indirectly from other non-Baha'i prisoners in Evin cannot be verified, but they are consistent with the state of the bodies that were later discovered.

Kamran Samimi

Le Monde newspaper in Paris, in its issues dated December 30, 1981, and January 1, 1982, provides a detailed account of the arrests and execution of this group. The authorities initially denied the story was true and claimed it represented a Zionist plot to disgrace the Islamic Republic.[5] Once the burial certificates issued by Evin Health Center were made public by the Baha'i international community, Ayatollah Ardebili said the group had been executed on grounds of "espionage for the benefit of foreign powers." Ardibili denied any religious motivation behind the killings.

The Baha'is were finally able to locate the burial sites in the section of the cemetery assigned to infidels, known as Kufrabad. As reported by Ramina Mahmudi, whose father and mother were executed in the first and second National Assemblies respectively, "some of the bodies had been thrown in a collective grave, and some families were not able to discover the location of their loved ones' bodies until they paid the authorities for the bullets used to execute them."[6]

Following the arrest and the execution of the second National Assembly, a third National Assembly was formed in January 1982 and served until it was disbanded in September 1983. On August 29, 1983, the prosecutor general of the Islamic Republic of Iran, Seyyed Husain Musavi Tabrizi, declared in a press interview that Baha'i religious organizations were illegal and participation in any administrative and community activities of the faith was a criminal act. The personal practice of the faith was allowable, he averred, but not its propagation. He provided no evidence of the alleged "agitation and sabotage" or the "transgression and disruption" that he claimed as the basis for his decision.

The statement effectively outlawed the third National Assembly, and 400 local assemblies. In keeping with the Baha'i principle of loyalty and obedience to the government, the National Assembly voluntarily disbanded all Baha'i institutions in a final letter addressed to the Baha'is of Iran. In the same letter, it asked them to continue to uphold their belief and not to dissimulate their convictions.

The National Assembly also released an open letter in response to the prosecutor general's statement, which was delivered to some two thousand government officials and prominent citizens in Iran. In this letter, the National Assembly expressed its compliance with the ban, but also detailed the abuses faced by the Baha'is in the Islamic Republic. It appealed to the government to halt the persecution and to end the arrests, imprisonment, torture, and executions of members of the faith. The letter refuted the government's allegations and appealed to common sense: "What kind of 'spy' is an eighty-five-year-old man from Yazd who has never set foot outside his village? . . . How could students, housewives, innocent young girls, and old men and women . . . be spies? . . . What secret intelligence documents have been found in their possession? What espionage equipment has come to hand?"[7]

The swiftness of the National Assembly's obedience in suspending administrative activities did not prevent the authorities from continuing to harass and intimidate the former members of the institutions as well as other Baha'is. By late 1983, over 750 Baha'is had been arrested without charge.[8]

Seven members of the third National Assembly were arrested and eventually executed. They were Jahangir Hedayati, who had served on the board of directors of Nawnahalan, the Baha'i Investment Company, before the revolution. He was arrested on June 30, 1984, and held in solitary confinement for eleven months, during which time he was tortured repeatedly to persuade him to appear on television and openly recant his faith. His wife was not permitted to visit him for a long time. Finally, she was granted one full minute. "Don't worry, I am all right," was the message he conveyed. On May 20, 1985, she went to see him again but was told he had been executed five days earlier.[9]

Shapur Markazi was arrested in September 1983. He had been much involved in organizing classes for Baha'i children, teaching both conventional studies and religious lessons in rural areas as well as towns. While imprisoned, his torturers broke his ribs and damaged one eye badly. He was executed on September 23, 1984.[10]

Ahmad Bashiri was arrested in July 1983, and after fifteen months of imprisonment and torture to force him to confess to being a spy, he was hanged on November 1, 1984.[11]

Dr Farhad Asdaqi went into hiding in 1983 but was arrested in June 1984. After four months of imprisonment and torture he was executed on November 19.[12]

Farid Behmardi was imprisoned for twenty-two months in Evin prison. During this time he was tortured and spent nearly nine months in solitary confinement. He was never allowed visitors. It is not certain whether he was executed or died under torture on June 10, 1986. He was buried during the night in the Kufrabad cemetery.[13]

Ardishir Akhtari and Amir-Husain Naderi were both arrested on September 11, 1984, and after extensive torture were executed together three years later, on September 28, 1987.[14]

ARRESTS AND EXECUTIONS OF LOCAL ASSEMBLIES

In Hamadan, seven members of the local Assembly were arrested and imprisoned. After several months of incarceration and torture, they

The members of the Local Assembly of Hamadan, pictured in prison prior to their execution. Front row, seated from left to right: Tarazollah Khozain and Husain Mutlaq. Standing from left to right: Sohail (Muhammad-Baqer) Habibi, Husain Khandel, Dr Naser Vafa'i, Sohrab (Muhammad) Habibi and Dr Firuz Na'imi.

were all executed on June 14, 1981. The bodies of the executed prisoners were returned to their families for burial.

The news of the executions and the signs of torture on their bodies quickly spread through the town. The hundreds of people who had been patients of Dr Na'imi and Dr Vafa'i could not believe the charges of espionage and spreading corruption on earth. The Baha'i international community publicized the evidence of torture, including photographs, around the world. Sixty-four-year-old Tarazollah Khozain's ribs had been crushed and his hands slashed. His legs and thighs had bayonet wounds. Sohrab Habibi's back had been branded with a hot ring—his own—and he had severe burns on his body. The fingers of Husain Khandel had been slashed and his abdomen had been cut open. Dr Na'imi's back had been broken and Dr Vafa'i's thighs had been cut open. Sohail Habibi's shoulders had been broken and smashed. Husain Mutlaq had not been tortured but his body had the greatest number of bullet wounds.[15]

The funeral for these seven individuals was attended by hundreds of people of Hamadan, Muslims and Jews as well as Baha'is, in protest against the brutality of their deaths.

On June 23 and 24, 1981, Badi'ollah Farid, Buzurg Alaviyan, Hashem Farnush—all members of the Local Assembly of Tehran—Yadollah Pustchi, the Assembly's office manager, and Dr Masih Farhangi, a member of the Board of Counselors, were arrested. After being tortured they were all executed by firing squad. Two other Baha'is, Farhang Mavaddat, a member of the local Assembly of Karaj, and Varqa Tebyaniyan were also executed alongside this group.

Meanwhile, ten Baha'is were arrested in Mashhad, two of whom, Kamal al-Din Bakhtavar and Nematollah Khatibpur Shahidi, were tried and executed by firing squad on July 26, 1981. Shahidi was the local representative of the Trustees Company, which administered Baha'i community properties, including sites of religious significance. Bakhtavar, a resident of Tehran, was a scholarly author and an eloquent speaker. Before the revolution, followers of the Hojjatieh and *Fada'iyan-e Islam* organizations, including Raja'i who later became president, created much trouble for him and disrupted

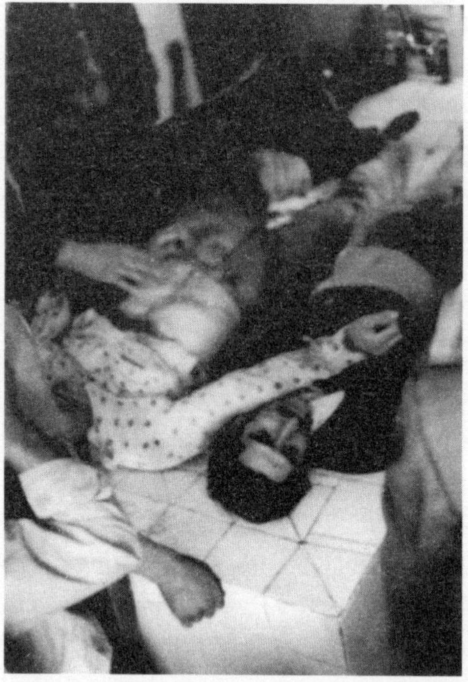

The members of the Local Assembly of Hamadan after execution, showing the signs of torture on the body of Sohrab Habibi who was burnt, presumably with his own ring.

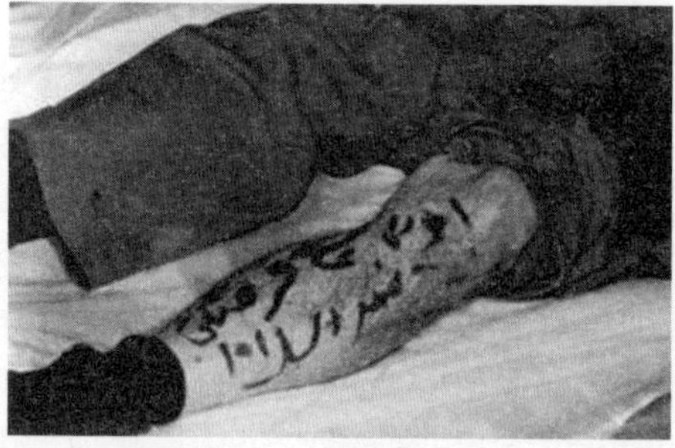

Dr Masih Farhangi's leg, on which has been written: Dr Masih Farhangi, anti-Islam.

meetings where he spoke about the Baha'i faith. The Islamic Revolutionary Court in Mashhad announced that Bakhtavar's trial would be broadcast by loudspeaker in the city's main square. Those who gathered to listen heard the prosecutor's accusations, but a few minutes after Bakhtavar's defense started, the judge ordered the loudspeakers turned off.

On July 19, 1981, seven members of the local Assembly of Tabriz, together with two others active in Baha'i institutions, were executed by firing squad. Their arrest and trial, like the others, were accompanied by the confiscation of books, documents, personal photographs, and interrogation about the activities of the Baha'is in Tabriz and Azarbaijan. As in other cases, their families were driven from their homes, and their property was confiscated. These individuals were: Allahverdi Mithaqi, Manuchehr Khaze'i, 'Abdul-'Ali Asadyari, Husain Asadollahzadeh, Dr 'Esma'il Zehtab, Parviz Firuzi, Mehdi Baheri, Habibollah Tahqiqi and Dr Mansur Dakhili.

In the summer of 1981, a number of Baha'is in over thirty hamlets around Isfahan were being pressed to recant their faith. During the attacks, some fled their farms and homes and went into hiding. Five were arrested and held for several months: 'Ezzatollah 'Atefi, a farmer, and his younger brother Bahman, both from the village of Afus; Gushtasb Sabet-Rasekh from Chegan, a young married man with a small child; 'Ata'ollah Rouhani from Faridan, married with seven children; and Ahmad Rezvani, also from Faridan with a large family. They suffered physical and psychological torture in prison, including death threats and inducements to recant. On one occasion the prisoners were permitted to return home for a few days, something which was intended to weaken their resolve by exposing them to their families. On September 11, the five Baha'is were taken from their cells at midnight, blindfolded, and told to run in the prison yard while shots were fired at their feet. Finally, they were riddled with machine-gun bullets. Relatives were informed that the prisoners had been shot while trying to escape, and were ordered to dig holes in which their loved ones could be buried. The corpses were interred in plastic bags and the families were not allowed to view the bodies or to hold memorial services.[16]

THE LOCAL ASSEMBLY OF TEHRAN

On January 4, 1982, less than a week after the executions of the National Assembly members, six members of the Local Assembly of Tehran were arrested, tortured and executed: Kurush Tala'i, Khosrou Muhandesi, Iskandar 'Azizi, Fathollah Ferdousi, 'Ata'ollah Yavari and Shiva Asadollahzadeh. Shidrukh Baqa, the hostess in whose home the meeting was held, was also arrested with the others and executed. This time, Ayatollah Gilani, head of the Central Revolutionary Courts, justified the executions by alleging that membership in the Baha'i community was synonymous with spying for a foreign power.[17] The Ayatollah did not explain what damage the country had suffered at the hand of the Baha'is, or in what manner they had been serving as spies, or what type of information they had communicated to "imperialist espionage organizations."

Throughout 1982, the arrests and executions of Local Assembly members of the towns of Kerman, Urumiyyeh, Karaj, Qazvin, Shiraz, Isfahan and Sari continued.

Towards the end of 1982, the attacks on the Baha'is of Shiraz intensified once again. As the birthplace of the faith and the Bab's home, Shiraz has always received special attention from those intent on eliminating the Baha'is.

On October 23, 1982, about forty-five Baha'is were arrested in Shiraz and taken to the Revolutionary Guards' prison for interrogation. In November, the public prosecutor's office ordered the arrest of an additional forty Baha'is. The grounds for the arrests were not made public. Some detainees were subsequently released, while others were held for nearly a year before being executed.[18] Both men and women were interrogated for days, during which time they were asked to reveal the names and addresses of the members of Baha'i institutions, to provide detailed accounts of their activities and those of their colleagues, to name the teachers of Baha'i children's classes, to state their contributions to the Baha'i fund, etc.

The Iran Human Rights Documentation Center has published a comprehensive report on the arrests and interrogations, entitled *A Community Under Siege: The Ordeal of the Baha'is of Shiraz.*[19] A section is devoted to the torture inflicted on these individuals, based on information provided by dozens of eyewitnesses. It was described by the interrogators as *ta'zir*, an Islamic legal term for discretionary punishment, and included lashing with whips and cables of the back, legs, and soles of the feet, repeated on unhealed and infected wounds of previous lashings, and psychological torture such as solitary confinement, sleep deprivation, and broadcasting the sounds of prisoners under torture over loudspeakers in the prison. The ultimate purpose was to force the detainees to admit to crimes they had not committed, and to obtain such confessions and public recantations of the Baha'i faith for broadcast on public media. As Mr Habibollah Hakimi observed:

> To fabricate their case [the interrogators] beat, injured, threatened and terrorized the prisoners to get [the statements] they were seeking... The foundation of their case rested on the international links of the Baha'i community, which they traced from the Local Assemblies to the National Assembly, from the National Assembly to the Universal House of Justice [in Haifa] and from that [institution] to Israel... Whoever tried to offer reason and logic or provide evidence and tell the truth was sent back to the *ta'zir* chamber and remorselessly lashed with cables or whips."[20]

To focus on one example only, Dr Bahram Afnan, a member of the Local Assembly of Shiraz, was separated from the other prisoners for several months. The fact that he was descended from the family of the Bab meant he received especially harsh treatment. News of his condition occasionally reached the Baha'i community through other non-Baha'i prisoners, which was how they learned Dr Afnan had suffered a heart attack while being lashed. His cellmate recounted that his unconscious body, torn and bloodied, was thrown into the cell. Two days later, he was again taken to the basement and suffered a second heart attack under torture. His resistance led to his torturers covering his wounds with cloths soaked in horse manure, resulting in severe infection and high fever. This time the prison authorities were forced to take him to the hospital.[21]

On February 22, the newspaper *Khabar-e Junub* reported that the Revolutionary Court of Shiraz had issued an order for the execution of twenty-two unnamed Baha'is. The court order provoked an international outcry, including an appeal from President Reagan to Ayatollah Khomeini that went unheeded.

Three Baha'i detainees—Tuba Za'erpur, Yadollah Mahmudnezhad and Rahmatollah Vafa'i—were executed on March 12, 1983. On June 16, Dr Bahram Afnan, 'Abd al-Husain Azadi, Kurush Haqbin, Jamshid Siyavashi and Bahram Yaldai, members of the Assemblies of Shiraz and Fars, and 'Enayatollah Eshraqi, were executed by firing squad. Every one of them had been tortured. No trial was held, and they were accused of no crime other than being Baha'is.

On June 18, 1983, ten Baha'i women, aged seventeen to fifty-four, were executed in Shiraz. Their crime was teaching Baha'i children's

Dr Bahram Afnan

The ten Baha'i women imprisoned and subsequently executed in June 1983. Top row (from left to right): Mona Mahmudnezhad, Mahshid Nirumand, Simin Saberi, Zarrin Muqimi-Abyaneh, Akhtar Sabet. Second row (from left to right): Shirin (Shahin) Dalvand, Ru'ya Eshraqi, 'Ezzat Janami Eshraqi, Tahereh Siyavashi, Nosrat Ghufrani (Yaldai).

classes. They were imprisoned for several months, and on four occasions, during prolonged interrogations, they were given the option to recant the Baha'i faith and embrace Islam. When none of them signed the forms that had been prepared for the denial of their faith the fourth time, the death sentence was issued by the Religious Magistrate in Shiraz. Their crime was stated as spying for Israel. The women executed were identified as Nosrat Yaldai, aged fifty-four, whose son had been executed two days earlier; 'Ezzat Janami Eshraqi, aged fifty, whose husband had been executed two days earlier; her daughter Ru'ya Eshraqi, aged twenty; Tahereh Siyavashi, aged thirty-two, whose husband had been executed three months earlier; Mona Mahmudnezhad, aged seventeen, whose father had been executed three months earlier; Zarrin Muqimi, aged twenty-four; Shirin Dalvand, aged nineteen; Akhtar Sabet, aged nineteen; Simin Saberi, aged twenty; and Mahshid Nirumand, aged eighteen.

Ten days later, Sohail Hushmand, aged twenty-four, was also hanged in Shiraz.

Following the executions in Shiraz during June 1983, *Khabar-e Junub* published an exclusive interview with Hojjat al-Islam Qazai, the religious magistrate and head of the Revolutionary Court of Shiraz.[22] Qazai's statement is typical of those made by religious magistrates of the Islamic Republic when issuing Baha'is' death sentences. It offers clear evidence of the religious motivation for the executions and the irrelevance of the allegations of espionage:[23]

> The Iranian nation has arisen in accordance with Koranic teachings and by the will of God is determined to establish the government of God on earth. Therefore, it cannot tolerate the perverted Baha'is who are the instruments of Satan and followers of the Devil, and who are mercenaries of the superpowers and their agents such as Israel's House of Justice. It is absolutely certain that in the Islamic Republic of Iran there is no place whatsoever for Baha'is or Baha'ism.

Jamshid and Tahereh Siyavashi who were arrested at the same time, and after enduring unbearable tortures, were executed three months apart.

Mr Mahmudnezhad and his daughter Mona who were executed within three months of each other.

A group of Baha'is of Shiraz, mourning the death of the executed members of their community.

ANTI-BAHA'I ACTIVITIES IN RURAL AREAS

Beyond the urban centers, the Islamic Republic exerted severe pressure on the Baha'is in rural villages to recant their faith. Efforts focused on hamlets and regions where all or a majority of the inhabitants were

Baha'is. The Baha'i villagers in Sangesar, Saysan (Azarbaijan), several hamlets near Qazvin, and other areas were subject to severe persecution. In Fars and Mazindaran provinces, the robbing of Baha'i homes, beatings, burning of harvests, and destruction of livestock became regular incidents. During late June 1983, 130 Baha'i men, women, and children were detained without food or water for three days outside the village of Ayval near Sari. When all efforts to force them to recant were exhausted, they were allowed to return to their homes. But on the night of their return, July 1, 1983, their homes were raided and they were forced to flee into the woods.

From August to November 1983, scores of Baha'is were arrested and detained throughout the country. Many were exiled to Khash or to remote regions such as Baluchistan.[24] The arrest of each individual would result in the confiscation of his or her home and belongings, leaving their spouse and children homeless.

Chapter 14

The Destruction of Baha'i Holy Sites and Community Resources

At the same time as the execution of the members of the Baha'i Assemblies, a separate crackdown focused on the confiscation or destruction of sites that held historical and religious significance to the Baha'i faith, as well as Baha'i community assets and economic resources. On March 6, 1979, just over a month after Khomeini's return to Iran, Ayatollah Qomi announced that the Baha'is were spies of Britain, Russia, the United States, and Israel, and as such the confiscation of their properties and demolition of sites belonging to their community was justified. The attacks started soon after his statement was published in the newspaper *Ettela'at*.

Two Baha'i companies, the Children's Savings Company (*Sherkat-e Naunahalan*) and the Trustees Company (*Sherkat-e Umana*), were seized. The former began as a savings company for Baha'i children, established in the early twentieth century, and was engaged in commercial activities and charitable functions. The Trustees Company was in charge of the Baha'i centers, cemeteries, and other properties throughout Iran. It was also responsible for the repair and maintenance of properties or lands entrusted to the community, often by Baha'is who died without heirs. Properties and sites that figured in the lives of the Bab and Baha'u'llah and other central figures, where significant events in the history of the faith had occurred, were also under the care of the Trustees Company.

The laying of the cornerstone of the Baha'i Center in Tehran in 1921, with a banner showing the Baha'i principles: Unity of Mankind, Investigation of Truth, Common Foundation of All Religions, Religion Must be the Cause of Harmony, Equal Rights For Men and Women, The Adoption or Creation of an International Auxiliary Language, Universal Education, Universal Peace, The Abolition of Extremes of Wealth and Poverty, Abolition of Prejudices, Harmony of Science and Religion, Justice and Truth. Despite the banner proclaiming the equality of the sexes, social conventions in Iran at the time did not allow women to attend such a gathering alongside men.

The seizure of the Trustees Company had far-reaching repercussions. A complete list of all Baha'i properties fell into the hands of the authorities. In April and May 1979 dozens of Baha'i Centers that had served as meeting places and administrative centers in cities, towns, and villages all across the country were either seized or demolished. The Tehran Baha'i Center (*Haziratul-Quds*) was occupied by the Revolutionary Guards in June 1979. Community properties such as

Muslim celebration in the occupied Baha'i Center. The announcement inviting people to that event reads: "The great Ayatollah Nuri has announced: From the scientific and Islamic point of view, we regard the Embassy of Israel and the *Haziratul-Quds* Baha'i Center as one and the same." A cloth banner raised at the entrance of the building reads: "The Temporary Center for Islamic Propagation, Islamic Open University, and Center for Islamic Studies. Under the supervision of Ayatollah Allameh Nuri." At present, the former Baha'i Center in Tehran is used for producing propaganda films for the Islamic Republic.

the youth recreation grounds in Tehran and Shiraz, the land and facilities of the Baha'i Summer Schools on the hills of northern Tehran, the Baha'i Publishing Trust in Tehran, the Hushangi Baha'i School in Yazd, and many other locations were all confiscated.

As soon as the list of properties held by the Trustees Company fell into the hands of the authorities, the seizure, desecration, and destruction of Baha'i holy sites followed immediately. During March and April 1979, properties of historic and religious significance that were confiscated included rooms in the town of Urumiyyeh where the Bab had stayed, the Black-Pit dungeon in Tehran where Baha'u'llah and a number of Babis were imprisoned during 1853, and the homes of renowned Baha'i martyrs. A house in Arak, where a family of five had been massacred in 1916 was demolished on July 24, 1979, and the remains buried there were exhumed and thrown out.[1] The Badasht garden, the site of the first Babi conference, where Qurrat al-'Ayn famously removed her veil in the summer of 1848, was demolished on September 9, 1979. Baha'u'llah's ancestral home in Mazandaran, where he had spent his youth, was razed to the ground in December 1981. The land was subsequently divided into small plots and sold.

One of the holiest of Baha'i historic sites was the small house in Shiraz where the Bab had lived with his wife and mother, where he had written his first works, and where his earliest followers had professed their faith more than 130 years before the start of the Islamic Revolution. It was an inconspicuous two-story home with an enclosed garden where an orange tree grew beside a small pool, one of many similar old houses in the winding alleys of the Shamshirgarha quarter in Shiraz. The neighboring houses all belonged to members of the Baha'i community.

The very existence of this building seemed a provocation to the leading clergy of Shiraz. In periodic outbreaks of violence during the Pahlavi era, windows were shattered and doors smashed, and other damage inflicted on the building. Each time, the Baha'i community would repair the damage, maintaining the architecture in the original form characteristic of the Qajar period. On April 26, 1979, the Revolutionary Guards seized the house, ostensibly in order to "protect" it from damage.

At that time, the Local Assembly of Shiraz and the National Assembly of Iran were still functioning and they appealed through all possible channels to the authorities of the Islamic Republic, requesting the return of the Bab's house to the Baha'i community. During that critical time, such actions required incredible courage. On September 1, 1979, a group of about 150 men, many of them armed, began the process of demolition. They were led by a *mullah* in a drama that played out over ten days. First they knocked down the wall of the adjacent building where the custodians of the Bab's house lived. Crowds gathered in the street and on neighboring rooftops to watch, and armed men from the local Komiteh milled about with walkie-talkies.

The demolition of the house of the Bab in Shiraz.

At the start of the demolition, Baha'i communities around the world mobilized to send hundreds of letters and telegrams appealing to Ayatollah Khomeini and the leaders of the regime. Kurush Tala'i, a Baha'i engineer who was present throughout the events, documented and videotaped the demolition meticulously and provided detailed reports to the Assemblies. Tala'i and the Local Assembly of Shiraz made repeated appeals, trying unsuccessfully with the police, the mayor, the public prosecutor, leading members of the Hojjatieh Society in Shiraz, and Ayatollah Mahallati, whose orders were ultimately responsible for the destruction. (Later, Tala'i would be elected to the Local Assembly of Tehran, and together with the other members of the Assembly was arrested in January 1982 and executed by firing squad.)

The Bab's home and all the surrounding houses were gradually razed to the ground, and the land leveled. In 1981, a road and public square were built over the site in front of the Mahdi Mosque that was then under construction.

Along with historical and holy sites, Baha'i cemeteries in many of the towns and cities of Iran were seized. Graves were dug open, bodies

The revolutionary students of Shiraz University joined hands with the clergy that had arrived from Qom, in demolishing the house of the Bab.

The Mahdi Mosque under construction. The white circle indicates the site of the house of the Bab.

exhumed, and tombstones broken. On December 5, 1981, Tehran's Baha'i cemetery, the *Gulestan-e Javid*, was seized, and thirteen employees of the cemetery were arrested and imprisoned.

Following the destruction of the Baha'i cemetery in Tehran, all cemeteries throughout the country were instructed not to bury the Baha'i dead. Likewise, all morgues and hospitals were ordered not to accept the corpses of deceased Baha'is, not even briefly. This created severe problems, especially in large cities. In one case, permission could not be obtained to bury the corpse of a nineteen-year-old who had died of cancer in the heat of summer. For several days his father laid the body in a van, covering it with ice, while he tried unsuccessfully to obtain a burial permit. Baha'i families had no choice but to bury their dead in their back yards, or in the mountains and plains outside town. Eventually, concern for hygiene led the government to allocate a site known as *Kufr-abad* ("Land of infidels") or *La'nat-abad* ("Land of damnation") in wasteland on the outskirts of Tehran for the Baha'is, as well as political prisoners such as the Mujahedin, to bury their dead. Meanwhile, the vast gardens of the former Baha'i cemetery in Tehran were used as the site for the construction of a cultural foundation named Khavaran Center.

The establishment of hospitals and the promotion of public health had been a focus of the Baha'i community since its inception, and the first Baha'i hospital, *Sehhat*, was founded in Tehran in 1908. It was open to patients of all religions, free for those without financial means, and renowned for the quality of care as well as its special women's section. Around 1949, the Misaqiyyeh Hospital was founded by a Baha'i donor and it expanded gradually into a large medical center and teaching hospital, with a nurses' training institute and Iran's first nursing home. It was subsidized by the Baha'i National Assembly of Iran and had ranked first in government assessments of hospitals before the revolution. Despite heroic efforts on the part of Dr Manuchehr Hakim, the hospital's director, and the Baha'i community, the hospital was taken over by the Revolutionary Committee, and all Baha'i medical staff were dismissed. The court order made familiar claims that the hospital was:

> a major center for Bahaism and anti-Islam propaganda. Through its illicit earnings, financial assistance is extended to the House of Justice of Israel, and ventures to protect the international Imperialist and Zionist interests. Baha'ism is the illegitimate product of the unlawful affair of two colonialists, Britain and Russia; and has no goal other than subjugating the agonized Muslim Iranian nation. Out of the 290 employees of the Hospital, the 123 Baha'is most probably have been responsible for advancing the interests of imperialism, and anti-Islamic Zionism.[2]

The Misaqiyyeh Hospital was renamed in honor of Khomeini's late son, and other Baha'i clinics and health services were also seized and renamed. Some time after the confiscation, assailants entered Dr Hakim's surgery on Takht-e Jamshid Avenue and shot him dead at his desk. The following day, trucks arrived at his home to remove his furniture and belongings.

PURGES AND ECONOMIC STRANGULATION

In the aftermath of the Islamic Revolution, the authorities initiated widespread action that was designed to strangle the economic life of the Baha'i community and extended far beyond the confiscation of property. "Purging" committees were formed in each government ministry, as well as other organizations and factories, with the aim of harassing Baha'is and forcing their removal. Baha'i employees who refused to return to Islam were fired and their pensions annulled.

Ayatollah Sadduqi, who proved particularly assiduous in his persecution of the Baha'i community in Yazd, was effectively a leader of anti-Baha'i actions throughout Iran. In his Friday sermons during the early months after the victory of the revolution, he demanded that all Baha'is be driven from their posts in government offices and brought before the authorities.

Following his appointment as minister of education and then later as prime minister, Muhammad Ali Raja'i intensified efforts to dismiss Baha'is from posts in the public education system. From early

1980 onwards, Iranian newspapers reported mass dismissals of Baha'i primary and high-school teachers, including fifty teachers in East Azarbaijan, forty-four in the province of Fars, and twenty-two in the Southern coastal province. Universities and cultural institutions were also gradually forced to take similar actions.

A government decree dated December 7, 1981, published in *Keyhan*, made the dismissal of all Baha'is employed in the public sector official government policy. All Baha'i doctors, nurses, teachers, and other government employees were dismissed. In most cases, they could be reinstated only by recanting their belief in the Baha'i faith and returning to Islam. The Baha'i international community estimates that more than 10,000 Baha'is were dismissed from positions in government and public education at this time.[3] In 1984, the community received yet another blow. The Islamic courts decreed that any salary paid to Baha'i employees had been illegal from the start and therefore former Baha'i employees had to pay back all wages and pensions that they had previously received. Those unable to repay such large sums were sent to prison.

Through measures such as closing bank accounts, the authorities excluded the Baha'is from normal participation in the economy. At the order of the government, it was forbidden for anyone to enter into a transaction with a Baha'i, and they were no longer allowed to hold passports.

Denial of inheritance rights was another weapon used by the government to force the Baha'is to recant their belief and accept Islam. This began with a ruling in 1980 by the Revolutionary Court in Yazd (Ruling 59/70) which empowered the local authorities to confiscate privately-held Baha'i property following the death of the owner. The actual text of the ruling has remained classified, although its implementation sheds light on its contents and on the type of legal contortions that were used to rationalize such practices. In the initial stages, individual Baha'is were summoned to the Revolutionary Court, where it was confirmed that they were indeed Baha'i and their property was identified. At that point, the property was considered confiscated, although the owner was allowed to remain in residence for the remainder of his or her life. At death, however, the property could not remain in the family unless it was inherited by a Muslim family member. In cases where the family members of a deceased Baha'i included a Muslim, he or she would be entitled to the entire inheritance, irrespective of the closeness of kinship. In the absence of any Muslim family member, ownership of the property was automatically transferred to the Imam Khomeini Relief Committee, led by Ayatollah Sadduqi. (This is one of the tax-exempt foundations, known in Persian as *bonyad*, that ostensibly operate as charitable organizations. They channel funds from a wide variety of sources to the Islamic Republic and now control an estimated 20 percent of Iran's GDP.)

In the case of Baha'is killed while serving the nation during the war against Iraq, the judicial system deprived their families of the benefits normally awarded to the families of war veterans. In some instances, they even ordered the confiscation of the assets of those family members.

The confiscation of Baha'i resources through the manipulation of inheritance laws and other mechanisms included agricultural land as well as urban properties. The hardship created for Baha'i farmers and villagers was often much harsher than that which resulted from the dismissal of Baha'i employees in towns and cities. Families who had subsisted for generations by working a plot of land were suddenly evicted and deprived of all means of livelihood.

In a recent example, during the presidency of Muhammad Khatami (1997–2005), a group of Baha'i farmers appealed their cases to the Constitutional Law Supervisory Board administered by the president's office. The Board made enquiries of the local county council in East Azarbaijan, which reported that the Friday prayer leader in Bustan-Abad had considered it impossible that Muslims and non-Muslims should live next to one another. Presumably he based his logic on "ritual impurity," as the Baha'is had actually lived together with the Muslims in that village for generations. As the Baha'i farmers refused to recant, they were banished from the village of Matanaq. Their lands were rented out by the same prayer leader for two years, after which time the Revolutionary Court took over. Finally, the land was auctioned off to the inhabitants of the village.

The confiscation of Baha'is' homes, their dismissal from private businesses, the closure of their factories and shops, and resulting problems would intensify and become even more widespread in later years, particularly during the presidency of Mahmoud Ahmadinejad. In a report dated June 29, 2006, Mr Miloon Kothari, the UN Special Rapporteur on adequate housing, offered detailed documentation that at least 640 Baha'i properties had been seized since 1980. Numerous additional cases, especially in remote locations, could not be easily documented. According to information received by the Special Rapporteur, "property confiscation in rural areas was often accompanied by threats and physical violence before and during related forced evictions."

Mr Kothari wrote of his concern about the clear evidence of discriminatory conduct with respect to Baha'i property: "In the last two years, there has been an increase in the number of Baha'i leaders or prominent people who have been arrested without any charge and then released with very high bail, and, the only way in which they can post this bail is to put their property as a guarantee. This seems to be another method of expropriation."[4]

Chapter 15

After Ayatollah Khomeini: The Escalation of Persecution

Following the death of Ayatollah Khomeini in June 1989, the Council of Experts elected Ayatollah 'Ali Khamenei, who had been president since 1981, as the new "Supreme Leader of the Islamic Republic."

The regime's sensitivity to international criticism of their treatment of the Baha'is led to a change of policy, with executions significantly reduced. The fate of Iran's Baha'i community has always been linked to broader political tides in the country. Whereas seventy Baha'is had been executed during the one year and eight months of Banisadr and Muhammad Ali Raja'i's presidencies, the eight years of Khamenei's presidency (with Prime Minister Mir Husain Musavi) saw 119 Baha'is killed by the regime—a substantial reduction in the pace of executions. And yet there was no easing of pressure on the Baha'i community, but only a masking of the most egregious offenses that were likely to draw international attention.

As Supreme Leader, Khamenei requested the Supreme Revolutionary Cultural Council to clarify policy on the Baha'i question and adopt a unified line of action. In a secret memorandum dated February 25, 1991, the Supreme Council informed Khamenei of the final decisions adopted in meetings held with then President Rafsanjani, and Khamenei signed the memorandum in approval. This document fell into the hands of the UN Special Representative on Human Rights, Reynaldo Galindo Pohl, and its contents were revealed in 1993. Initially, the Islamic Republic claimed that the document was forged, but it has since referred officially to its provisions. Its core points are:

A. General status of the Baha'is within the country's system:
1. They will not be expelled from the country without reason.
2. They will not be arrested, imprisoned, or penalized without reason.
3. The government's dealings with them must be in such a way that their progress and development are blocked.

B. Educational and cultural status:
1. They can be enrolled in schools provided they have not identified themselves as Baha'is.
2. Preferably, they should be enrolled in schools which have a strong and imposing religious ideology.
3. They must be expelled from universities, either in the admission process or during the course of their studies, once it becomes known that they are Baha'is.
4. Their political (espionage) activities must be dealt with according to appropriate government laws and policies, and their religious and propaganda activities should be answered by giving them religious and cultural responses, as well as propaganda.
5. Propaganda institutions (such as the Islamic Propaganda Organization) must establish an independent section to counter the propaganda and religious activities of the Baha'is.
6. A plan must be devised to confront and destroy their cultural roots outside the country.

C. Legal and social status:
1. Permit them a modest livelihood as is available to the general population.

2. To the extent that it does not encourage them to be Baha'is, it is permissible to provide them the means for ordinary living in accordance with the general rights given to every Iranian citizen, such as ration booklets, passports, burial certificates, work permits, etc.
3. Deny them employment if they identify themselves as Baha'is.
4. Deny them any position of influence, such as in the educational sector, etc.

From the time of the memorandum onwards, anti-Baha'i activities were conducted under the direct supervision of the Supreme Leadership, which in turn had at its disposal the services of the judicial department, the police, the military and the Revolutionary Guards, the paramilitary militia known as *basij*, the Ministry of Information, and the national radio and television services. Daily

A man signs a scroll demanding combat against the Baha'is.

newspapers such as *Keyhan* and *Jumhuriy-e Islami*, as well as the IRNA News Agency, also played a major role in the persecution of the Baha'is.

The recommendations made by the Supreme Council of the Islamic Revolution, and honed subsequently by the Supreme Leader's office, were not substantially different from policies that had been implemented by the regime over the years since the revolution. The provisions of the memorandum were so vaguely expressed that any interpretation or crackdown was possible, and its positive aspects were cosmetic and meaningless in practice. For example, Article 1 states that Baha'is will not be expelled from the country without reason. In reality, the harsh treatment they receive is such that many Baha'i families have had no option but to flee the

Slogans written on the homes of the Baha'is calling them Zionist, infidels and *najes* (religiously unclean). Below, scenes show a Baha'i graveyard after gravestones were broken and trees uprooted.

country. Article 2 maintains that Baha'is will not be arrested, imprisoned, or penalized without reason, yet false charges of espionage have served as sufficient reason.

The memorandum intensified the process by which the Ministry of Culture and Islamic Guidance had sought the dismissal of Baha'is from the private sector. Business licenses of Baha'is could not be renewed. Some private organizations that relied on the expertise of Baha'i employees requested exemptions, only to be then threatened by the government. Members of the clergy were positioned in some offices to ensure all Baha'i employees were dismissed. The greatest number of dismissals from the private sector occurred during the presidency of 'Ali Akbar Rafsanjani (1989–97).[1] Following a brief pause during Khatami's presidency (1997–2005), these measures were resumed with an even greater intensity once Ahmadinejad became president in 2005.

THE EXCLUSION OF BAHA'IS FROM HIGHER EDUCATION

In the purge that immediately followed the revolution, all Baha'i university professors had been fired, and any students recognized as Baha'is were expelled from universities, regardless of how long they had been studying. Some students were only one examination away from obtaining their degree.

Similarly, according to a circular letter addressed to all elementary schools and high schools throughout Iran in 1979, one of the conditions for admission was a student's affiliation with Islam or one of the recognized religious minorities. This circular was aimed purely at denying Baha'is access to education and included a questionnaire on the religious beliefs of students and their parents. One question enquired whether the student or either parent was a Baha'i. If the answer was yes, the next question was whether they would be willing to recant. The reply given to these questionnaires would be the deciding factor in the child's future education.

Statistics on the number of Baha'i students expelled from primary and secondary schools are not available. Because of the war with Iraq

(1980–88), the policy was not rigidly enforced and was mainly applied to Baha'is who were recognized as such in smaller town and villages. Due to international pressure, from 1990 onwards Baha'i primary and secondary students were once again admitted to school.

Following the resolutions adopted by the Supreme Council, students were asked to identify their religion on university admission forms. The intention was to exclude Baha'i students, as the authorities knew very well that Baha'is would not conceal their faith even when they knew why the question was being asked.

The government's campaign to deny hundreds of Baha'i students access to higher education led the Baha'i community to establish a private university. An abundance of scholars and educators in the community made such a project viable. Starting as a covertly run university, classes were initially held in individual homes and basements, with a limited number of courses. These classes gradually expanded and developed into a fully-fledged university. From 1987, when the university started functioning, until 1998, the Baha'i Institute for Higher Education (BIHE) had over 900 students, a faculty of more than 150 academics and instructors, offering courses in ten subject areas. The degree awarded by the BIHE has since been recognized by many universities in Europe and the United States, and graduates have been accepted for postgraduate and doctoral programs outside Iran.

In October 1998, in a series of raids on five hundred Baha'i homes where classes were held, thirty-six professors of the BIHE were arrested. Textbooks, computers, laboratory equipment, and university records were confiscated. These attacks, carried out during Khatami's term as president, were condemned by the UN Commission for Human Rights and by universities worldwide. Academics from many universities throughout Britain and the United States signed an open letter in support of the right of the Baha'is to access higher education in Iran. The *New York Times* wrote:

> The materials confiscated were neither political nor religious, and those arrested were not fighters or organizers. They were lecturers

in subjects like accounting and dentistry; the materials seized were textbooks and laboratory equipment.[2]

Following appeals to government authorities by the Baha'i community, and because of the response that these attacks provoked internationally, the BIHE was once again able to resume its activities, but under more difficult circumstances. From 2001 to 2002, classes were again closed down. In the midst of an examination, the papers of students in Mashhad and Shiraz were confiscated by the Revolutionary Guards.[3]

As a result of the large number of messages of protest sent to the government and to international authorities, the Supreme Revolutionary Cultural Council finally passed a resolution on December 16, 2003, removing the question that identified an applicant's religion from university admission forms. Instead, as part of the entry exams, the student had to be examined on one of the following religions of his or her choice: Islam, Judaism, Zoroastrianism and Christianity.[4]

This news was welcomed in the Baha'i community. A thousand Baha'i students took part in the university entrance exams the subsequent year (2004), and 900 successfully passed the examination. As most Baha'i students had a good knowledge of Islam, they chose that religion to be examined on. After receiving their admission letters from the National Organization for Educational Testing, the Baha'i students were surprised to find out that they were registered as Muslims. In reply to their objection, the authorities stated that it was presumed that the selection of Islam for the entrance exam indicated the religion of the applicant. The Baha'i students did not agree with this reasoning and the community wrote a letter of protest to President Khatami. Following these complaints, the students were given the option of filling in amended forms that had no entry for religion, which most students submitted. With the exception of ten, all Baha'i students were registered as Muslims.

When they protested again, the Baha'i students were denied access to university education that year too. In solidarity with their fellow believers, the ten students who had been admitted returned their papers to the admissions office. Events unfolded in the same fashion the following academic year. When Ahmadinejad came to office, the December 2003 resolution was overturned, and all hopes for Baha'i students' access to higher education were suspended.

Chapter 16

Efforts at Reform under President Khatami

Muhammad Khatami took the presidential oath on August 3, 1997. His election raised much hope among Iranians, who expected reforms and better regard for civil rights and citizens' liberties. His promotion of a "Dialogue Among Civilizations" in his talks and writings presented him in international circles as open-minded, with progressive views. This gradually led to a more positive image of Iran internationally. But the Khatami administration met with problems in enforcing constitutional law and implementing its policies. As a result of obstruction and parliamentary censure in the *Majlis*, as well as the covert and overt hostility of fundamentalists who resisted its reformist ideas, the government came to a standstill.

Dr Husain Mehrpour, who served as advisor to the president and chairman of a commission tasked with implementing constitutional law, provides an insightful commentary on the condition of the Baha'is during Khatami's presidency. In 2005, Mehrpour published a book entitled *The Challenging Task of Monitoring the Implementation of Constitutional Law*,[1] of which one full chapter deals with the rights of the unrecognized religious minorities—in other words, the Baha'is. It documents his correspondence on Baha'i civil rights with President Khatami and various ministries and departments of the government, reflecting the continuing tension between the expectations of those determined to maintain *Shari'at*, or religious law, and what he calls "the demands of reality"—the need for Iran's government to function effectively in the modern world and honor its commitments under international law.

In the letters, written in his official capacity as chairman of the commission on constitutional law, Mehrpour refers to the many appeals made by the Baha'i community to international organizations, and their protests addressed to various Iranian institutions such as the Islamic Commission for Human Rights and the Constitutional Supervisory Board. The appeals and protests mentioned cover such abuses as dismissals from the public sector, the suspension of pensions and attempts by the government to reclaim past salaries, cancellation of business and trade licenses, being barred from access to higher education, difficulties in registering their children at schools, the refusal of authorities to register their marriages, and problems in obtaining passports and travel permits. He also includes judicial verdicts for the confiscation of property and death sentences based solely on individuals' membership of the Baha'i faith.

Against these abuses, Mehrpour invokes the constitution, Article 14 of which specifies that "the government of the Islamic Republic of Iran and all Muslims are duty-bound to treat non-Muslims in conformity with ethical norms and the principles of Islamic justice and equity, and to respect their human rights." He quotes Imam Khomeini's statement that non-Muslims, including those not recognized under Islamic law as well as the recognized minorities, "are under the shelter and protection of Islam, and the laws of Islam are equally applicable to them as to the Muslims. The shedding of their blood is not permissible [*mahqun al-dam*] and their properties are to be respected."[2] He notes that the dismissal of Baha'is from government and private employment, and their exclusion from trade unions and professional associations that control necessary work permits, are in violation of Article 28 of the constitution, which states that "everyone has the right to choose any occupation he wishes, if it is not contrary to Islam and the public interests, and does not infringe the rights of others. The government has the duty, with due consideration of the need of society for different kinds of work, to provide every citizen with the opportunity to work, and to create equal conditions for obtaining it."[3]

Mehrpour also notes Iran's commitments under international agreements such as the International Convention on Civil and Political Rights, the International Convention on Economic, Social, and Cultural Rights, and Convention 111 of the International Labor Organization. In making his case he further invokes President Khatami's many public addresses asserting that the civil and basic rights of all Iranians, irrespective of race, tribe, religion or belief, will be fully safeguarded.

The response of various officials to the letters, including those forwarded with expressions of concern to the president himself, reveal the intractable nature of the conservative forces opposing any progressive change. The methods of their resistance range from bureaucratic deflection and legalistic obscuration to the forthright exclamation that Ayatollah Shahroudi, head of the judiciary, inscribed at the foot of one letter: "In the Name of God! It has been stated on several occasions that interfering in judicial matters and cases is not the concern or responsibility of that Board."[4]

There were rare victories. On February 21, 2000, in response to Mehrpour's communications and after months of delay, the Interior Ministry issued a circular to the public notary offices in all provinces, stating that there was no objection to the registration of the marriages of non-Muslims, including marriages of the unofficial religious minorities.[5] More typical were the continuing resolutions from various governmental bodies and judicial decisions on court cases that defied the constitution and sparked more objections from Mehrpour's office.

A particularly charged exchange took place between Mehrpour and Ayatollah Makarem Shirazi, who wrote to President Khatami to express his concern about the dangerous privilege that the Baha'i community enjoyed in higher education and "the activities of the Baha'is in international assemblies"—as he described the actions taken by the international Baha'i community, and statements released by the UN Commission on Human Rights, the European Parliament, and other international organizations in defense of Baha'is in Iran. On behalf of Khatami, Mehrpour responded:

> It would be most appropriate if the all-knowing *ulama* would clarify this issue from the religious and canonical point of view, and would define the stance of the government in this respect. It is necessary that they elucidate the limits to which the civil rights of the followers of this sect, and in general of those who do not belong to one of the religious minorities recognized by the Constitutional Law may be observed. Do the members of this group actually have the right to life, and are they entitled to the basic rights that are the requirement for living in present day society, or not? Is it possible that all the members of a sect or group who have a certain belief, even if erroneous, and who are all citizens of the Islamic Republic of Iran, be deprived of their civil rights such as going to school or university, merely on the supposition that they are supported by foreign enemy powers and that some may even be spying for those powers? The fact is that these individuals pay taxes just as any other citizen of this country; they are called to military service just as any other Iranian. Obviously, spying for a foreign power is a crime, and a grave one, irrespective of whether it is committed by a Muslim or a non-Muslim. But crimes and punishments are personal issues. When it is established that an individual has committed such a crime, he or she should be held responsible and must pay the consequences. Is it honestly possible to issue a general ruling and to state that all members of a certain belief system are spies? Can we justify the deprivation of all such members of a sect of their basic social rights known as the civil rights of a nation, such as the right to education? It is truly befitting that the distinguished *ulama* seriously clarify this issue and adopt a proper ruling on this matter so that the government would know where it stands in relation to its legislative, judiciary, and executive decisions.[6]

Mehrpour's correspondence as a whole stands as an indictment of the Islamic Republic. In a country where the clergy regard themselves as above the law, the creation of a commission to monitor the implementation of the constitution, and the appointment of one of the president's closest advisors as its chairman, was an innovative challenge to the status quo. The effort demonstrated Khatami's best intentions, but was ultimately unsuccessful.

Even during Khatami's presidency, the destruction of Baha'i historic sites continued. During the spring of 2004 in Babul, the tomb of Quddus, one of the first disciples of the Bab, was razed to the ground. Two months later, the home of Mirza Buzurg Nuri, the father of Baha'u'llah, was demolished by bulldozers in Tehran. Beyond its historic value to the Baha'i community, this beautiful house was considered a masterpiece of Qajar architecture with great cultural and artistic significance.

In addition to statements of protest from the international Baha'i community as well as Iranian Baha'is, the demolition raised an outcry in two of Tehran's major newspapers. Both *Hamshahri* and *E'temad* published articles about the historic and artistic value of the building, protesting its demolition. The *E'temad* article referred to the house as "a matchless masterpiece of art, spirituality, and architecture," and its destruction as a tragic national and cultural loss.

In September 2004, Baha'i communities around the world published a statement entitled, "Cultural Cleansing: Destroying a Community and Erasing its Historic Memory." Describing the cruelty and injustice suffered by the Baha'is in Iran, the statement declares:

> The hatred of the extremist mullahs for the Baha'is is such that they, like the Taliban of Afghanistan who destroyed the towering Buddhist sculptures at Bamiyan, intend not only to eradicate the religion, but even to erase all traces of its existence in the country of its birth.[7]

The historic house of Mirza Buzurg Nuri, father of Baha'u'llah, in Tehran. It was demolished in spite of public protests to preserve this historic house from the Qajar period.

Chapter 17

Escalating Repression under President Ahmadinejad (2005–13)

The election of Mahmoud Ahmadinejad as president of the Islamic Republic of Iran on July 25, 2005, opened a new chapter in the persecution of the Baha'i community. Large sums of money were allocated for anti-Baha'i propaganda in a continuation of policies established while Ahmadinejad was mayor of Tehran. Four days after his election as president, *Keyhan*, closely linked to the office of the Supreme Leader, initiated the publication of a series of anti-Baha'i articles, repeating the familiar accusations of Baha'i ties to Israel, accusations of espionage, and allegations of immorality. A glance at the titles of articles on the Baha'i faith published in *Keyhan* during 2005 and 2006 is revealing:

The Bab in Jewish Doctrine, 7/8/1384 SH
Contradictory teachings in Baha'ism, 19/8/1384 SH
Propagator of Terrorism, 28/8/1384 SH
The Helper of Zionism, 19/1/1384 SH
The Imam's Warning against the Infiltration of the Baha'is, 3/9/1384 SH
The Mire of Corruption, 8/9/1384 SH

In January 2006, *Keyhan* once again dedicated a few issues to the story of the murder of an innocent woman in Abarqu that had occurred in 1950 and was unjustly blamed on the Baha'is.[1] From June to October 2006, the newspaper published in serial the book *The Grim Shadow*, the memoirs of Mahnaz Raufi, who claimed to come from a Baha'i family and to have returned to Islam. She presented the Baha'i administration as an organization seeking power and money.

Dozens of books were published during this time by anti-Baha'i organizations with the principle aim of distorting the religion in the eyes of the public and linking it to foreign powers. The quarterly journal, *Ayyam*, dedicated its twenty-ninth issue, entitled "Bahaism, As It Is," to such material. The quarterly journal *Historical Studies* (*Mutali 'at-e Tarikhi*) assigned two issues to the same topic. Even children's books on combating the Baha'i faith were published, and the Islamic Propaganda Organization produced anti-Baha'i literature and distributed it free of charge among the population.[2] Some bookstores included a section specifically for "books against the wayward sect," and a special booth was assigned to the topic in Tehran's annual book fair.

Radio and television programs on national media also constantly attacked the Baha'i faith. The common thread in all of these publications, books and talks is the avoidance of any discussion of the teachings and principles of the faith. Their efforts are based on depicting the Baha'i faith as a monster that collaborates with Russia, Britain, and the United States, that associates with Israel and yet lives in Iran. They aim to create fear at the mere mention of its name. Baha'i writers have refuted these accusations, both on websites and in books published outside Iran.[3] But although anti-Baha'i literature is widely distributed and made available free of charge in Iran, the opposite is true when it comes to Baha'i literature. Even being in possession of a Baha'i book is a crime with heavy penalties.

Immediately after Ahmadinejad's election, the Supreme Leader Ayatollah Khamenei instructed the chief of staff of the Armed Forces to prepare a detailed report identifying all Baha'is in Iran and to monitor their activities. A copy of the secret report fell into the hands of Asma Jahangir, Special Rapporteur on freedom of religion appointed by the UN Commission on Human Rights. In August 2006, the Ministry of the Interior instructed all political and intelligence deputies of municipalities throughout the country to "carefully and subtly monitor and control the social activities of the Baha'is." A form was created to gather information on Baha'is, including their income and profession, social relationships and conflicts, political activities and any relationship with Baha'i assemblies outside Iran.

The government demanded that all guilds provide the names of the Baha'is who were members of their association. In April 2007, the headquarters of the Intelligence and Public Security Forces sent a circular to local commanders and chiefs of police throughout the country, requesting that they identify Baha'is and gather information and detailed statistics on them. The same circular instructed them to prevent Baha'is from being employed in high-income occupations, and to limit their work permits to jobs that would only allow them "a mediocre income." The areas of trade where Baha'is were not permitted to be employed included newspapers and periodicals; jewelry, goldsmithing, and watchmaking; print shops; tourism, hotels, and car rentals; publishing; tailoring training schools; photography and film-making; internet gaming; computing and internet cafes.

The circular letter also identified professions that required "ritual purity," where Baha'is could not by law be employed, including catering, restaurants, and food service; supermarkets and grocery stores; pastry shops and bakeries; and "all businesses where the Baha'i owner is successful and the business is highly profitable." Moojan Momen writes:

> As a result of these and probably other orders that have not come to light, during the course of 2007 the pressure on smaller Baha'i businesses intensified and a large number of Baha'i businesses in all parts of the country. . .were forced to close either by refusal of licenses, withholding of supplies, boycotts or eviction from premises. Where Baha'is were in business in partnership with Muslims, the business was pressured to force the Baha'is out of the company.

> As well as urban businesses, Baha'i farmers had their farms and orchards forcibly occupied, their crops seized and their property confiscated. They cannot get supplies for their farms and cannot sell their produce. Many Baha'i peasant farmers in small villages have been forced to leave their villages and their livelihood behind and move to the cities. This has even occurred in villages where Baha'is were the majority of the population. Entire villages have been cleared of Baha'is in acts of 'ethnic cleansing' reminiscent of what occurred in Bosnia. The Baha'i villagers are then forced to move to cities where they live as refugees, dependent on the charity of other Baha'is. Previously this had occurred only in villages where there were known to be a large number of Baha'is, but since 2005 it has become much more systematic, affecting villages with both large and small Baha'i populations.[4]

Presently, a Baha'i has no rights under the Islamic Republic. For example, a Baha'i who is dismissed from work may resort to renting out his property to earn a living. The tenant then has the right to refuse to pay the rent, and can be certain that no action will be taken if the landlord complains to the authorities. If a fair-minded Muslim wishes to pay the rent, he will be notified by authorities that the rent can only be paid to a charitable foundation or to the town's prayer leader.

If a Baha'i brings a complaint to the police or to court, he or she may be immediately arrested. Night-time raids on Baha'i homes by security officers, resulting in the confiscation of books, computers, and documents, are a normal practice. Other forms of harassment include the prevention of burials, the demolition of Baha'i cemeteries, and the felling of their trees. Many Baha'is are arrested on unsubstantiated charges and then temporarily released on bail having paid an exorbitant fee or pledged their property as collateral. The individual Baha'i has no idea why he was arrested, and the officer in charge has no explanation to offer. The purpose is simply to disrupt the lives of the Baha'is and to strip away the community's assets.

With the coming to power of President Ahmadinejad, the persecution, which had been less extreme under President Khatami, once again intensified. There were night-time raids involving Molotov cocktails thrown at Baha'i homes and walls bulldozed. Anti-Baha'i graffiti was sprayed on walls and threatening leaflets were distributed. Baha'i students were expelled from high schools, and in some primary schools Baha'i students were segregated from others and bullied in the playground.

Arson attacks against Baha'i-owned homes and cars were the newest form of violence to emerge. Between July 2007 and July 2008, at least twelve such cases of arson were reported. In one horrifying attack, a fifty-three-year-old businessman in Shiraz was assaulted by a mob in the street and chained to a tree. They poured kerosene on him and tried to set him on fire by throwing matches at him. Wind blowing out the matches prevented him catching fire before bystanders interfered and set him free.

In Karaj, a section of the cemetery allocated to the Baha'is as "infidels" was set on fire.[5] Another cemetery in the village of Ayval near Semnan, where local Baha'is have buried their dead for a hundred years, was put up for auction by the "Headquarters Properties Office." It was in the same village where twenty Baha'i farming families had been arrested in 1983. They had initially been detained in the local mosque and pressured unsuccessfully to recant their faith. After a few days, they were all expelled from the village. Since then, they have been allowed to come to the village and their homes once a year to harvest crops by presenting written permission from the police and the judiciary. For twenty-six years, their efforts to return to the village permanently, including appeals to the courts and complaints to the authorities, bore no results. In June of 2010, four bulldozers were brought to the village. Fifty Baha'i homes were demolished and set on fire, some totally razed to the ground.[6]

There were no executions under Ahmadinejad, but the comments made by a religious judge to a Baha'i who was unjustly sentenced to prison were indicative of the new government policy: "At the start of the revolution we were clumsy and amateurish in killing your lot, and in providing you with the excuse to raise mayhem in the international media. I will make sure that you suffer in prison in such manner that you will long for death a hundred times a day."

THE CASE OF A BAHA'I PHYSICIAN IN NAJAFABAD

Bureaucracy itself has become a tool to deny Baha'is their legal rights and marginalize them. A policy of postponing their queries, sending them on wild goose paper chases with files being continuously "lost" in offices has one aim: harassing the Baha'is into submission.

One example of many shows how deliberately convoluted patterns of harassment have been used to demoralize and wear down the Baha'i community. A period of anti-Baha'i activities in the town of Najafabad began with raids on the Baha'i cemetery: tombstones were smashed, trees and plants were cut down or uprooted. The attacks continued with threats to the Baha'i traders and shopkeepers, and anti-Baha'i graffiti defacing their shops and homes.

One of the victims was Dr Homa Agahi, a well-regarded physician who had served the people of Najafabad for twenty-eight years. The harassment started in late September of 2007 when a mob covered her clinic's noticeboard with black paint, wrote anti-Baha'i messages on the walls of the complex where her clinic was located, and broke the windows. One of the messages read: "*Dr Homa Agahi, Baha'i, spy for Israel, enemy of Islam and the Quran*". Dr Agahi took note of the hostility and cleaned up the graffiti with the help of her relatives. She then made a total of fifty-six visits to the authorities as bureaucratic procedure became a form of harassment, sketched here very briefly.

Her landlord initially sympathized and expressed his hope that the commotion would subside and she would be able to return to her clinic and continue practicing. But then the landlord was threatened and pressured to evict Dr Agahi. He asked her to close the clinic temporarily, but when the threats intensified he became apprehensive and finally sold the property.

The local police station advised Dr Agahi to submit a complaint to the city court. She did so and the prosecutor instructed the police to investigate the case. On her next visit to the prosecutor she learned that the case file had been sent to the Intelligence and National Security Bureau in Najafabad, which had jurisdiction over all the problems related to the Baha'i community.

Dr Agahi then appealed to the prayer leader in Najafabad, who claimed that the offenders were not in his control, and that they had criticized him for not confronting the Baha'is more aggressively. After appealing to the chief of the Medical Council in Najafabad, Dr Agahi was told that the council had already shown their support a few years earlier when they had renewed her work permit over the objections of the authorities. In this particular case they could do nothing.

The Intelligence Bureau informed Dr Agahi that the main reason for the violent attacks were the Baha'i activities of her husband and children. Her husband had, for example, uploaded a report on the internet about the desecration of the Baha'i cemetery in Najafabad. She was warned not to voice her complaint to the ministries or to the United Nations, as it would eventually come back to the Intelligence Bureau. Any final decision would be made locally. The Intelligence Bureau in Najafabad did however advise her to take her case to the headquarters of the Intelligence Office of the province of Isfahan, where they initially refused to meet with her or discuss the matter. When she persisted, the person in charge of Baha'i affairs raised the subject of her family members' religious activities, and stated that the attacks were a retaliation for those activities. He reiterated that the perpetrators belonged to a group that was beyond the control of the Intelligence Office and therefore their reactions to Baha'i teaching activities could not be prevented. Finally, he emphasized that he should never be contacted directly in future, and that any further communication should be done through the Member of Parliament for Najafabad.

The Member of Parliament initially received Dr Agahi cordially. On a second meeting, he became formal and distant, and defended the position of the Intelligence Bureau in Isfahan, pointing out that they were one of the most moderate offices! In closing, he promised that he would discuss the matter further with the Intelligence Bureau and referred Dr Agahi back to the Intelligence Office of Isfahan.

Meanwhile, lawyers at the Bar Association in Tehran expressed sympathy but indicated that the Intelligence Bureau held the authority in this matter, and they could not help. They suggested that she take her case to the chief of the judiciary for the region. He in turn stated that the activities of the paramilitary *Basijis*, the apparent offenders, were beyond his jurisdiction. He could not interfere. He too suggested that she return to the Intelligence Bureau, as all affairs of the Baha'i community and other minorities were under the supervision of that office.

On meeting with the governor of Najafabad, Dr Agahi was abruptly told, "You are all the trusted spies of foreign powers." The governor added that there was also graffiti about him, and that it was a sign of democracy and freedom in the country. He finally told her to go to the judiciary, to appeal to the Intelligence Bureau, and that this matter was of no concern to him. The runaround continued in this manner until Dr Agahi was forced to close the clinic where she had been practicing medicine for twenty-eight years. The financial pressures on the family were great. Her husband was a distinguished engineer who had lost his job at the beginning of the revolution, and the family's only source of income was her medical practice.[7] Night raids followed, with Molotov cocktails thrown at their home, and a notice was distributed in town threatening her and advising her to leave her home town for ever.

THE ARREST AND CONVICTION OF FIFTY-FOUR BAHA'I YOUTH IN SHIRAZ

In 2006, a group of Baha'i and Muslim youth obtained permission from the city council to undertake a humanitarian project in one of the impoverished suburbs of Shiraz. They gathered a group of destitute children, taught them to read and write, and offered education on hygiene and ethics.

The project made no reference to any religious teachings, yet security officials claimed it was incompatible with the principles of Islam. They arrested those involved on charges of conspiring against national security. The Muslim members of the group were released immediately, while the fifty-four young Baha'is remained in custody. Fifty-one were soon released on bail, but the other three, who were regarded as the ringleaders, were kept for a further month and a half before being freed.

But the matter did not end there. The young Baha'is were all summoned again and charged with conspiring against national security. Fifty-one of them received a suspended jail sentence with compulsory attendance of Islamic education classes. The remaining three received sentences of four years' imprisonment. They appealed. After being rejected by many defense attorneys, a lawyer finally accepted their case.

Even before the hearing, the three youths were summoned and told that their appeal had been denied. Haleh Ruhi, Ruha Sabet and Sasan Taqva each got five years in prison on November 20, 2007.

The incident was reported widely in international media, and following numerous appeals and protests by their families, a legal advisor was assigned to investigate the case. In a written report dated

From left: Haleh Ruhi, Sasan Taqva and Ruha Sabet.

June 16, 2008, the advisor stated emphatically that in all testimonials gathered, there was no mention of the Baha'i faith in the classes held. The advisor described the meetings he had with the accused and with their parents, and conveyed his findings in support of their innocence. He gave an account of his conversation with a colonel retired from law enforcement who was familiar with the group's activities and described the classes in painting, writing, hygiene, and ethics as humanitarian and altruistic in spirit, with no mention of any religious or political matters. "Ever since these youths came to Mahdi-abad, their manners, social behavior, and standards have had a positive effect on the children of the area, creating a progressive and positive change. This has caused much hope and optimism among the parents for the future of their children." Other witnesses conveyed the same sentiments when questioned by a representative of the Shiraz's Friday prayer leader.

This report was distributed in Iran by human rights activists, and presented to the UK Commission for Human Rights. Nevertheless, the verdicts and prison sentences remained in place. A letter written from prison by Haleh Ruhi described the conditions that the three endured:

> During these eighteen months, I have been deprived of any contact with others and of the social interaction that is the right of any prisoner. I am allowed a five-minute visit with my family once a week. I have been denied telephone communication, which is the right of any prisoner. During the first eight months, I was not allowed any books. Leave permits which are also prisoners' rights—allowing them five days of leave every twenty-five days of prison—have also become an issue for my family and myself. The Intelligence Office and the judiciary require unnecessary and useless visits to various offices for my family to obtain permission for the leaves. The time between the leaves has stretched to three or four months, and at times even longer. We need to spend even longer time in court to obtain permission for extending a five-day leave to a week.

> A prisoner should be kept in prison, but I have been at a detention center. The center is a closed building. They leave my food behind the door. I am not allowed to leave my prison cell. I spend the whole day in a closed cell. If I need to come out for any reason, I have to be blindfolded.
>
> I am allowed ten to twenty minutes a day to walk in a small yard. The duration of the walk is fixed by the guard. At times I am called out at eight in the morning, at other times at noon. The time cannot be extended. Are ten minutes of open air sufficient for a person who spends twenty-four hours in a closed cell?
>
> I am not allowed to use a telephone. Prisoners have the right to make calls. I am overlooking all that has happened prior to the verdict, but now, if I am a prisoner, treat me as a prisoner. If I am a prisoner, then take me to a prison, give me the right to fresh air, allow me to use the phone, let me be in contact with others.[8]

THE ARREST AND TRIAL OF THE "YARAN OF IRAN"

The term "*Yaran* [Friends] of Iran" refers to an informal group of Baha'is who are elected to tend the affairs of the Iranian Baha'i community in the absence of the banned Baha'i administration. The group was formed during Khatami's presidency with the government's approval. It initially consisted of five members, and two more were added later. Their activities have been in the open and were known to the government as they worked under the supervision of the Intelligence and Security authorities of the Islamic Republic.

On March 5, 2008, one member of the group, Mahvash Sabet, was arrested in Mashhad, and then on May 14 the remaining six members of Yaran were arrested at their homes in Tehran and imprisoned: Fariba Kamalabadi, Jamal al-Din Khanjani, Afif Naʿimi, Saʿid Reza'i, Behrouz Tavakoli and Vahid Tizfahm.

During the first seven months of their incarceration, all seven members were held in solitary confinement and underwent lengthy interrogations. Finally, the judicial authorities of the Islamic Republic announced their crimes: spying for Israel, blasphemy against Islam, and offenses against the Islamic Republic. The attorney general accused them of gathering information, "intrusive activities," and subverting the foundation of people's belief.

The trial date was announced as March 28, 2009. The Nobel Peace Laureate Shirin Ebadi, together with a few colleagues, agreed to defend the Yaran. However, they were never allowed proper access to the prisoners' files, nor were they allowed to meet with their clients. As the presidential elections approached, the media spread negative propaganda about the Yaran, accusing them of responsibility for a bombing in Shiraz and spying for foreign powers.

The trial was postponed three times and the prisoners' relatives were informed that the accused would be tried as *mahdur al-dam*—those whose blood may be shed without penalty—on charges of being *muharib ba khuda*, or enemies of God, a capital offense punishable by death. Finally, on January 12, 2010, a brief court session was held

Each member of the Yaran, the group administering the affairs of the Baha'i community of Iran, suffered ten years of imprisonment 2008–18. Seated from left: Sa'id Reza'i, Behrouz Tavakoli. Standing from left: Fariba Kamalabadi, Vahid Tizfahm, Jamal al-Din Khanjani, Afif Na'imi and Mahvash Sabet.

without any public attendance. As a result of political tensions in Iran, Shirin Ebadi was subsequently forced to leave the country. The trial was resumed in three sessions over February, April and June of 2010. Neither members of the public nor the relatives of the accused were allowed in any of the court sessions, except for the last, when the verdict was announced. Eventually, the lawyers were notified in August that each of the accused was sentenced to twenty years in prison, reduced to ten years on appeal. The sentences were met with widespread international protests, which were ignored by the Iranian authorities.

Chapter 18

An Obsession with Conspiracy Theories in the Islamic Republic

We have seen the Iranian susceptibility to conspiracy theories and the role that accusations of espionage played in the persecution of the Baha'is in earlier periods. Under the Islamic Republic, that same impulse has escalated into a paranoid obsession with conspiracy. In the government's view, the country is beset by anti-revolutionary agents and surrounded by foreign enemies. Those who do not blindly support the regime are seen as devious conspirators who oppose the system, even if subtly. The fear of enemies within and without, both real and imaginary, has been the pretext for relentless crackdowns on many strata of Iranian society, whether women, students, politicians, the intelligentsia, or non-Muslim Iranians. To justify the repression, the regime needs to provide excuses that are acceptable to the masses, and to achieve this aim it resorts to falsification and invents its own conspiracies.

History testifies to the role that such paranoid thinking has played in genocides, mass murder, forced labor camps, terror, and repression. The Nazi holocaust, China's cultural revolution under Mao Tse-Tung, the genocide in Cambodia, and the massacres in Sarajevo during the Bosnian war were all fueled by government-controlled media spreading lies and half-truths in which conspiracies played a large role.

For years, Iran's clergy have claimed that the repression of the Baha'i community is in fact a fight against foreign colonialism—against Israel, the United States, and Britain. Constant accusations are broadcast in the media and in the speeches of government authorities. To justify the allegations against the Baha'is and shore up baseless charges, the regime has launched enterprises such as the Institute for Iranian Contemporary Historical Studies and the Political Studies and Research Institute. A considerable portion of these institutes' publications are dedicated, directly and indirectly, to revealing secret conspiracies that have supposedly shadowed the lives of a multitude of victims for centuries, and are only now being exposed by the Islamic Republic.

Some of the most interesting examples are to be found in the work of 'Abdollah Shahbazi, the first director of the Political Studies and Research Institute, and one of the main figures behind the Institute for Iranian Contemporary Historical Studies. Shahbazi has taken the art of conspiracy theories to newly convoluted depths. He interprets the anti-Semitic fabrication known as the *Protocols of the Elders of Zion* as a false flag effort, authored by "Jewish plutocrats" to promote the idea that conspiracy theorists are pathologically paranoid. Thus, when the document is eventually revealed to be counterfeit they can discredit their enemies as the source of baseless conspiracy theories that implicate them in various plots against humanity. Similarly, he confirms that the *Memoirs of Dolgorukov* (see Chapter 4) are a forgery, but he asserts that it was commissioned by the British Secret Intelligence Services as part of a deeper conspiracy against Iran and Islam.

He links Baha'is to Zionism and "Jewish plutocrats" at the very inception of the religion. In his book *The History of Bahaism in Iran (Justar ha-i az tarikh-e Bahaigari dar Iran)*, published in 2003 by the Institute for Iranian Contemporary Historical Studies, Shahbazi claims that his own research reveals that when the Bab was working as a merchant in Bushehr, it was Anglo-Jewish companies operating in that region who convinced him to make his declaration of the new faith.[1]

In his book, Shahbazi goes as far as providing a novel interpretation of the Allahdad incident that occurred in Mashhad in 1839, when a number of Jews were killed in attacks on the Jewish quarter, and some 400 Jewish families, in fear of their lives, forcibly converted to Islam. Those who were forced to abandon their religion were called the *Anusim*, which translates as the "coerced ones." Contrary to all evidence, Shahbazi claims that the conversions took place without any pressure, in anticipation of the advent of the Bab in 1844, so that these crypto-Jews could then pretend that they were Muslims joining the new religion.[2] The abundance of similarly outlandish claims makes Shahbazi's book a twenty-first century equivalent of the *Memoirs of Dolgorukov*, with a more professional tone.

The endorsement and dissemination of such literature by the propaganda organs of the Islamic Republic is harmful to the intellectual and psychological health of Iranian society. During the past few years, accusations of a Jewish-Baha'i conspiracy against Shi'i Iran has proved troublesome even for the most prominent officials operating within the Islamic regime itself. In 2007 Shahbazi claimed that Saeed Emami, a leading figure in the Intelligence Ministry who died mysteriously in prison after revealing information about the assassinations of political prisoners, was an agent of the Jewish-Baha'i conspiracy. Shahbazi further accused Ruhollah Husainian, a friend of Saeed Emami and a close associate of President Mahmud Ahmadinejad, of being a Baha'i. These allegations implied that Iran's intelligence agency was now being directed by Baha'i-Zionist infiltrators. Shahbazi also suggests that the increasing harassment and persecution of the Baha'is during recent years are part of a conspiracy by the Iranian Intelligence Office to attract attention and support for the Baha'is.

However, Shahbazi's wild allegations are tame compared to those put forth in 2009 by Dr Mahdi Khaz'ali, son of Ayatollah Khaz'ali, on his website. Khaz'ali explicitly states that Mahmud Ahmadinejad is a crypto-Jew, or *anusi*, as is Ayatollah Mesbah Yazdi, the prominent Shi'i cleric and Ahmadinejad's patron, and that both are effectively acting in Israel's best interests.[3] Similarly, spokesmen for the regime's propaganda machine claimed in media broadcasts that the demonstrations of millions of Iranians who took to the streets to protest the June 2009 elections were actors in a conspiracy devised by the Baha'is.

Today more than ever, Iranian society needs to turn its back on this illusory world of hatred and deceit, and reassess many of the assumptions that shadow its world view. During the past few years, strong first steps have been taken in this direction by a number of statesmen and liberal-minded intellectuals as well as members of the general public. Still, there are those who prefer the familiar darkness of their own illusory world to a more complex and colorful reality. Iran's government spokesman still asserts that the Baha'i movement is "an organized set-up linked to alien powers, especially the Zionists," and the attorney general insists that the Baha'i administration is "evidently affiliated with Israel."

Chapter 19

Systematic Humiliation: Being Labeled Ritually Unclean (*Najes*)

From the beginning of the Islamic Revolution, official and semi-official discourse used polarized language to divide Iranians. Those idealized were labeled as combatants, revolutionary, committed, and faithful; the loathed others were called spreaders of corruption, members of the shah's secret police (SAVAK), traitors, anti-revolutionaries, and Baha'is. Mass media repeatedly linked Baha'is with SAVAK, whose very name provoked hatred and fear before the revolution, so that there is now a general misperception that most, if not all, SAVAK members were Baha'is, ignoring the fact that minorities would have been ineligible for the vast majority of positions in SAVAK, especially those involving torture, due to the highly sensitive nature of the work.

During the 2005 presidential elections in Iran, the conservative Qadiri Abyaneh debated with a reformist opponent. In the debate, broadcast by the Iran Labor News Agency (ILNA), Abyaneh posed the question: "Among those who hold an Iranian identity card, there are some who are spreaders of corruption. In your view, should a Baha'i, an ex-SAVAK member, or a homosexual be given permission to run for the presidency?"[1] This casual association, demonizing whole sections of the population in a public forum, is typical of efforts to manipulate public sentiment in the Islamic Republic.

The labeling of the Baha'is as *najes* has been one of the most pernicious violations of their dignity. According to Shi'i jurisprudence, certain objects, animals (dogs and pigs), and infidels are regarded as *najes*, and all contact with them must be avoided by Muslims. The idea that Babis and Baha'is were *najes* took hold during the Qajar period, but faded during the Pahlavi era. In environments where association with Baha'is was commonplace, whether through marriage, friendship, in the workplace or universities, many Iranians came to ignore such discrimination. But since the establishment of the Islamic Republic, the practice was officially implemented in places such as in prisons where Baha'is and non-Baha'is came into contact. Leftist political prisoners who were not Baha'i were also treated as ritually unclean. Reza Afshari, professor of history at Pace University, describes the conditions of the victims of such labeling who endure a different type of persecution and psychological torture:

> Unparalleled in the history of modern prisons, one traditional cultural practice became an official policy, compounding the problem of the over-crowded prisons and creating a novel punishment for prisoners. The traditional Shi'i Muslims always considered a non-Muslim to be *najes* (physically and spiritually unclean, polluting). In prisons, the category of the untouchables covered the entire leftist population. Of course, the Baha'is were the *najes* people par excellence. In the 1970s, when the Islamists were themselves prisoners of the shah's regime, they insisted that their infidel inmates (the Marxists) should not "touch their things." In the 1980s when they became prison officials they imposed the cultural-religious proscription as a prison rule. As shown in other instances, the Islamic Republic and ancient prejudices fed on each other. Such a practice underscores the relevance of a traditional culture as mainly a negation of the notion of equal concern and respect for all human beings.[2]

The repentant prisoners (*tawaban*), taking their cues from the zealot guards, particularly objected to being placed in the proximity of the *najes* leftists. The Islamists forbade the *najes* prisoners to touch anything that was moist or wet, like a teacup, since the traditional Shi'i Muslims considered water to be the main conduit of *nejasat* (impurity). In 1984, Raha[3] was transferred to Evin's ward 4,

> where the mainly leftist inmates, with a few Baha'i women clustered in a corner, lived in rooms 4 and 6. According to Raha, the female leftists' relationships with the Baha'is in the ward appeared normal, even cordial, and in Raha's case very friendly. Together they constituted the *najes* population of the ward. They were painfully reminded of their humiliating status during those designated nights when the showers had water. They were always the last group to use the showers, since good Muslims refused to follow the *najes* individuals in an area tainted by impurity. A Baha'i woman in ward 6 had a beautiful three-year-old daughter. She was also petite *najes*, not allowed to stroll into other rooms or even play with a Muslim child in the ward. Azadi's description of prison in the provincial city of Shiraz showed that the problems created for the *najes* prisoners were even more egregious than those experienced in Tehran's prisons.[4] Azadi saw the humiliating epithet of *najes* "was used as a psychological torture." It caused, in Raha's words, "daily torment and pain."[5] [6]

This issue was not limited to prisons. Before Baha'i workers were excluded and dismissed from factories, the supervising *mullahs* ordered special work areas to be allocated to the Baha'is, separating them from their non-Baha'i co-workers. They had to eat in separate rooms, and had to bring their own dishes and cutlery to avoid contaminating their Muslim colleagues.

A treatise entitled *Replies to Inquiries about the Practical Laws of Islam*,[7] written by Ayatollah Khamenei, deals with rulings on which the Constitutional Law of the Islamic Republic is based. These rulings also form the basis of the regime's policies regarding religious minorities, as well as guidelines for the behavior of government officials and others towards those minorities. They are available to the public on Khamenei's official website. A section concerning Baha'is follows:

> **Q 327**: Please answer the following questions:
>
> 1. What is the rule for Muslim students intermingling and shaking hands with students belonging to the deviant Baha'i

sect at the primary, secondary, and high school levels, irrespective of whether they are boys or girls, *mukallaf* [accountable] or *non-mukallaf*, within or outside the school?

2. What should be the behavior of teachers vis-à-vis students who either declare that they are Baha'is or are known to be such?
3. Third, what is the rule pertaining to things used by all the students, such as drinking-water taps, latrine taps, pitchers, soap, etc., knowing that the body and hands are wet?

   A: All members of the deviant Baha'i sect are considered *Najes* and their coming into contact with something requires observing the rules of purity (*taharat*) in cases where *taharah* is required. But the behavior of the headmasters and teachers with Baha'i students should be in accordance with the regulations and Islamic ethics.

Q 328: Please elucidate the duty of the believing men and women vis-à-vis the deviant Baha'i sect and the impacts that arise due to the presence of the followers of this sect within Islamic society?

> **A:** It is obligatory for all believers to counter the deceit and corruption of the deviant Baha'i sect and to stop others from being misled by this deviant sect or following it.

Q 329: At times the followers of the deviant Baha'i sect bring us food or something else. Is it permissible for us to use them?

> **A:** Any sort of association with the deviant and misleading Baha'i sect should be avoided.

Q 330: A large number of Baha'is live in our neighborhood and often visit our home. Some say that the Baha'is are *Najes* while others say that they are clean. These Baha'is also exhibit good morals. Are they *Najes* or clean?

> **A:** They are *Najes*, enemies of your religion and faith. So beware of them, my dear friends.[8]

In this same treatise, Khamenei argues that the People of the Book—those who follow revealed scripture, including Jews, Christians and

Zoroastrians—are not *Najes*. He disregards the fact that Baha'is also consider themselves People of the Book, recognizing the divinely ordained mission of the prophets of these faiths, and valuing Christian, Jewish, Zoroastrian and Islamic holy books as their own.

As the Guardian and Supreme Leader, Ayatollah Khamenei's view forms the basis for the government's official policies regarding religious minorities, although there are dissenting Shi'i legal views which are more progressive. In his treatise on *Questions and Answers*,[9] among a variety of subjects, Ayatollah Montazeri addresses the issue of the ritual impurity of the minorities. In reply to a question about the civil rights of a non-Muslim citizen (a follower of one of the recognized religious minorities) living in an Islamic state, he replies:

> Every citizen has social rights that have been stated in the Constitutional Law, and those rights are not confined only to Muslims. . . In my opinion, if the People of the Book have not been accidentally defiled through the consumption of alcohol or pork, or through contact with other impurities, they are not intrinsically *Najes* (impure).

Similarly, Ayatollah Jannaati declares on his official website the intrinsic purity of all human beings:

> Non-Muslims of any group (People of the Book, polytheists, and atheists) are intrinsically, physically and bodily clean. And if they stay away from things that are considered *najes* (impure) by Muslims, they will not have accidental uncleanness either.[10] [11]

It must be pointed out that the view expressed by Khamenei and Montazeri, that non-Muslim People of the Book are not *najes* or impure, is a positive shift in the outlook that some Muslim jurists have traditionally held on this issue. In traditional Shi'i belief, even non-Muslim People of the Book were considered, by some, as *najes*; and there are some who regard them as such to this day. Other restrictions on non-Muslims living in an Islamic state, such as the *dimmi* laws that required Christians, Jews, and Zoroastrians to pay an annual poll tax, were gradually abandoned in the late nineteenth century. Reports written by Western visitors to Iran and memoirs of some of the followers of the minority faiths convey painful accounts of the discrimination that prevailed. Napier Malcolm, the Christian missionary who lived in Yazd during the early years of the twentieth century, writes about the Parsi, or Zoroastrian, community:

> Up to 1895 no Parsi was allowed to carry an umbrella. Even during the time that I was in Yezd they could not carry one in town. Up to 1895 there was a strong prohibition upon eye-glasses and spectacles; up to 1885 they were prevented from wearing rings; their girdles had to be made of rough canvas... Up to 1891 all Zoroastrians had to walk in town, and even in the desert they had to dismount if they met a Mussulman of any rank whatsoever... Up to about 1860 Parsis could not engage in trade. They used to hide things in their cellar rooms, and sell them secretly. . . Up to 1870 they were not permitted to have a school for their children.[12]

But this prevailing repression of non-Muslims was not always the case historically. The magnificent civilization that bloomed in the Islamic world during the eleventh and twelfth centuries was a time when Islam stood apart from these corrosive prejudices. Muslims, Jews, Zoroastrians, even Buddhists and atheists, lived in peace and harmony within the Islamic societies that spread out from Andalusia in Spain to Persia and China. They each had their own places of worship, but there was no segregation, and non-Muslims could even hold high posts in government. If they were encouraged to embrace Islam, it was based on observing the tolerant and humane manners of Muslims. That was the Islam that prepared the grounds for the flourishing of science, a far cry from the divisive and malicious rulings that are pronounced by the grand ayatollahs of our time.

Chapter 20

The Perspectives of Iran's Grand Ayatollahs on the Baha'i Faith

The ayatollahs and the highest Shi'i legal authorities (*maraji'e-taqlid*) do not all share the same view on the Baha'i faith. While none of them regard this religion as rightful, their outlook on the Baha'i community is shaped by the extent of their open-mindedness, liberal world views, and goodwill, as opposed to fanaticism and bias.

AYATOLLAH KHOMEINI

One of the tactics used effectively by Ayatollah Khomeini in bringing down the shah's regime was his claim that Baha'is had participated in the shah's government, that they had ties to Israel and Zionism, and posed a threat to Islam. Although persecution and executions of the Baha'is began immediately in the aftermath of the revolution, the genocide that was feared as a result of Khomeini's earlier statements did not materialize, and the killings that did occur were not initiated by him. It is not known whether access to the confidential documents of the shah's government and army disabused him of his earlier beliefs, or if he had been aware of the reality even before the revolution.

Throughout the history of the religion, the attacks on the Baha'is had been instigated by local clergy or fanatical private citizens, and not resulted from central government policies. Now that the clergy held ultimate power, the persecution of the Baha'is was problematic. They could not all be executed on charges of heresy, but neither could the new regime leave them in peace.

After coming to power, Ayatollah Khomeini realized that it would be impossible to govern the nation according to strict Islamic law in the twentieth century, and that the educated and liberal-minded Iranian middle class would not tolerate atrocities carried out in the name of religion. Therefore, and in response to political struggles within the regime, the Ayatollah issued his famous *fatwa* on "the prior need of safeguarding the regime, even at the price of overruling certain Islamic requisites."[1] This *fatwa* allowed him to stand up to those members of the clergy who aimed to create a Taliban-type Islamic government, though it did not substantially change his course of action towards the Baha'is in the early years of the revolution. After Khomeini's death and the election of Ayatollah Khamenei as the Supreme Leader, the regime would gradually become more conservatively religious, and the persecution of the Baha'is would come under the supervision of a center commanded directly by the Supreme Leader and the Ministry of Information.

The journalist Roger Cooper observed in 1982 that, "despite his reputation for outspokenness Ayatollah Khomeini has not made any inflammatory anti-Baha'i remarks since his return to Iran."[2] One of the rare comments that Khomeini did make about the Baha'is came in reply to President Reagan, who had appealed for the lives of twenty-two Baha'is—more than half of them young girls—who were accused of espionage by the head of the Revolutionary Court in Shiraz and sentenced to be executed on February 21, 1983. The court order had provoked severe international outcry, including that direct plea from the US president. Khomeini responded in a speech that, as Dr Reza Afshari notes, mocked Reagan's humanitarian intentions but fell short of the harsh anti-Baha'i statements of the head of the Revolutionary Court:

> Mr Reagan says that these poor, calm Baha'is are silently doing their prayers and religious ceremonies; and that Iran has arrested them only because our beliefs are against their beliefs. Were these people not spies, you would not be raising your voices! You are doing this because you benefit from them. . . Baha'is are not a religious group, they are a party which was previously supported by the British, and now is being supported by the United States. They [the Baha'is] are spies like them [the Americans and British].[3]

Dr Afshari believes that Khomeini was fully aware of the non-political nature of the Baha'i faith, and that the sharpest edge of his rhetoric during his first years in power was directed at the royalists, the secular leftists, and the Mujahedin. The fact that Khomeini's early attacks on the Baha'is under the shah were not repeated after the revolution suggest that he was convinced that the Baha'is posed no political or security threat to the new regime.[4]

The record of the Islamic Republic's attempts to exterminate groups that threatened its existence, including the prison executions of the Mujahedin, confirms Dr Afshari's view that had the "Baha'i problem" been perceived as a threat to state security, the results would have been far more bloody and destructive than they were.[5] In some instances the actions of high-ranking authorities confirm this view. For example, when the Baha'is of Sangesar were attacked and harassed in the early years of the revolution, a group visited Ayatollah Khomeini in Qom to appeal for his support, and he ordered that the harassment be stopped. This order did not reflect a new policy for the entire country; it was regional and temporary.[6] It was only a week later that the house of the Bab in Shiraz was seized by the Revolutionary Guards and finally demolished.

Similarly, after the arrest and imprisonment of the members of the Baha'i Local Assembly of a village near Karaj, their wives appealed to Ayatollah Taleqani, who ordered the release of the prisoners. At the same time, violent crimes against the Baha'is of Karaj were being organized by the prayer leader there, and the persecution continued in other localities.

An important statement by Khomeini that reflects on the rights of Baha'is was either forgotten or deliberately ignored by clerics who regarded the harassment and persecution of the Baha'is as part of their duties:

> In reply to a question raised by the Higher Judicial Council regarding the non-Muslims who were members of People of the Book and those who were not, Imam Khomeini replied: "the mentioned non-believers are under the protection of Islam and the rules of Islam are applied to them the same as other Muslims. They are protected by the law[7] and their property is also respected." (Mehrpour 1384: 598)[8]

The reference to "those who were not" members of the People of the Book clearly referred to the Baha'is. Khomeini was fully cognizant of the intention of this question, and his reply explicitly ruled that the lives and property of the Baha'is were protected and respected by Islam. Nevertheless, the ruling is not mentioned in any other source, and was never implemented.

DISSENTING VOICES

Following Bazargan's removal from office on November 6, 1979, as the head of the temporary government, the affairs of the country fell under the control of the Supreme Council of the Revolution, whose members were unknown to all but a few. The persecution of the Baha'is and the executions during that period reached unprecedented levels. When their initial appeals were ignored, the National Assembly of the Baha'is appointed representatives to meet with high-ranking members of the clergy and government authorities.

In these meetings, Ayatollah Shari'atmadari was the only authority who received the representatives cordially. For forty-five minutes, he listened to their report and expressed interest through his questions. The spokesman of the National Assembly, Ruhi Roushani, was from Azarbaijan, and spoke to the Ayatollah in his native Turkish. At the end of the meeting, the Ayatollah expressed his regret at being unable to help as he was under house arrest and could only pray for the Baha'is.[9] Three days later, Ruhi Roushani was kidnapped and never heard of again.

Ayatollah Husain-Ali Montazeri was also placed under house arrest and denounced by Khomeini for disagreeing with the regime's policies. In 2008, in a courageous *fatwa* issued during a critically sensitive time for the Baha'i community, Montazeri declared that Iranian Baha'is deserve full rights as citizens. This *fatwa* was issued by the highest Shi'i authority in Iran in response to the unlawful arrest and imprisonment of the seven leaders of the Baha'i community known as Yaran-e Iran.[10]

This view was not new. Ayatollah Montazeri (*Resale-ye Istifta'at*, vol. I, and on his web page) had issued a similar *fatwa* several years earlier, without using the word "Baha'i." It stated that a rightful citizen would be protected from harassment by security forces, their lives and livelihood would be safe, and they would be entitled to education and employment.

While fully aware that this decree would not affect the government's policy, the Baha'i community responded to Montazeri's intervention joyfully, and Persian language media outside Iran reported it positively. It was a historic, courageous, and humanitarian act,

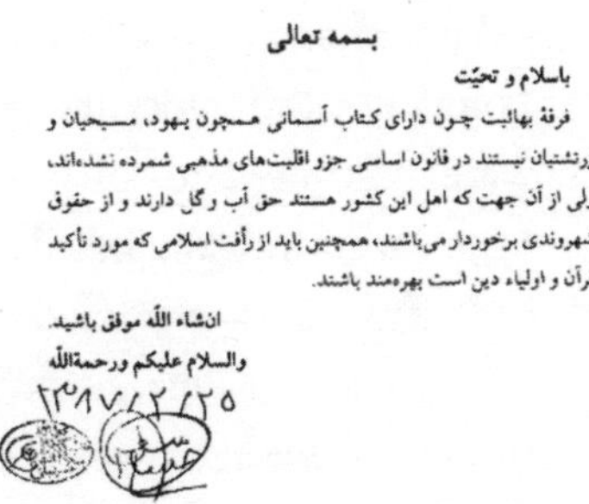

بسمه تعالی

باسلام و تحیّت

فرقۀ بهائیت چون دارای کتاب آسمانی همچون یهود، مسیحیان و زرتشتیان نیستند در قانون اساسی جزو اقلیت‌های مذهبی شمرده نشده‌اند، ولی از آن جهت که اهل این کشور هستند حق آب و گل دارند و از حقوق شهروندی برخوردار می‌باشند، همچنین باید از رأفت اسلامی که مورد تأکید قرآن و اولیاء دین است بهره‌مند باشند.

انشاء الله موفق باشید.

والسلام علیکم ورحمة‌الله

۱۳۸۷/۲/۲۵

The Persian text of the *fatwa* (judicial decree) issued by Ayatollah Montazeri declaring that Baha'is should have the same civil rights as other Iranian citizens.

especially coming from such a notable figure, and an indication of Montazeri's insight and fair-mindedness in a mature transformation of his judgment on the Baha'is.[11]

Among dozens of commentaries in response to this ruling, human rights journalist Akbar Ganji wrote:

> The recent ruling of Ayatollah Montazeri on the citizenship rights of the Baha'is is regarded as a step forward within the mentality of the Shi'a clergy. This ruling provides the liberal and the fair-minded with a chance to evaluate the attitude of the Iranians, the religious supreme legal authorities (*maraji'-e taqlid*), the learned divines, the clergy, the religious intellectuals, and the government of the Islamic Republic towards the Baha'is and to review their behaviour towards that community. This very ruling, in itself, speaks of deplorable brutalities such as deprivation from education, barring from employment, prohibition to hold religious activities, detention and imprisonment, pressure to recant, and finally death. Two examples follow:
>
> 1. In his book *Sar o tah yek karbas*, Jamalzadeh writes that when he was a child passing through the bazaar in Isfahan, he remembers incidents when suddenly someone would shout out: "Babi, Babi". People would then pour out a barrel of kerosene on the victim, and set him on fire.
> 2. During the early days of the Revolution, an elderly lady, the sister of one of the renowned intellectuals of the nation, was beheaded under the pretext of her belief in the Baha'i faith.
>
> If an irrationally hostile view did not exist, and were it not for the prevailing inhumane conduct towards the Baha'is, such a ruling would not have been necessary, nor would it have been viewed as a courageous act by one of the highest Shi'i clerics. Such a move is only regarded as a heroic one by those who are aware of the mentality of the Shi'a authorities.

Ganji continues: "The right to be present in the public domain is a logical consequence of the right to live and to be regarded as a citizen. If the Baha'is are entitled full citizenship rights, they must also be able to—like other citizens—freely present their views and beliefs, and to enter discussions with others." He notes how Iranian intellectuals have neglected to defend the rights of the Baha'is, and ends by posing a question to Ayatollah Montazeri:

> When speaking about the citizenship rights of the Baha'is, what exactly does the Grand Ayatollah mean by "citizenship" and "rights"? Can citizens be rightfully divided into unbelievers. . . and believers? When one enters the domain of citizenship, does that mean leaving behind the religious division of the civil community? Can the beliefs of citizens be categorized as "wayward" and "guided"? Or, should their beliefs, as well as their varied and different lifestyles be respected? Ayatollah Montazeri's reply to these questions would pave the way towards a peaceful society.[12]

In an interview with the Persian section of Radio France, while analysing the legal and religious implications of Montazeri's *fatwa*, Hasan Yousefi Eshkevari, himself a former religious leader, underlines where traditional perspectives are in conflict with the world at present:

> Given that Ayatollah Montazeri's decree clearly places Iranian Baha'is alongside other Iranian tribes and religions, and grants them citizenship rights together with all other peoples of Iran, it should be regarded as a step forward. In view of his religious authority and the traditional principles of Islamic jurisprudence that he follows, it is a great step that must be considered a highly significant ruling with positive bearing on the sociopolitical situation in Iran, and on the issues of human rights and freedom in the country. In my view, the framework of traditional Islamic Law does not allow for a defense of personal freedom, human rights, and citizenship rights in a similar manner that these rights are

regarded by the world today, as presented by the Charter of Human Rights, or discussed in the modern democratic or judicial systems in the world. That framework contains contradictions that would lead to possible problems or ambiguities.

At the same time, we should not forget that the traditional Islamic principles governing Iran at present, principles that Ayatollah Montazeri also follows and issues his rulings based on them, do create these ambiguities, and may raise new questions... Ayatollah Montazeri has written: "However, since the Baha'is are people of this land, they deserve to have the right to live in this country and enjoy full citizenship rights." Ayatollah Montazeri's stance towards the Baha'is may even be regarded as a most innovative turning point, for it marks the first time that a central religious Shi'a authority defends the national rights of the Baha'is, and what is more, before a religious state founded by the Shi'a clergy.

As such, this innovative action taken by Ayatollah Montazeri further adds to the complexity and the ambiguity of the human rights issue as well as the rights of citizenship from the viewpoint of Shi'a jurisprudence: Firstly, the Ayatollah has, indirectly, made a distinction between the citizenship rights and the human rights of an individual, as if there are no logical, historical, cultural, or political relationships between the two domains. As such, Ayatollah Montazeri's decree implies that it is possible for one—like the Baha'is—to be deprived of basic human rights, but to enjoy citizenship rights. Secondly, Ayatollah Montazeri has based the recognition of a set of beliefs as a religion upon the necessary condition of the existence of a Holy Book. He has accordingly excluded the Baha'i Faith from the group of religions, and furthermore, he has defined the deprivation of its followers from the basic human rights in the constitutional law as a direct consequence of such a characteristic. Thirdly, following this reasoning, Ayatollah Montazeri has specified one's affiliation to religious beliefs as the only condition, or at least as one of the most important conditions, for the granting of human rights to an individual.

In this same interview, Mehdi Mozaffari, professor of political science at Aarhus University in Denmark, explains that Montazeri's *fatwa* is consistent with Article 14 of the constitution, which states that the government of the Islamic Republic of Iran and all Muslims are duty-bound to treat non-Muslims in conformity with ethical norms and the principles of Islamic justice and equity, and to respect their human rights:

> So, he has not stepped that much further from the context of the Constitutional Law. My disagreement with his decree is that he has issued it out of sympathy and pity. That is to say, well, the Baha'is are people who anyhow belong to this land; a statement that has no clear legal or even religious meaning... The point of view that they are pitiful and must benefit from Islamic compassion is in fact contrary to the principle of citizenship... The concept of citizenship was created through the French Revolution in pluralistic republics. It means that all the people of a country, irrespective of their beliefs and religions are equal before the law. As Mr Eshkevari has clearly stated, this no longer depends on who is a Baha'i and who is not. The point is that we must not wait for the courageous but yet much limited measures taken by Islamic jurists and scholars. As mentioned by Mr Eshkevari, these two groups are also not in agreement between themselves. Ayatollah Montazeri has issued a decree; another equally influential Ayatollah may well contradict it in another ruling tomorrow. The issue is thus not resolved. It will just become more ambiguous.
>
> I believe that the fundamental issue is the need for the separation of religion from the state. That is to say, human rights, constitutional law, the state, government organizations, and the educational system must be based on other elements and not on religious assumptions and principles.[13]

During his election campaign in spring of 2009, the presidential candidate Mehdi Karrubi expressed the need for understanding and tolerance on a national level that would incorporate all minorities, explicitly including the Baha'is: "The Baha'is must also enjoy citizenship rights, like all others."[14] His spokesperson Jamileh Kadivar also defended the rights of the Baha'is in one of her campaign speeches.[15]

AYATOLLAH KHAMENEI AND OTHERS

It is not clear where exactly those Grand Ayatollahs who have remained silent concerning the Baha'i faith stand on constitutional questions. What is clear, however, is that many of them are well known enemies of the Baha'is. Since their early years of seminary training, many have wholeheartedly used their power and influence, both openly and secretly, to suppress the Baha'is, and they have identified such acts as the religious and even national duty of members of a Muslim society.

Ayatollahs Boroujerdi, Kashani, Khamenei, Mesbah Yazdi, Mahallati, Dast-Gheib, Makarem Shirazi, Rabbani Shirazi, Sadduqi . . . and tens of others fit into this group. Many were involved with the anti-Baha'i Hojjatieh society and are proud of their persecution of the Baha'is.

It is also not clear whether they are at all familiar with the religious and social teachings of the Baha'i faith, or if their judgments and the decrees that they have issued for executions of Baha'is and the confiscation of their properties are based on their own findings, or simply the result of incitement by those around them.

Chapter 21

The Appeals of International Organizations and the Iranian Diaspora

When harassment and persecution started at the beginning of the revolution, the Baha'i community tried to make its voice heard by writing to various Iranian organizations and the authorities of the new regime. These letters went unanswered, and gradually the authorities even refused to accept them, threatening or arresting the Baha'is who tried to approach influential individuals or offices.

The Baha'is were left with no choice but to appeal to international organizations. The Office of the Baha'i International Community at the United Nations (an NGO that collaborates with the UN) submitted the appeals of the Baha'i community to the UN Commission on Human Rights (UNCHR). Through its office in Brussels, it also informed the representatives of the European Community of the reports they had received.

Baha'is all over the world made contact with members of their own governments and other authorities in their countries. In each case, they provided documents and evidence of persecution and killings, and requested the support of those individuals in appealing to the government of Iran.

Many countries and international bodies have been most sympathetic towards the situation of Iranian Baha'is. The UNCHR has issued over thirty resolutions concerning violations of human rights in Iran, most of which referenced the terrible situation of the Baha'is there.

The UN General Assembly has also issued some twenty resolutions on the subject, and many more have followed from the European Parliament and other international organizations. Further information on these resolutions may be found on the web page of the Baha'i International Community,[1] and in the detailed and well documented publication, *Human Rights, the UN and the Baha'is of Iran*, by Nazila Ghanea.[2]

In reply to these protests and appeals, the Iranian representatives to the UN have repeated the same allegations: that the Baha'i faith is not a religion, that it was fabricated by Russia and Britain, that the Baha'is are spies for Israel, and that the movement was created to cause problems in Iran.

Although the Iranian regime claims that it pays no attention to international pressure, it published a booklet in English called *Bahaism – Its Origins and Role*, and distributed it to the members of the third committee of the UN General Assembly on November 18, 1982. Twelve pages of this thirty-two-page document were dedicated to answering the protests of the representatives of the Baha'i International Community regarding human rights violations against Iranian Baha'is. On page thirty, it states: "The beliefs of a few hundred followers of the Baha'i sect are of no logical or political-ideological value to us, and we do not regard it as dangerous."[3] Nevertheless, the Islamic Republic continues to cling to their pretext of the danger that the Baha'i community poses to Islam, and their allegations of espionage for Israel and Zionism.

Since the 1980s, following the rising wave of suppression and executions in Iran, the UNCHR appointed Special Rapporteurs with the mandate to investigate and monitor human rights violations in the country. These individuals traveled to Iran and prepared reports for the UNCHR. The first such representative, appointed in 1984, was Andrés Aguilar of Venezuela. After his resignation, the UNCHR appointed Ronaldo Galindo Pohl, a professor of law and human rights. In 1994, he was replaced by Maurice Copithorne, a Canadian lawyer. The reports submitted by all three confirmed that there had been widespread violations of the Iranian Baha'is' human rights.

From 2002 until 2011, the mandate of the Special Rapporteur on human rights in Iran was not renewed. This decision was made as part of a policy of creating a space for dialogue with Iran, during which the situation of Iranian Baha'is deteriorated and the UN protests and resolutions were ignored by the Iranian authorities. In July 2011, the UN appointed Mr Ahmad Shahid as its Special Rapporteur, who served until September 2016. In November 2016, Ms Asma Jahangir, a well-known human rights lawyer from Pakistan, was appointed to the post. After her sudden death in February 2018, the UN appointed Professor Javaid Rehman, a British-Pakistani lawyer, on July 6, 2018.

THE RESPONSE OF IRANIAN AUTHORS AND INTELLECTUALS TO THE BAHA'IS

The deadly silence of Iran's liberal intelligentsia in the face of the clergy's systematic persecution of the Baha'is constitutes a dark chapter in Iran's social history. Since the beginnings of the Babi and Baha'i movement, only very rarely have articles been published protesting their oppression. When a number of dramatic incidents shocked the nation during the reign of Muhammad Reza Shah, such as the murder of Dr Berjis and the Falsafi upheavals in 1955, a few protests were voiced. Otherwise, the general policy of the intellectuals and academics of the country has been total silence and to avoid even mentioning the word "Baha'i."

More recently, however, with a new wave of persecution and the increase in the worldwide protests against these injustices, Iranian authors and intellectuals have joined with other humanitarian and human rights advocates around the world in speaking out. The atrocities perpetrated against the Iranian Baha'i community are openly discussed on Persian-language media in Iranian diaspora communities around the world, and their rights defended. In the Persian section of international broadcasters such as Radio France, the BBC, and the Voice of America, liberal-minded Iranians have begun to speak alongside other experts in interviews and commentaries on human rights violations against the Baha'is.

Several brave theologians and lawyers in Iran have examined the case of the Baha'is in the context of Islamic law and Iranian constitutional law, and have declared that the injustices committed against the Baha'is cannot be justified by either legal system.

In an interview broadcast on Radio Zamaneh on January 7, 2009, Dr Seyyed Muhammad Hashemi, professor of law at Shahid Beheshti University of Tehran, stated in reference to the "People of the Book" that the religions referred to in the Quran, and used as a basis for the "recognized religions" in the Iranian constitution, are defined as such only because at that time in Arabia no other religions were known but those of the Jews, Christians, Sabaeans, and Zoroastrians. Dr Hashemi cited other verses of the Quran that declare the faithful are recognized as pious individuals who also believe in God and in the Day of Resurrection. In reference to his view that the Baha'is must be granted work permits, the right to study, and to have their marriages recognized and registered, Dr Hashemi said:

> I am not talking about the historical roots of Baha'ism, neither do I care if the Baha'is consider themselves as [true] Muslims or not, and I do not share their beliefs either. But, the Baha'is are also human beings, and as such must be entitled to human rights. These people have their own beliefs, and the inquisition of people's beliefs is not allowed. No one should be reprimanded or punished because of a certain belief. Consequently, they are entitled to the right to live and to enjoy human rights. As a matter of fact, the Constitutional Law contains an Article that includes this group as well as other groups. That is Article number 14. . . They are entitled to the opportunities and means that life offers. They need food and clothing, and in order to obtain such necessities, they have to work. As such, working is their right. Finally, in this day and age, illiteracy is not a feasible condition, so they are entitled to education in all aspects and levels that is offered.
>
> These people may not be officially recognised, [but] their existence as human beings is obvious. They may not be entitled to government posts, but they can be employed as workers, as labourers, as physicians and lead a normal life. When they go to the

> market, the Muslim and Christian shopkeepers must sell their goods to them. These all fall within the range of human rights. The Constitutional Law includes this interaction with the unbelievers as mentioned in Article 13. So, according to the Constitutional Law itself, these people must be entitled to their human rights.[4]

In this same program, the interviewer Saraj al-Din Mirdamadi asked Muhammad Amjad, an expert on Islamic and human rights issues, and a seminary graduate, for his view on this topic. Amjad replied:

> Citizenship rights is a newly coined term, and Islamic jurists must treat it as a new concept. It cannot be assessed according to the pre-modern religious laws. Freedom of religion, of belief, of speech, the right to live, to education, the right to hold religious or political gatherings or parties, as well as all other freedoms and rights that a citizen must enjoy, apply to any person that is living in the present day world.
>
> Once an Islamic state feels bound to enforce justice, and when it recognises that human rights and the implementation of those rights have a greater bearing on the realization of justice than their absence would, then, according to the provisions of the Charter for Human Rights, that state should necessarily respect the citizenship rights of the Baha'is who live within its jurisdiction.[5]

Theologians such as Mohsen Kadivar and Hasan Yousefi Eshkevari have written similar articles in support of the citizenship of the Baha'is.[6] The open letter reproduced below was written and signed by over 250 prominent Iranian academics, writers, artists, journalists, and activists around the world, and addressed to the Baha'i community.

> In the name of goodness and beauty, and in the name of humanity and liberty!
>
> As Iranian human beings, we are ashamed for what has been perpetrated upon the Baha'is in the last century and a half in Iran.
>
> We firmly believe that every Iranian, "without distinction of any kind, such as, race, colour, sex, language, religion, politics or other

opinions," and also without regard to ethnic background, "social origin, property, birth or other status," is entitled to all the rights and freedoms set forth in the Universal Declaration of Human Rights. However, from the very inception of the Baha'i Faith, the followers of this religion in Iran have been deprived of many provisions of human rights solely on account of their religious convictions.

According to historical documents and evidence, from the commencement of the Babi Movement followed by the appearance of the Baha'i Faith, thousands of our countrymen have been slain by the sword of bigotry and superstition only for their religious beliefs. Just in the first decades of its establishment, some twenty thousand of those who stood identified with this faith community were savagely killed throughout various regions of Iran.

We are ashamed that during that period, no voice of protest against these barbaric murders was registered.

We are ashamed that until today the voice of protest against this heinous crime has been infrequent and muted.

We are ashamed that in addition to the intense suppression of Baha'is during its formative decades, the last century also witnessed periodic episodes of persecution of this group of our countrymen, in which their homes and businesses were set on fire, and their lives, property and families were subjected to brutal persecution – but all the while, the intellectual community of Iran remained silent.

We are ashamed that during the last thirty years, the killing of Baha'is solely on the basis of their religious beliefs has gained legal status and over two hundred Baha'is have been slain on this account.

We are ashamed that a group of intellectuals have justified coercion against the Baha'i community of Iran.

We are ashamed of our silence that after many decades of service to Iran, Baha'i retired persons have been deprived of their right to a pension.

We are ashamed of our silence that on account of their fidelity to their religion and truthfulness in stating this conviction, thousands of Baha'i youth have been barred from education in universities and other institutions of higher learning in Iran.

We are ashamed that because of their parents' religious beliefs, Baha'i children are subjected to denigration in schools and in public.

We are ashamed of our silence over this painful reality that in our nation, Baha'is are systematically oppressed and maligned, a number of them are incarcerated because of their religious convictions, their homes and places of business are attacked and destroyed, and periodically their burial places are desecrated.

We are ashamed of our silence when confronted with the long, dark and atrocious record that our laws and legal system have marginalized and deprived Baha'is of their rights, and the injustice and harassment of both official and unofficial organs of the government towards this group of our countrymen.

We are ashamed for all these transgressions and injustices, and we are ashamed for our silence over these deeds.

We, the undersigned, ask you, the Baha'is, to forgive us for the wrongs committed against the Baha'i community of Iran.

We will no longer be silent when injustice is visited upon you.

We stand by you in achieving all the rights enshrined in the Universal Declaration of Human Rights.

Let us join hands in replacing hatred and ignorance with love and tolerance.[7]

The freedoms enjoyed by the Iranian diaspora community outside Iran, and the open communication possible on the internet today, have had a very positive effect on the discourse concerning human rights in Iran. The radically different position taken by the diaspora community online can be seen in the writing of a young freelance journalist, Khosrou Shemirani:

I Am a Baha'i Too!

I want to cry out: "I am a Baha'i! For as long as belief in the Baha'i Faith is viewed as a crime, consider me a Baha'i too! For that, you can end my meagre pension, you can stop me from going to university, and you can abuse me in grade school and high school! You can seize me, bind me, imprison me, torture me, separate me from my family, burn my house, confiscate my tools through your religious laws, prevent me from earning bread for my children, execute me and at the end, expel me from Iran – my sacred land!"

For more than 150 years, leaning on the Shi'i clerical establishment, the governmental apparatus of Iran has been determined to suppress the Baha'is of that land. At times these suppressions have been so extremely intense that they border on criminal insanity and at other times they have been more subtle and insidious – but always, always they have been present.

The fact that rulers, desiring to maintain their power, and religious priests, fearing the loss of their demagogical influence, have ordered and issued verdicts to suppress [the religious minorities] perhaps is not surprising. Most of the prominent men of history have sacrificed humanity for the sake of more power. And to protect their materialistic domain and riches, with utmost deviousness, the ecclesiastics bereft of spirituality have always and in all parts of the world, turned to corruption and the killings of the innocents. Unfortunately this historical trend is not surprising either. What causes astonishment is the silence of the society – a society which at times actively collaborates with these barbaric deeds. It is no secret that what has befallen the followers of the Baha'i Faith in Iran has often come about through our own hands. In response to every authority that issued an order or every *akhund* that produced a religious verdict, tens, hundreds, nay, thousands, of us proceeded to perpetrate harm upon the Baha'is and on occasions reddened our hands with their blood. But, why?

The collaboration of various sectors of society with the centers of power and the religious authorities can be attributed to ignorance, and one could say that every society has its share of ignorant individuals, who are used and exploited by influential and powerful elements or its ecclesiastic orders. But what about those that call themselves progressive, intelligent, on the intellectual vanguard, supporter of the people, and such names, and whose claim to moral authority has filled every ear?

Should we close our eyes to the truth that almost every political organization, whether on the left or the right, religious or secular, nationalistic or otherwise, in the most self-serving way has colluded in this suppression? Was not providing the theoretical justification for this suppression [of the Baha'is] the best support of the oppressors?

One of the most widespread notions for justifying suppression of the Baha'is was: "The Baha'i creed is not a religion, but a political organization in service of imperialism." Did we ever ask: Based on what evidence, what document, do we formulate such an absurd claim? The Tudeh Party of Iran was one of the most prominent promoters of the above notion, though it was never able to produce a single document in support of its claim. However, the manufacturing of this undocumented theory prompted the silence – and at times the supportive silence of the intellectuals – over the suppression of the Baha'is after the Islamic Revolution. The painful truth is that such a theory not only gained currency among the supporters of the [Tudeh] Party, but it also received widespread acceptance among the groups opposing the Tudeh... The purpose of this essay and raising the points above is to say: Now that we have begun to understand the concept of human rights, then even if we thought "the Baha'is are a political organization in the service of imperialism," we have no right to condemn them without proof and substantiated documentation... If we truly are defenders of the right of all humans, now is the time to raise our voice in unison and cry aloud: "For as long as the followers of the Baha'i Faith are suppressed and imprisoned for their religion and convictions, we are all Baha'is!"[8]

Beyond the efforts of individual Iranians advocating for the rights of the Iranian Baha'i community, recent years have witnessed numerous publications and statements from Iranian political, social, and human rights organizations in support of the rights of the country's Baha'is. For example, in a letter addressed to the Secretary-General of the

United Nations in 2008, the *Association des Chercheurs Iraniens*, headed by Dr Husain Lajevardi, noted several incidents of injustices inflicted upon the Baha'i community and requested the United Nations to investigation and intervene.

Nobel Peace laureate Shirin Ebadi has on numerous occasions courageously defended the rights of Iranian Baha'is. In 2008, Ebadi and five other women Nobel Peace laureates issued a joint statement requesting the immediate release of the seven Baha'is known as the Yaran of Iran.[9] Ebadi also agreed to defend the Yaran in court, but the regime made things so difficult for her that after traveling abroad she was unable to stay in Iran for the trial, such as it was (see Chapter 12). Other groups that have issued statements defending the human rights of the Baha'is include the International Organization of Human Rights Defenders in Iran, the Iran Human Rights Documentation Center, the Iranian Community Organization of Australia, the United Republicans of Iran, the Constitutionalist Party of Iran, the Worker-Communist Party of Iran, the Organization of Iranian People's *Fedaian* (Majority), the Organization of Iranian Socialists, the National Salvation Movement of Iran, the Iranian Human Rights Activist Groups in Europe & North America, the Human Rights Activists in Iran, and the Human Rights Organization of Kurdistan.

Epilogue

Ten years have passed since the publication of this book in Persian. Now, when assessing the situation of the Baha'i community in Iran, two parallel processes stand out. One is the intensified crackdowns during the presidency of Mahmoud Ahmadinejad (2005–13) and their continuation during the term of office of President Rouhani (2013–). The other is the wave of empathy and sympathy towards the Baha'is that has grown among intellectuals, artists, and the general populace.

Despite the lapse of forty years since the establishment of the Islamic Republic, the schemes used for the suppression of the Baha'is have remained unchanged. Group after group of Baha'i men and women have been arrested and condemned to short and long-term prison sentences with allegations such as "acting against national security," "propaganda against the regime," and "blasphemy." Hundreds of Baha'i men and women have been given five-or ten-year jail sentences after being judged in courts where the prosecutor and the judge were one and the same person, and where no defense attorney was allowed to enter. Those convicted testify that some of these trials barely lasted five minutes, and the judge would not even look at the file. Faced with objections to their lack of investigation in such cases, the judges have typically responded by saying: if the answer given by the accused as to whether or not he or she is a Baha'i is affirmative, that is sufficient evidence to justify a five-year prison sentence.

In addition to the confiscation of the homes and properties of the Baha'is during the previous four decades, the last ten years have also witnessed seizures of the agricultural lands of farmers in towns such as Semnan, Yasuj, and Qaem-Shahr, as well as in the villages of Kata in Boyer-Ahmad Province and Ayval in Mazandaran. The Baha'is in these localities had been farmers for generations; but with the expansion of the towns, and the rise in price of agricultural land, greed led local authorities, including the *mullahs* leading Friday prayers (*Imam-jom'eh*), and security and administrative officials, to take over their properties. The prevalent scheme used by the authorities has been to first incite the hatred of the local population against the Baha'is by spreading negative propaganda from the pulpit and the local press. They would then drive the Baha'is out of their homes and expel them from the region, using threats, military force, beatings, and insults. Eventually, the authorities would divide the vacant lands between themselves. Naturally, any complaint or appeal made by the farmers to the judicial authorities, who themselves have a hand in all this, is of no avail.

In a series of new raids that were carried out on May 21, 2011, targeting the Baha'i Institute for Higher Education (BIHE),[1] all the books and computers were confiscated and twelve of the professors were arrested. These individuals, whose only crime had been to educate young Baha'is who had been barred from entering university, were each accused of "propaganda against the regime" and sentenced to four or five years' imprisonment.[2]

Dozens of organizations for Islamic propaganda, heavily funded by the government, focus on the task of persecuting the Baha'is and claim spreading hatred against them is their most significant achievement. The continued campaign of hate and false accusations against the Baha'is in the media aims to justify the persecution. In principle, it is not different to the anti-Semitic propaganda of the Nazis. Such inflammatory provocations have tragic consequences. A recent example is the case of Mr 'Ata'ollah Rezvani, a Baha'i businessman residing in Bandar-Abbas, who was kidnapped on August 24, 2013,

Professors from the Baha'i Institute for Higher Education who have been imprisoned.

by an unknown gang while leaving his home. He was driven to an uninhabited area outside the city limits and shot in the head from behind. The assassins were never identified. The murder was not reported in the Iranian newspapers, and did not raise any protest, except among prisoners of conscience at Rejaee prison, including some Baha'is, who condemned the assassination in a statement, and demanded that the murderers be identified and brought to justice.[3]

Concurrent with the inauguration of the Baha'i Temple in Santiago, Chile, in October 2016, two brothers, incited by the *Imam-jom'eh* in Yazd, attacked Farhang Amiri outside his home, stabbing him to death in front of his wife and children. The killers confessed to the murder and added that they would not refrain from killing other Baha'is in the future. Both were absolved of all charges by the courts of Yazd.

'Ata'ollah Rezvani

Farhang Amiri

Also consider the following incident, which occurred in the spring of 2016. It created a frenzy in Iran and reveals how great the regime's hostility towards the Baha'is remains.

Mrs Fariba Kamalabadi, one of the seven members of the Yaran who was serving a ten-year prison sentence (see Chapter 17), had been given a three-day break to visit her family, after she had been deprived for seven years of every legal right and temporary leave that prisoners are entitled to. During these three days, she was visited by Mrs Faezeh Rafsanjani who, some years earlier, had shared the same cell with her for three months. A photograph of this visit, taken with the permission of Mrs Rafsanjani, surfaced online and on social media.

The event per se was of no particular significance, but as Faezeh Rafsanjani was the daughter of Ayatollah Rafsanjani—one of the founders of the Islamic Republic and an influential political figure—this visit sparked outrage among the nation's religious and political leaders. Her action was denounced by her father immediately. Ayatollah Makarem Shirazi called the visit an "absolute abomination" and a "prosecutable crime." The clerics unanimously demanded that Ms Rafsanjani repent and apologize for her sin. She refused, and said that she regarded her act as a friendly and humanitarian gesture. Naturally, such a response, especially coming from a woman, was not well received by the clerics, especially as it indicated that their forty years of negative propaganda against the Baha'is had had no effect on an ayatollah's daughter.

The Iranian prosecutor general pronounced that the Baha'i faith had been created by Israel, and warned that "those individuals who contact the followers of this sect should await the judicial consequences of their action." A senior theologian declared that any friendship with the Baha'is constitutes a "betrayal to Islam and to the Revolution", while another official announced that "any association and socializing with the Baha'is is contrary to the teachings of Islam." To document all the hostile comments, threats, and accusations heaped upon the Baha'is is beyond the scope of this section. But suffice to say that this turned out to be one of those rare occasions that all the various factions of the Islamic Republic, whether hardliners or reformists, agreed with each other and condemned this natural and brave gesture of friendship by Faezeh Rafsanjani.

Just as these attacks continue, the ban on Baha'i students entering universities remains in effect, despite protests from within the country and abroad. If Baha'i students at universities are discovered then they are expelled, no matter whether they are in their first year or their last. Many Baha'i scholars and writers suffer in much the same way: they cannot publish their work, knowing that if they do the books are likely to be seized by the authorities. Whether their work is scientific research, a translation of a philosophical work, a poetry collection, or a story with absolutely no relation to the Baha'i faith. Even when a non-Baha'i author or translator publishes a work, the Baha'i faith can only be mentioned in the context of expressing contempt for its beliefs. Active censorship is complemented by self-censorship. Before sending any book to the relevant authorities for approval, publishers automatically observe this red line.

In commemoration of the events in the history of their faith, Baha'is abstain from work on nine days in the course of the year. Such a "demonstration of faith" is disagreeable to the Islamic Republic. The Baha'i shops that are closed in observance of their religious holy days are sealed by the authorities, and often the business licenses of the owners are revoked. Naturally, such closures disrupt the lives of families whose only source of income is their shops, but they also have a negative effect on business relations with other traders and banks. Some shopkeepers have been threatened and forced to sign an official pledge specifying the dates that the shop will be closed. According to Iranian Trade Law, business owners are allowed to close their shops for up to fifteen days a year, but the authorities do not allow any of the Baha'i holy days to be included in these dates. This is just another part of the government's effort to weaken Baha'i families, reduce the community to an insignificant minority, disable it economically and educationally, and force it into social exile.

Over the past decade, the General Assembly of the United Nations has issued forty statements expressing its concern over human rights in Iran, especially when it comes to the Baha'i community.[4] Similar statements have been issued by the European Union. The response of the Iranian authorities to such protests has often been silence, but when a response has been deemed necessary, the facts have been refuted and the existence of freedom of religion in Iran asserted.[5]

EXPRESSIONS OF SYMPATHY WITH THE BAHA'IS FROM WITHIN IRAN

The intensity of crackdowns on members of the Baha'i community has raised a range of protests and expressions of sympathy among the Iranian population. This indicates that many ordinary Iranians are convinced of the innocence of the Baha'is and the unfounded nature of the accusations leveled against them by the government.

The non-violent resistance and resilience of the Baha'is in the face of forty years of oppression and tyranny has placed them in the vanguard of the enlightened forces seeking freedom, and on the front lines of the struggle against injustice and authoritarian oppression. It is thus natural that when speaking of state repression and tyranny, and the long, peaceful struggle of the Iranian people, that the Baha'is and women of Iran come to mind.

An International Symposium on "Intellectual Othering and the Baha'i Question in Iran" was held from July 1–3, 2011, at Toronto University and was attended by a large audience. At the invitation of Professor Mohamad Tavakoli-Targhi, over thirty scholars and human rights activists from North America and Europe gave talks[6] concerning the persecution of Iran's Baha'is.

That same year the documentary film *Iranian Taboo*, directed by Reza Allamehzadeh, was released. The film provided a glimpse of the persecution suffered by the Baha'is of Iran, their forced exile from their homeland, the seizure of their land, and various other systematic discriminations against them.

Another film, *The Gardener*, directed by Mohsen Makhmalbaf, was released in 2013. It depicts the journey of a father and his son to Israel to learn more about the Baha'i faith. After speaking to a Baha'i gardener from Papua New Guinea, the father discovers that his own ideas have much in common with those of the gardener, and in fact to the belief system of the Baha'i faith itself, and also to the views of great thinkers such as Gandhi and Mandela. Yet his son holds all religions responsible for the chaotic state of the world.[7] This film portrays the current situation in Iran, where the older generation continues to believe in religion but many young people have severed themselves from it.

In July 2013, the human rights activist Mohammad Nourizad visited the home of Kamran Rahimian and his wife, who are both serving prison sentences for their involvement with the Baha'i Institute for Higher Education. During that visit, Mr Nourizad kissed the feet of their four-year-old son, Artin, who is being cared for by his grandmother. He wrote a moving account of the meeting and posted it on his blog with a photo of him kissing the boy's feet. Nourizad explained that he'd done this to apologize, as a Shi'i Muslim, for all the injustices suffered by the Baha'is over many years. He added that apologies from the nation's leader and its religious and non-religious authorities were also owed to the country's Baha'i community. It should be noted that Artin's grandfather was executed by a firing squad in 1984 for being a Baha'i.

Nourizad's visit was strongly criticized in the media, but at the same time a wave of approval arose for him and his courage in supporting the Baha'is. Mehrangiz Kar, a prominent lawyer and human rights activist in the United States, wrote:

> when Mohammad Nourizad bestowed a kiss on the foot of a child, he threw the whole contemporary political and social history of Iran into turmoil and challenge. . . When he kissed the foot of a Baha'i child recently, he sent a message much stronger and louder than tens of books and stories on the subject. . . The history of Iran is blood-stained with its Babi and Baha'i killings. What a difference there is between bestowing a kiss upon the feet of a Baha'i child, and the social and political nature of contemporary Iranian history.[8]

Mehdi Khalaji, a scholar of Islamic studies and a political analyst, wrote:

> The fact that Mohammad Nourizad visited a Baha'i child whose parents are serving prison sentences due to their belief in the

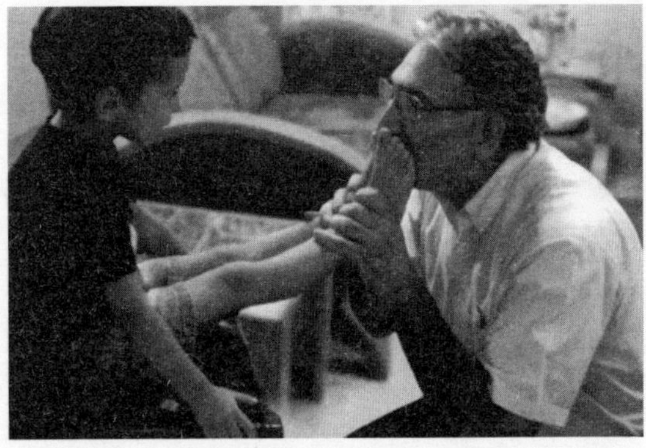

Mohammad Nourizad kissing Artin Rahimian's feet.

> Baha'i faith, or that Mohsen Makhmalbaf makes a film about the Baha'is, is an indication that the icy frost of our Shi'i conscience might thaw and change under the heat of the sun of justice. During my years of study and mingling with the Baha'is, I have read and heard stories of their sufferings, the remembrance of which makes me shudder with shame and fury.[9]

Later that year, Mohammad Nourizad and Dr Muhammad Maleki, the first president of the University of Tehran since the revolution, visited the home of Taraneh Taefi on September 23, 2013. Taraneh was a seventeen-year-old girl who had been banned from entering university because of her faith. Her mother, a professor of psychology, had been sentenced to five years' imprisonment because of her involvement with the Baha'i Institute for Higher Education. On that same day, the two men visited an elderly lady who had two sons, Amir Keyvan and Amir Kamran, and a daughter-in-law, Faran, in prison serving five-year sentences for the crime of teaching at the Baha'i home-university.

During early 2014, in a bold and unprecedented move, Ayatollah Masoumi Tehrani presented the Baha'i community of Iran with an exquisite work of calligraphy of an excerpt from Baha'u'llah's *Kitab-i-Aqdas* (*Most Holy Book*). Part of the chosen passage reads "Consort with all religions with amity and concord." This gesture was followed by a massive wave of support. A number of prominent religious leaders who were gathered at a conference in New Delhi commended the action, and stated that it represented a profound appeal for religious coexistence. This was accompanied by a statement calling for an end to the persecution and discrimination against the Baha'is of Iran.

On February 10, 2018, *The Times* published the text of an open letter addressed to Muhammad Javad Larijani, the head of the High Council for Human Rights in Iran. Signed by twenty-five prominent international lawyers and human rights activists from various countries, it was an appeal for an end to the regime's persecution and discriminatory treatment of the Baha'is and a call for them to be given equal rights as citizens of Iran. The letter mentions the false statements made by Larijani in the assessment session of the United Nations Universal Periodic Review of human rights records in Iran, held in October 2014. During that meeting, Larijani claimed that "Baha'is are [a] minority in Iran. . . they are dealt [with] under the so-called citizenship contract. So under this citizenship contract, they enjoy all the privileges of any citizen in Iran." The letter also calls upon Larijani to examine the recently launched Archives of Baha'i Persecution in Iran website. It contains thousands of documents, all translated into English, demonstrating the extent of the human rights violations committed by the Iranian state.[10]

WHAT THE FUTURE HOLDS FOR THE BAHA'IS IN IRAN

It is always difficult to predict the future, especially in a country such as Iran that has experienced significant political, economic, and social crises since the beginning of the revolution. Now, forty years after the establishment of the Islamic Republic, the greatest opposition force facing the regime is the generation that was born after the revolution—a generation that does not see the state's oppressive ideologies as compatible with its own ambitions and aspirations for a free and prosperous country.

The best to be hoped for is that the nation's discontent will eventually force the state to review its policy and to end the suppression of minority voices, whether religious, ethnic, or political, so that the Baha'is too will enjoy citizenship rights, and their lives, properties, and security will be protected by the legal system. This, however, will only be realized when a large number of open-minded individuals and writers in Iran, together with the masses, declare that Baha'is must be given the rights to which they are entitled, recognizing that the Baha'i community is, and always has been, a part of Iranian society, and that, as their fellow citizens, they must stand up for the Baha'i community in the face of cruelty and oppression. It is also to be hoped that progressive clerics in religious centers such as Qom will recognize and value the religious and irreligious alike, and allow believers, unbelievers, and apostates of any tradition or doctrine to benefit from full human rights in their own country. Unless and until such changes occur, despite any aspiration of the government for reform, history may repeat itself and what happened during the Constitutional Revolution may very well recur. Without the support of others, the Baha'is and other marginalized groups in the country will continue to remain as outsiders.

In anticipating such a future, the possibility of repeated, bloody assaults on the Baha'i community during another revolution, a war, a military coup, or similar, should not be ignored. This book has demonstrated that at times of great upheaval in Iran, including the assassination of Naser al-Din Shah, the Constitutional Revolution, the transition from the Qajar to the Pahlavi regime, the 1953 coup d'état, and the Islamic Revolution, the Baha'is have been subject to the greatest threats and attacks. The extent to which such events can be prevented, or their severity reduced, is directly related to the awareness and mindfulness of the people of Iran, and dependent upon their persistence in securing the social and citizenship rights of all religious and tribal minorities of the country.

In the midst of all this, and despite all that has happened to the Baha'i community and all that they continue to face, they should turn their gaze towards the future. Taking strength from expressions of sympathy and mutual understanding from among their fellow compatriots, they must continue to bring down the walls that have separated them from others. The destiny of the Baha'is in Iran lies in the hands of the people of Iran.

Postscript

The resurrection of anti-Baha'i violence that began with the Islamic Revolution of 1979 continues unabated to this day. Even as the Iranian government grapples with ever more challenging problems confronting the Iranian people, it maintains its obsessive hate propaganda and systematic discrimination against its largest non-Muslim religious minority, denying their fundamental human rights, especially freedom of conscience and belief.

The philosopher George Santayana famously said that "those who cannot remember the past are condemned to repeat it." This book is an attempt to bring the historical truth to the surface so that we can perhaps conceive of a different and brighter future, liberated from the darkness and atrocities of the past. The root of all evil is the dehumanization of others, portraying victims as aggressors and justifying injustice as a glorious demonstration of divine virtue. Equally, the root of all good is to speak truth to power, speak of a shared humanity, and demonstrate that we are all worthy of respect because of our inherent dignity.

It has been an enormous challenge to convey such a history merely through episodes and epochs, neatly divided and categorized for the reader in a coherent, analytical fashion. The problem has not been a dearth of facts. On the contrary, the evidence of widespread cruelty is overwhelming. The problem has been how to express the reality of this inhumanity for those who suffered it, often for generations. No pen can adequately describe the lasting wounds for those whose families have been shattered, homes looted, and loved ones imprisoned, tortured, or hanged. The deeper meaning of these unspeakable atrocities, exacerbated by calumny and denial, is best expressed by recognizing that it can never be adequately captured in words.

Yet, just as the vicious persecution of the innocent is overwhelming, so too is the astonishing spiritual resilience of this long-suffering community. Despite more than a century and a half of ceaseless and ruthless persecution, the fanatical forces that today have the vast resources of a government at their disposal have manifestly failed to destroy the Baha'is. The encounter between perpetrator and victim is of course a universal story in the history of many different nations and cultures. The strong seek to dominate and destroy the weak, perhaps out of political calculation, or through simple fear and ignorance. An identity built on hatred and the scapegoating of others to build a false sense of self is an easy and appealing escape from shortcomings and failures, or simply an opportune means of acquiring power. Either way, the Baha'is have stood firm throughout their history and withstood untold trials and tribulations, rather than giving in to the dictates of their tormentors. Their resistance has not, however, been through violence, because that would run counter to their essential belief that just as human beings are capable of cruelty, so too are they capable of spiritual transformation and service to humankind. The resistance of the Baha'is has been through remaining true to their beliefs, by continuing to spread compassion and justice, even among their fellow inmates in the notorious prisons of Iran, where they became a source of inspiration for those in the most desperate conditions. Their unshakeable integrity and legendary heroism has shown people, in the most striking manner, that the power of the human spirit is far greater than the power of hatred and violence.

It is this resilience that has moved so many prominent Iranians, from human rights champions to famous artists, and from dissident Islamic clerics to former supporters of the Islamic Revolution, to raise their voices in defense of the Baha'is, demanding respect for their human rights. The historical tide is turning, and awareness of the historical truth is a central ingredient of this emerging emancipatory consciousness that seeks to build a new Iranian identity free from the poison of hatred and fanaticism.

Dostoyevsky famously said: "There is only one thing that I dread: not to be worthy of my sufferings." The heroes whose stories have been related in this book have certainly been worthy of their sufferings. In the face of the worst expressions of human nature, they have demonstrated the highest potential of humankind for compassion and love; they have been shining lamps in the midst of darkness, confident that within these sacrifices lay the seeds of a better future.

When the Nazis were at the height of their power, few could have imagined that one day Holocaust memorials and remembrances would become prevalent. The same could be said of so many other historical injustices around the world, from Argentina and Chile to Cambodia and Rwanda. Iran's day will come too, and one day school children will learn the truth about what was done to the Baha'is, and how they remained steadfast and true to their beliefs even in the worst of times. Hopefully this book will make a small contribution to that day when the memory of the courageous men and women whose lives were so horribly extinguished will be remembered and celebrated in a new and glorious Iran.

Appendix

The Names of the Baha'is Executed Since the Start of the Islamic Revolution Until the Present Time, 1978–2018

(SH = Solar Hijri calendar)

1978 / 1357 SH – During the revolution

1. Ahmad Esma'ilí (Jahrom)
2. Ruhollah Teymúrí (Birjand)
3. Zia'ulláh Haqíqat (Jahrum)
4. Mír-Muhammad Azízí (Khurmuz)
5. Hátam Rúzbehí (Búyer Ahmad)
6. Ján-Alí Rúzbehí (Búyer Ahmad)
7. Shír-Muhammad Dast-Písh (Búyer Ahmad)
8. Sefatolláh Fahandezh (Shiraz)
9. Avaz-Gul Fahandezh (Shiraz)
10. Parvíz Afnání (Míyánduáb)
11. Khosrou Afnání (Míyánduáb)

1979–80 / 1358 SH – During the premiership of Bázargán

12. Ebráhím Ma'naví (Hesár)
13. Husain Shakúrí (Ushnavíyeh)
14. Muhammad Muvahhed (Tehran)
15. Bahár Vujdání (Mahábád)
16. 'Alí Sattárzádeh (Búkán)
17. 'Alí-Murád Dávúdí (Tehran)

18. ‘Azamat’ulláh Fahandezh (Shiraz)
19. Rúhí Roushaní (Tehran)

February 1980 to June 1981 / Bahman 1358 to Khurdád 1360 SH

During the presidency of Banisadr and premiership of Rajá’í

20. Habíbolláh Panáhí (Urúmíyyeh)
21. ‘Abd al-Husain Taslímí (Tehran)
22. Húshang Mahmúdí (Tehran)
23. Ebráhím Rahmání (Tehran)
24. Husain Nají (Tehran)
25. Manúher Qá’em-Maqámí (Tehran)
26. ‘Atá’olláh Muqarrebí (Tehran)
27. Yúsef Qadímí (Tehran)
28. Bahíyyeh Náderí (Tehran)
29. Kámbíz Sádeqzádeh Mílání (Tehran)
30. Yúsef ‘Abbásíyán (Tehran)
31. Heshmatolláh Rouhání (Tehran)
32. Ghulám-Husain A‘zamí (Tehran)
33. Badí‘olláh Yazdání (Tehran)
34. ‘Alí-Akbar Mu‘íní (Tehran)
35. ‘Alí-Akbar Khursandí (Tehran)
36. Parvíz Bayání (Tehran)
37. Mír-Asadolláh Mukhtárí (Bírjand)
38. Hasan Ismá‘ílzádeh (Sanandaj)
39. Yúsef Subhání (Tehran)
40. Farámarz Samandarí (Tabríz)
41. Yadolláh Ástání (Tabríz)
42. ‘Alí-Dádásh Akbarí (Rasht)
43. Yadolláh Mahbúbíyán (Tehran)
44. Zabíh’olláh Mumení (Tehran)
45. Núrolláh Akhtar-Khávarí (Yazd)
46. Mahmúd Hasanzádeh (Yazd)
47. ‘Azízolláh Zabíhíyán (Yazd)
48. Fereydún Farídání (Yazd)
49. ‘Abd al-Vahháb Kázemí Manshádí (Yazd)

50. Jalál Mustaqím (Yazd)
51. 'Alí Mutahharí (Yazd)
52. Rezá Fírúzí (Tabríz)
53. Muhammad-Husain Ma'súmí (Núk, Bírjand)
54. Shekar-Nesá Ma'súmí (Núk, Bírjand)
55. Behrúz Saná'í (Tehran)

1981

56. Manúchehr Hakím (Tehran)
57. Mehdí Anvarí (Shiraz)
58. Zabíh'olláh Dehqání (Shiraz)
59. Núráníyyeh Yársháter (Tehran)
60. Yadolláh Vahdat (Shiraz)
61. Sattár Khushkhú (Shiraz)
62. Ehsánolláh Mehdízádeh (Shiraz)
63. Sohráb (Muhammad) Habíbí (Hamadán)
64. Husain Khándel (Hamadán)
65. Tarázolláh Khozain (Hamadán)
66. Fírúz Na'ímí (Hamadán)
67. Náser Vafá'í (Hamadán)
68. Sohail (Muhammad-Báqer) Habíbí (Hamadán)
69. Husain Mutlaq (Hamadán)
70. Buzurg Alavíyán (Tehran)
71. Háshem Farnúsh (Tehran)
72. Farhang Mavaddat (Tehran)
73. Masíh Farhangí (Tehran)
74. Badí'olláh Faríd (Tehran)
75. Yadolláh Pústchí (Tehran)
76. Varqá Tebyáníyán (Tehran)

1 August 1981 to 30 August 1981 / Murdád-Shahrívar 1360 SH

During the presidency of Muhammad-Alí Rajá'í and premiership of Ayatollah Báhunar

77. Kamál al-Dín Bakhtávar (Mashhad)
78. Nematolláh Khatíbpúr Shahídí (Mashhad)

79. Alláhverdí Míthâqí (Tabriz)
80. Manúchehr Kháze'í (Tabriz)
81. 'Abdul-'Alí Asadyárí (Tabriz)
82. Husain Asadolláhzádeh (Tabriz)
83. 'Esmá'íl Zehtáb (Tabriz)
84. Parvíz Fírúzí (Tabriz)
85. Mehdí Báherí (Tabriz)
86. Habíbolláh Tahqíqí (Tabriz)
87. Mansúr Dakhílí (Tabriz)
88. Husain Rastegár Námdár (Tehran)
89. Habíbolláh Azízí (Tehran)

September 1981 to October 1981 / Shahrívar to Ábán 1360 SH

During the premiership of Ayatollah Mahdaví Kaní

90. 'Atá'olláh Rouhání (Dárán, Isfahán)
91. Ahmad Rezvání (Dárán, Isfahán)
92. Gushtásb Sábet-Rásekh (Dárán, Isfahán)
93. 'Ezzatolláh 'Átefí (Dárán, Isfahán)
94. Bahman 'Átefí (Dárán, Isfahán)

October 1981 to August 1989 / Mihr 1360 to Murdád 1368 SH

During the presidency of Ayatollah Khamene'í and premiership of Mír-Husain Músaví

95. Yadolláh Sepehr Arfa' (Tehran)
96. Kámrán Samímí (Tehran)
97. Zhinús Mahmúdí (Tehran)
98. Mahmúd Majzúb (Tehran)
99. Jalál 'Azízí (Tehran)
100. Mehdí Amín-Amín (Tehran)
101. Sírús Roushaní (Tehran)
102. 'Ezzatolláh Furúhí (Tehran)
103. Qudratolláh Rouhání (Tehran)
104. 'Atá'ollah Haqqání (Tehran)
105. Asadollah Zaidí (Miyándoáb)

106. Ebráhim Ma'naví (Hesár Khorasán)
107. Ebráhím Kheyrkháh (Babolsar)
108. 'Alí Na'ímián (Urúmíyyeh)

1982

109. Kúrush Talá'í (Tehran)
110. Khosrou Muhandesí (Tehran)
111. Iskandar Azízí (Tehran)
112. Fatholláh Ferdousí (Tehran)
113. 'Atá'olláh Yávarí (Tehran)
114. Shívá Asadolláhzádeh (Tehran)
115. Shídrukh Amír-Kíyá Baqá (Tehran)
116. Husain Vahdat-Haqq (Tehran)
117. Ehsánolláh Khayyámí (Urúmíyyeh)
118. 'Azízolláh Gulshaní (Mashhad)
119. Askar Muhammadí (Rahím Khán)
120. Mahmúd Furúhar (Karaj)
121. Ishráqíyyeh Furúhar (Karaj)
122. Badí'olláh Haqq-Paykar (Karaj)
123. Ágáh'olláh Tízfahm (Urúmíyyeh)
124. Jalálíyyeh Mushta'el Uskú'í (Urúmíyyeh)
125. Írán Rahímpúr (Hamrá'í) (Dezfúl)
126. Sa'dolláh Bábázádeh (Khání-Ábád)
127. Nasr'olláh Amíní (Khání-Ábád)
128. Muhammad Mansúrí (Qazvín)
129. Jadíd'olláh Ashraf (Qazvín)
130. Muhammad Abbásí (Qazvín)
131. Manúchehr Farzáneh Mu'ayyad (Qazvín)
132. Manúchehr Vafá'í (Tehran)
133. Abbás-Alí Sádeqpúr (Shiraz)
134. 'Habíbolláh Aují (Shiraz)
135. Zabíh'olláh Ahrárí (Shiraz)
136. Husain Nayyerí Isfahání (Isfahán)
137. Guldáneh Yúsefí Alípúr (Sárí)

1983

138. Hedáyat Síyávashí (Shiraz)
139. Yadolláh Mahmúdnezhád (Shiraz)
140. Rahmatolláh Vafá'í (Shiraz)
141. Túbá Zá'erpúr (Shiraz)
142. Jalál Hakímíyán (Tehran)
143. Sohail Safá'í (Isfahán)
144. Bahrám Afnán (Shiraz)
145. Abul-Hasan Ázádí (Akbar-ábád, Fárs)
146. Kúrush Haqq-Bín (Marv-Dasht, Fárs)
147. Enáyatolláh Eshráqí (Shiraz)
148. Jamshíd Síyávashí (Shiraz)
149. Bahrám Yaldá'í (Shiraz)
150. Shírín (Shahín) Dálvand (Shiraz)
151. 'Ezzat Jánamí Eshráqí (Shiraz)
152. Ru'yá Eshráqí (Shiraz)
153. Moná Mahmúdnezhád (Shiraz)
154. Zarrín Muqímí-Abyáneh (Shiraz)
155. Mahshíd Nírúmand (Shiraz)
156. Símín Sáberí (Shiraz)
157. Táhereh Arjumandí Síyávashí (Shiraz)
158. Akhtar Sábet (Shiraz)
159. Nosrat Ghufrání Yaldá'í (Shiraz)
160. Sohail Húshmand (Shiraz)
161. Ahmad-Alí Sábet Sarvestání (Shiraz)
162. Muhammad Eshráqí (Tehran)
163. Akbar Haqíqí (Khuy)
164. Bahman Dehqání (Muhammadíyeh, Isfahán)
165. 'Abd al-Majíd Mutahharí (Isfahán)
166. Rahmatolláh Hakímíyán (Kermán)

1984

167. Ghulám-Husain Hasanzádeh Shákerí (Tehran)
168. Muhsen Razaví (Tehran)

169. Nosratolláh Zíyá'í (Báft, Kermán)
170. Kámrán Lutfí (Tehran)
171. Rahím Rahímíyán (Tehran)
172. Yadolláh Sáberíyán (Tehran)
173. Asadolláh Kámel-Muqaddam (Tehran)
174. Maqsúd Alízádeh (Tabriz)
175. Jalál Payraví (Tabriz)
176. Jahángír Hedáyatí (Tehran)
177. 'Alí-Muhammad Zamání (Tehran)
178. Nosratolláh Vahdat Nezamí (Tehran)
179. Ehsánolláh Kasírí (Tehran)
180. Manúchehr Ruhí (Bujnurd)
181. Amínolláh Qurbánpúr (Tehran)
182. Rustam Varjávandí (Tehran)
183. Shápúr (Húshang) Markazí (Tehran)
184. Fírúz Pordel (Mashhad)
185. Ahmad Bashírí (Tehran)
186. Yúsuf Nawrúzí Íránzád (Karaj)
187. Ziá'olláh Mani'í Uskú'í (Tabriz)
188. 'Alí-Rezá Níakán (Tabriz)
189. Farhád Asdaqí (Tehran)
190. Fírúz Atharí (Karaj)
191. Ghulám-Husain Farhand (Karaj)
192. 'Enáyatolláh Haqíqí (Karaj)
193. Jamál Káshání (Karaj)
194. Jamshíd Púr-Ustádkár (Karaj)
195. Rúholláh Ta'lím (Kermánsháh)

1985

196. Rúholláh Husúrí (Yazd)
197. Rúholláh Bahrámsháhí (Yazd)
198. Nosratolláh Sobhání (Tehran)
199. Abbás Ídelkhání (Tehran)
200. Rahmatolláh Vujdání (Bandar-Abbás)

201. Núr al-Dín Tá'efí (Pahlaví-Dezh, Mázindarán)
202. 'Azízolláh Ashjárí (Tabriz)

1986

203. Peymán Subhání (Saráván)
204. Iraj Mehdínezhád (Bandar Abbas)
205. Mehrdád Maqsúdí (Urúmiyyeh)
206. Serrolláh Vahdat Nezámí (Tehran)
207. Fedros Shabrukh (Záhedán)
208. Faríd Behmardí (Tehran)
209. Habíbolláh Muhtadí (Tehran)
210. Bábak Tálebí (Karaj)
211. Íraj Mehdí-Nezhád (Bandar-Abbás)

1987

212. Ahmad Káveh (Isfahán)
213. Sorúsh Jabbárí (Tehran)
214. Abu al-Qásem Sháyeq (Tehran)
215. Ardeshír Akhtarí (Tehran)
216. Amír-Husain Náderí (Tehran)

1988

217. Behnám Pásháʹí (Tehran)
218. Íraj Afshín (Tehran)

August 1989 to August 1997 / Murdád 1368 to Murdád 1376 SH

During the presidency of Alí-Akbar Háshemí Rafsanjaní

1992

219. Bahman Samandarí (Tehran)
220. Rúholláh Qedamí (near Qom)

1995

221. Shervín Falláh (Arák)

August 1997 to August 2005 / Murdád 1376 to Murdád 1384 SH

During the presidency of Seyyed Muhammad Khátamí

1997

222. Mansúr Doulat (Kermán)
223. Shahrám Rezá'í (Rasht)
224. Másháolláh 'Enáyatí (Isfahán)
225. Rúholláh Rouhání (Isfahán)

August 2005 to August 2013 / Murdád 1384 – Murdád 1396 SH

During the presidency of Mahmud Ahmadinejad

2005

226. Rúholláh Mahramí (Yazd)*

August 2013 / Murdád 1396 SH

During the presidency of Hasan Rouhání

2013

227. 'Atáolláh Rezvání (Bandar Abbas)

2016

228. Farhang Amírí (Yazd)

* Instead of the usual announcement that a member of the Baha'i faith had been executed for "being a spy," it was declared that Mahramí had died from a heart attack after being poisoned in prison.

Glossary

'Abdul-Baha	(1844–1921) the eldest son of Baha'u'llah and his successor.
Akhund	A low-ranking cleric.
Aqa	Sir, Mr (honorific title).
Ayatollah	The highest-ranking and most prestigious member of the *ulama*.
Bab	The Bab (1819–1850) was the founder of the Babi religion, a religious movement that shook Iran in the middle of the nineteenth century. The Bab claimed to be the promised one, *Mahdi* (see below), expected by all Muslims. His independent (albeit shortlived) Babi religion eventually formed the foundation of the Baha'i faith. He was condemned to death by the Shi'i clergy and executed by firing squad in Tabriz on July 9, 1850.
Babi	A follower of the Bab.
Baha'u'llah	(Tehran 1817–Akka 1892) the prophet-founder of the Baha'i faith, considered by adherents to be the one who has ushered in a new age of world unity. He was banished from his homeland to Baghdad in 1853 and finally imprisoned in the fortress of 'Akka in Palestine in 1868. His spiritual and social teachings form the basis of the Baha'i religion.
Bast	Inviolable sanctuary; asylum.
Fatwa	A decree or ruling in Islamic law that is issued by a *mujtahid* or Ayatollah.
Haji	A Muslim who has made the pilgrimage to Mecca.
Hojjat al-Islam	A high-ranking cleric.
Ijtihad	Judgment, diligence, studiousness, reason (see *mujtahid*).
Imam-jom'eh	A clergyman who leads the congregational prayer on Fridays.
Mahdi	The title of the twelfth imam who, according to Shi'i Muslims, is in occultation and will appear to establish peace and justice in the world.

Mujtahid	A high-ranking cleric who exercises *ijtihad* (judgment) in religious rulings.
Mullah	An honorific title. Traditionally, a teacher knowledgable in religious matters.
Nastaliq	An exquisite style of calligraphy.
Pahlavi	The ruling dynasty of Iran, 1925–1979.
Qajar	Turkish tribes who ruled Iran 1795–1925.
Seyyed	An honorific title for someone claiming to be a descendant of the Prophet Muhammad.
Shaykh	An honorific title for elders of a tribe or group.
Shi'i	One of the two main branches of Islam, dominant mainly in Iran and in some parts of the Middle East.
Shoghi Effendi	(1897–1957) the grandson of 'Abdul-Baha, and his successor (1921–1957).
Ulama	A body of learned Muslim scholars, specialists in understanding and interpreting the Islamic texts.

Select Bibliography

WORKS IN EUROPEAN LANGUAGES

Abrahamian, Ervand. *The Iranian Mojahedin.* New Haven: Yale University Press, 1989.

________. *Tortured Confessions: Prison and Public Recantations in Modern Iran.* Los Angeles: University of California Press, 1999.

A Faith Denied: The Persecution of the Baha'is of Iran. Iran Human Rights Documentation Center. New Haven, http://www.iranhrdc.org/english/.

Affolter, Friedrich. "The Specter of Ideological Genocide: The Bahá'ís of Iran," in *War Crimes, Genocide, & Crimes against Humanity*, vol. 1, nr. 1, 2005.

Afshari, Reza. *Human Rights in Iran: The Abuse of Cultural Relativism.* Philadelphia: University of Pennsylvania Press, 2001.

________. "The Discourse and Practice of Human Rights Violation of Iranian Baha'is in the Islamic Republic of Iran," in Brookshaw and Fazel, 2008.

Akhavi, Shahrough. *Religion and Politics in Contemporary Iran: Clergy–State Relations in the Pahlavi Period.* Albany: State University of New York Press, 1980.

Amanat, Abbas. *Resurrection and Renewal: The Making of the Babi Movement in Iran, 1844–1850.* New York: Cornell University Press, 1989.

________. *The Pivot of Universe: Nasir al-Din Shah Qajar and the Iranian Monarchy 1831–1896.* Oakland: University of California Press, 1997.

________. "The Historical Roots of the Persecution of Babis and Baha'is in Iran," in Brookshaw and Fazel, 2008.

Amanat, Mehread. "Messianic Expectation and Evolving Identities: The Conversion of Iranian Jews to the Baha'i Faith," in Brookshaw and Fazel, 2008.

Ashraf, Ahmad. "Conspiracy Theories," in *Encyclopaedia Iranica* vol. IV, Costa Mesa: Mazda Publishers, 1993.

________. "The Appeal of Conspiracy Theories to Persians," *Princeton Papers: Interdisciplinary Journal of Middle Eastern Studies*. Princeton: Markus Wiener Publishers, 1997.

Baha'i Question, The: Cultural Cleansing in Iran. Baha'i International Community, Geneva. At http://question.bahai.org/001.php.

Baha'u'llah. *Tablets of Bahá'u'lláh Revealed After the Kitáb-i-Aqdas*. Wilmette: Bahá'í Publishing Trust, 1988.

________. *Gleanings from the Writings of Bahá'u'lláh*. Wilmette: Bahá'í Publishing Trust, 1988.

Brookshaw, Dominic P. and Fazel, Seena B. (eds). *The Baha'is of Iran: Socio-historical Studies*. Abingdon: Routledge, 2008.

Browne, Edward. G. *Persian Revolution of 1905–1909*. Cambridge: Cambridge University Press, 1893 (rep. 1926).

________. *A Year Amongst the Persians: Impressions as to the Life, Character, & Thought of the People of Persia Received during Twelve Months' Residence in that Country in the Years 1887–1888*. London: A. & C. Black Ltd, 1893 (rep. 1927).

________ (ed. and trans.). *The Táríkh-i-Jadíd, or New History of Mírzá 'Alí Muḥammad the Báb, by Mírzá Ḥusayn of Hamadán*. Cambridge: Cambridge University Press, 1893.

________. *Materials for the Study of the Bábí Religion*. Cambridge: Cambridge University Press, 1918.

Chehabi, Houchang E. "Anatomy of Prejudice: Reflections on Secular Anti-Baha'ism in Iran," in Brookshaw and Fazel, 2008.

Cole, Juan R. I. *Modernity & the Millennium: The Genesis of the Baha'i Faith in the Nineteenth-Century Middle East*. New York: Columbia University Press, 1989.

Conolly, Arthur. *Journey to the North of India, Overland from England, Through Russia, Persia, and Affghaunistaun*. 2 vols. London: Richard Bentley, 1834.

Cooper, Roger. *The Baha'is of Iran*. London: Minority Rights Group Ltd., 1982.

Ghanea, Nazila. *Human Rights, the UN and the Bahá'ís in Iran*. Oxford: George Ronald, 2002.

Gobineau, Arthur de. *Les Religions et Les Philosophies dans l'Asie Centrale*. Paris: Ernest Leroux Éditeur, 1900.

Ivanov, Mikhail S. *Babidskie Vosstaniya v Irane (1848–1852)*. Moscow: Trudy Instituta Vostokvedeniya XXX, 1939.

Kazemi, Farhad. "The *Fada'iyan-e Islam*: Fanaticisms, Politics and Terror," in *From Nationalism to Revolutionary Islam* (ed. S. Amir Arjomand). Albany: State University of New York Press, 1984.

________. "State and Society in the Ideology of the Devotees of Islam," in *State, Culture, and Society*, Vol. 1, No. 3. New York: Sprinter Publishing, 1985.

Kazemzadeh, Firuz. *Russia and Britain in Persia 1864–1914: A Study in Imperialism*. New Haven: Yale University Press, 1968.

Keddie, Nikki R. *Roots of Revolution: An Interpretive History of Modern Iran*. New Haven: Yale University Press, 1981.

Labib, Muḥammad. *The Seven Martyrs of Hurmuzak* (trans. M. Momen). Oxford: George Ronald, 1981.

Malcolm, Napier. *Five Years in a Persian Town*. New York: Dulton, 1908.

Martin, Douglas. "The Persecution of the Baha'is of Iran, 1844–1984," in *Baha'i Studies*, vols. 12 & 13. Ottawa: Association for Baha'i Studies, 1984.

Milani, Abbas. *The Persian Sphinx: Amir Abbas Hoveyda and the Riddle of the Iranian Revolution*. Washington, DC: Mage Publishers, 2000.

________. *Eminent Persians: The Men and Women Who Made Modern Iran, 1941–1947*. New York: Syracuse University Press, 2008.

Momen, Moojan. *The Bábi and Bahá'í Religions, 1844–1944: Some Contemporary Western Accounts*. Welwyn: George Ronald, 1981.

________. "The Role of Women in the Iranian Baha'i Community during the Qajar Period," in Robert Gleave (ed.), *Religion and Society in Qajar Iran*. Abingdon: Routledge, 2005.

________. "The Babi and Bahá'í Community of Iran: A Case of 'Suspended Genocide'?" in *Journal of Genocide Research*, vol. 7. New York and London: Routledge, 2005.

________. "Economic Strangulation of the Baha'i Community," at http://www.iranpresswatch.org/post/1578.

Momen, Moojan and Mottahedin-Mavaddat, Mehraeen. "Alavíyyih Khánum (c. 1885–c. 1918), and 'Alí Ján, Mullá (1846–83)," in *The Bahá'í Encyclopedia* at http://bahai-library.com/bahai_encyclopedia_alaviyyih_khanum.

Mottahedeh, Negar. "The Mutilated Body of the Modern Nation: Qurrat al-'Ayn Ṭahirah's Unveiling and the Iranian Massacre of the Babis," in

Comparative Studies of South Asia, Africa, and the Middle East, The Emergence of Modernity and Nationalism in Iran, XVIII, 2. Duck University Press,1998.

Sadri, Mahmoud. "Hojjatiya," in *Encyclopaedia Iranica*, vol. XII. Costa Mesa: Mazda Publishers, 2004.

Sanasarian, Eliz. *Religious Minorities in Iran*. Cambridge: Cambridge University Press, 2000.

Shahvar, Soli. *The Forgotten Schools: The Baha'is and Modern Education in Iran, 1899–1934*. London and New York: I. B. Tauris, 2009.

Shoghi Effendi. *God Passes By*. Wilmette: Baha'i Publishing Trust, 1965.

________. *The World Order of Bahá'u'lláh*. Wilmette: Bahá'í Publishing Trust, 1991.

Tavakoli-Targhi, Mohamad. "Refashioning Iran: Language and Culture during the Constitutional Revolution," in *Iranian Studies* 23, 1–4. Abingdon: Taylor and Francis, 2001.

________. "Anti-Bahá'ísm and Islamism in Iran," in Brookshaw and Fazel, 2008.

Vahman, Fereydun. "The Conversion of Zoroastrians to the Baha'i Faith," in Brookshaw and Fazel, 2008.

WORKS IN PERSIAN

'Abdul-Baha. *Majmú'e-ye khatábát-e hazrat-e 'Abdul-Baha*. Germany: Baha'i Verlag, 1984.

Adamiyat, Fereydun. *Andísheh-ye taraqqí va hokoumat-e qánoon dar 'asr-e Sepahsalar*. Tehran: Kharazmi Publishers, 1972/1351.

________. *Amír Kabír va Iran, yá varaqí az táríkh-e síyasá-e Iran*. Tehran: Kharazmi Publishers, 1999/1378.

Ajúdaní, Masha'alláh. *Yá Marg, Ya Tajaddod, Daftarí dar she'r va adab-e mashrouteh*. London: Fasle Ketáb, 2002/1381.

________. *Buf-e Kur va Nasionalism*. Tehran: Khavaran, 2006/1385.

________. *Mashrouteh-ye Irani. Píshzamínehá-ye nazariyyeh-ye veláyat-e faqíh*. London: Fasle Ketáb, 1977.

'Álikháni, 'Alinaqi (ed.). *Yad-dashthá-ye 'Alam*. Washington, DC: Ibex Publishers, 1992, 1995.

Amanat, Abbas and Vahman, Fereydun. *Az Tehran Tá Akká: Bábíyán va Bahá'iyán dar asnád-e dourh-ye Qajar*. Copenhagen & New Haven: Áshkár Publishers, 2016.

Amanat, Musa. *Baha'iyán-e Káshán*. Madrid: Nehal Publishers, 2012.

Anahid, Aram. "Baha'is, the Sole Targets of Conspiracism?" at http:// iranpresswatch.org/post/1407/.

Banáni, Amin. " 'Asr-e Táhereh," in *Khúsheh-há'i az kharman-e adab va honar*, vol. 3. Darmstadt: 'Asr-e jadíd, 1992.

Dámghani, Muhammad Taqi. *Jáme-ye Álúdeh dar Áftáb*. Tehran: 2003/1382.

Davani, 'Ali. *Zendegi-námeh-ye za'im-e bozorg-e 'alam-e tashayo' Ayatuolláh Borujerdí*. Tehran: printed by Motayyar, 1991/1370.

Djazayeri, Ezzat. *Strangers in their Native Land*. Uppsala: Baha'i Publishing Trust of Sweden, 1987.

Eghbal, Abbas. "Hujjat al-Islam Haj Muhammad Baqer Shafti," in *Yádgar*, 5, 10. Tehran: 1949/1328.

Falsafi, Muhammad Taqi. *Kháterát va mobarezát-e hojjat al-Islam Falsafi* (ed. 'Ali Davani). Tehran: Markaz-e setád-e enqelab-e Islami, 2003/1382.

Fashahi, Muhammad Reza. *Az shahriyárí-ye Áryá'i be hokoomat-e eláhí-e sámi*. Stockholm: Baran, 2000.

Fazel Mazandarani, Asadulláh. *Zuhúr al-Haq*, vol. 8. Tehran: 1975/1354.

Fo'ádi-Boshrou'i, Hasan. *Tarikh-e diánat-e Baha'i dar Khorasa*. Darmstadt: 'Asr-e jadíd, 2007.

Ghani, Mahdi. "Avvalin mo'menán-e secular", *Máhnámeh-ye jáme'e-ye nou*. Vol. 21. Tehran: 2004/1383.

Ishraq-Khávari, Abd al-Hamid. *Mohazerát*, vol. 3 (ed. Vahid Ra'fati). Hofheim: Baha'i Verlag, 2009.

Ja'fariyan, Rasoul. *Jarayán-há va sázmánhá-ye mazhabi-siasi-ye Iran 1320–1357*. Qom: 2006/1385.

Karbáschi, Gholam Husain. *Tárikh-e shafáhí-ye Enqelab*. Qom: 2001/1380.

Kasravi Tabrizi, Ahmad. *Bekhánand va dávarí konand*. Tehran: Parcham Publications, 1944/1323.

Khubruy-Pák, Manuchehr. "Tahavolat-e qavánín-e Iran dar báreh-ye aqalyyathá-ye díní az dourh-ye Qajar tá emrouz," in *Khúsheh-há'i az kharman-e adab va honar*, vol. 16. Darmstadt: 'Asr-e jadíd, 2008.

Mahdavi, 'Abd al-Reza Hushang (ed.). *Guftuguhá-ye man bá Shah, khaterát-e mahramáneh-ye Asadolláh 'Alam*. Tehran: Tarh-e Nou Publications, 1992.

Mahingostar, Iraj. *Khoon va gol-e sorkh, baláyá-ye várdedeh bar Bahá'iyán-e Iran, 1320–1368*. California: Shrkat-e Ketab, 2008.

Majd al-Islam Kermani, Ahmad. *Tárikh-e-Enhetát-e Majles*. Isfahan: Isfahan University Press, 1972/1351.

Málamárí, Muhammad Táher. *Tarikh-e shohadá-ye Yazd* (reprint). Kerachi: 1979.

Mansouri, Firuz. *Negáhí Nou be Safar-námeh-ye Naṣer Khusrau*. Tehran: Chapakhsh Publishers, 1993/1372.

Mashhouri, Deláram. *Rag-e Ták*. Paris: Khávaran, 1983.

Mehrabkhani, Ruhollah. "Shahádat-e doctor Berjís," in *Áhang-e Badi'* vol. 4. Tehran: 1949/1328.

Mehrpour, Husain. *Vazífe-ye dushvár-e nezárat bar ejráy-e qánún-e asásí*. Tehran: Nashr-e Sáles, 2005/1384.

Milani, Abbas. *Tajaddod va tajaddod satizí dar Iran*. Tehran: Nashr-e Átiyeh, 1999/1378.

Montazeri, Husain 'Ali (Ayatollah). *Matn-e kámel-e kháterat*. Paris: Ettehadiyyeh-ye násherán-e Irani dar Europa, 2000/1379.

Motahhari, Murteza (Ayatollah), *Nur-e Malakout-e Qur'án*, vol. 4. Qom: n.d.

Muhajer, Náser, "Kárd-ájin kardan-e doctor Berjís," in *Baran Journal* 19 and 20. Stockholm: 2008.

Najafi, Muhammad Baqer. *Baháíyán*. Tehran: Tahouri, 1978/1357.

Nateq, Homa. *Iran dar ráhyábí-ye farhangi*. London: Payam Publications, 1988.

________. "Rouhániyyat az parákandegí tá qodrat 1828–1908," at http://www.iran-resist.org.articles4482#nb15.

Nateq-Adamiyat. *Afkár-e ejtemá'í va siyási va eqtesádi dar 'ásár-e montasher nashodeh-ye douran-e Qajar*. Germany: Navid Publishers, 1989.

Nikusefat, Sohrab. *Kankáshi dar Bahá'i satízi*. Germany: Navid Publishers, 2006/1385.

Raha, M. *Haqiqat-e Sadeh, khaterati az zendánhá-ye zanán-e jomhourí-ye Islami*. Germany: 1992.

Rejál-e 'asr-e Pahlavi: Amir Abbas Hoveyda be raváyat-e SAVAK. Tehran: Keyhan Publishers, 2007/1386.

Rezvani, Homa. *Laváyeh-e Aqá sheykh Fazlolláh Nuri*. Tehran: 1963/1362.

Sáber Tabrizi, 'Ali Akbar. *Hop-hop Námeh*. Baku: 1941.

Saberi, Reza. "Sofalíneh-í bi arzesh," in *Iranshenasi*, vol. 16. Meriland: 2004/1383.

Sayyáh Mahallátí, Muhammad Ali. *Khâterat-e Sayyáh yá doureh-ye khouf va vahshat*. Tehran: 1980/1359.

Shahbazi, 'Abdollah, *Jostarha-i dar tarikh-e Bahá'igari dar Iran*. Tehran: 2003/1382.

________. *Zohour va soqut-e selseleh-ye Pahlavi*, vol. II. Tehran: 1991/1370.

Tavakoli-Targhi, Mohamad. "Bahá'i satízi va Islamgará'í," in *Iran Nameh*. Bethesda: 2001/1380.

Turkamán, Muhammad. *Rasá'el, e'lámiyyeh, Maktubát va Rooznámeh-ye sheikh-e shahíd Fazlollah Nuri*. Tehran: 1372/2013.

Y. P. *Haqáyeq-e Guftani dar píramún-e hádese-ye nangín-e Shahroud va koshtár-e Bahá'iyán*. Tehran: Parcham Publications, 1944/1323.

Zarrinkoob, 'Abd al-Husain. *Do qarn Sokoot*. Tehran: Elmi Publishers, 1965/1344.

Notes

INTRODUCTION: THE "ENIGMA" OF THE BAHA'I RELIGION IN IRAN

1. Banáni, Amin. "'Asr-e Táhereh," *Khúsheh-há'i az kharman-e adab va honar*, 3. Darmstadt: 'Asr-e jadíd, 1992, p. 83.
2. Mashhouri, Deláram. *Rag-e Ták*, Paris: Khávaran, 1983, p. 262.
3. Fashahi, Muhammad Reza. *Az shahriyárí-ye Áryá'i be hokoomat-e eláhí-e sámi*. Stockholm: Baran, 2000, p. 56.
4. Quoted from the Center for the Islamic Revolution Documents: http://irdc.ir/article.asp?id=472.
5. Tavakoli-Targhi, Mohamad. "Bahá'i satízi va Islamgaráí," *Iran Nameh*, Bethesda 2001/1380, p. 114. The translation of the whole article can be found in: Brookshaw and Fazel, *The Baha'is of Iran, Socio-Historical Studies*, Abingdon: Routledge, 2008, pp. 204–25.
6. Ghanea, Nazila. *Ethnic and Religious Groups in the Islamic Republic of Iran: Policy suggestions for the integration of minorities throughout participation in public life*. London: University of London, Institute of Commonwealth Studies, 2003. Available at: https://www.academia.edu/11798253/Driving_while_Bah%C3%A1_%C3%AD_A_Typology_of_Religious_Discrimination_pp.53-70.
7. http://archiv.iran-emrooz.net/archiv.html 11/6/2008.
8. Tavakoli-Targhi 2001/1380, pp. 80, 81.
9. See Chapter 21.

CHAPTER 1: WHY WERE THE BABI AND BAHA'I FAITHS SUPPRESSED IN IRAN?

1. Eghbal, Abbas. "Hujjat al-Islam Haj Muhammad Baqer Shafti," *Yádgar*, 5, 10, Tehran 1949/1328, p. 20.

2. Ajúdaní, Masha'alláh. *Mashrouteh-ye Irani*. London: *Fasle Ketab*, 1977, p. 58.
3. Sayyah 1359, pp. 57–58.
4. Nateq, Homa. *Iran dar ráhyábí-ye farhangi*. London: Payam Publication, 1988, p. 54, with reference to *Nasekh al-tavarikh*.
5. Fashahi 2000, p. 54.
6. Amanat, Abbas. *Resurrection and Renewal, The Making of the Babi Movement in Iran, 1844–1850*. New York: Cornell University Press, 1989, p. 406.
7. Amanat 1989, pp. 406–7.
8. Baha'u'llah. *Gleanings from the Writings of Baha'u'llah*. Wilmette: Bahá'í Publishing Trust, 1988, p. 259.
9. Momen, Moojan. "The Role of Women in the Iranian Baha'i Community during the Qajar Period," in Robert Gleave (ed.) *Religion and Society in Qajar Iran*. Abingdon: Routledge, 2005, pp. 359–60.
10. The Roshdieh school of Tabriz that was founded in 1898 was destroyed soon after by a mob incited by the clerics. For more information on Roshdieh and his schools, see Ajúdaní 1977, pp. 253–62.
11. Momen, Moojan. "The Babi and Baha'i Community of Iran: A Case of Suspended Genocide?" *Journal of Genocide Research*, vol. 7., Routledge, 2005, pp. 220–46.
12. Rezvani, Homa. *Laváyeh-e Aqá sheykh Fazlolláh Nuri*. Tehran, 1984/1362, p. 28.
13. Shahvar, Soli. *The Forgotten Schools: The Baha'is and Modern Education in Iran, 1899–1934*. London and New York: I. B. Tauris, 2009, p. 106.
14. Momen 2005, p. 228.
15. See Chapter 3.
16. Momen and Mottahedin-Mavaddat, Mehraeen. "Alavíyyih Khánum (c. 1885–c. 1918), and 'Alí Ján, Mullá (1846–83)," in *The Bahá'í Encyclopedia 2009*: http://bahai-library.com/bahai_encyclopedia_alaviyyih_khanum.
17. For more see: Momen, Moojan: http://bahai-library.com/bahai_encyclopedia_alaviyyih_khanum
18. See the two following articles: Amanat, Mehread. "Messianic Expectation and Evolving Identities: The Conversion of Iranian Jews to the Baha'i Faith," pp. 6–30, and Fereydun Vahman, "The Conversion of Zoroastrians to the Baha'i Faith," pp. 31–49, both in Brookshaw and Fazel, 2008.
19. Zarrinkoob, 'Abd al-Husain. *Do qarn Sokoot*, Tehran: Elmi Publishers, 1965/1344, pp. 173, 228–300.
20. Motahhari, Morteza (Ayatollah), *Nur-e Malakout Qur'án*, vol. 4 Qom, n.d., p. 160ff.
21. 'Abdul-Baha. *Majmú'e-ye khatábát-e hazrat-e 'Abdul-Baha*. Germany: Baha'i verlag, 1984, pp. 10–11.
22. Ibid., p. 12.
23. Fashahi 2000, p. 56.

24. Turkamán, Muhammad. *Rasá'el, e'lámiyyeh, Maktubát va Rooznámeh-ye sheikh-e shahíd Fazlollah Nuri*. Tehran, 1372, p. 108.
25. Nateq, Homa. *Rouhaniyyat az parakandegi ta qodrat 1828–1908*, 2008. http://www.iran-resist.org.articles4482#nb15.

CHAPTER 2: THE VIOLENT REPRESSION OF THE BABIS AND BAHA'IS DURING THE QAJAR PERIOD

1. Sayyáh Mahallátí, Muhammad Ali. *Khaterat-e Sayyáh yá doureh-ye khouf va vahshat*. Tehran, 1980/1359, p. 57.
2. Ibid., p. 272.
3. Ibid., pp. 57–8.
4. Majd al-Islam Kermani. *Tárikh-e-Enhetát-e Majles*. Isfahan: Isfahan University Press, 1972/1351, pp. 214–19.
5. Malcolm, Napier. *Five Years in a Persian Town*. New York: Dulton, 1908, pp. 88, 89, 104.
6. Ibid.
7. Ibid.
8. Málamárí, Muhammad Táher. *Tarikh-e shohadá-y Yazd*. Kerachi, 1979, pp. 241–7.
9. Ibid., pp. 241–7.
10. Fo'ádi-Boshrou'i, Hasan. *Tarikh-e diánat-e Baha'i dar Khorasan*. Darmstadt: 'Asr-e jadíd, 2007, pp. 237–8.

CHAPTER 3: THE BAHA'IS DURING THE REIGN OF REZA SHAH PAHLAVI

1. Momen, Moojan. *The Babi and Baha'i Religions, 1844–1944: Some Contemporary Western Accounts*. Welwyn: George Ronald, 1981, p. 463.
2. Also known as 'Abdul-Baha, who was the leader of the Baha'i community at that time.
3. Keddie, N. R. *Roots of Revolution: An Interpretive History of Modern Iran*, New Haven: Yale University Press, 1981, p. 143.
4. This section is based on the report dated 10 August 1924 by Mr W. Smith Murray, the chargé d'affaires of the American Embassy in Iran addressed to the US Ministry of External Affairs, and an article published in the *New York Times* dated 24 July 1924.
5. Momen 1981, pp. 465–72; *The Baha'i World*, vol. II, *1926–28*, pp. 287–99.
6. Momen 2005, pp. 220–46; for comprehensive details of these schools see Sháhvar 2009.
7. Momen 2005, p. 228.
8. *Baha'i World 1934–1936*, pp. 28–31.

CHAPTER 4: BAHA'IS IN THE REIGN OF MUHAMMAD REZA SHAH PAHLAVI

1. Kasravi Tabrizi, Ahmad. *Bekhánand va dávarí konand*. Parcham publication, 1944/1323, pp. 66–7.
2. Rabbani Shirazi. *Dá'iratul-Ma'arif-e Ulama-ye Mujahed*: http://www.irdc.ir/personage.asp?id=325.
3. Montazeri Husain 'Ali (Ayatollah). *Matn-e kámel-e khúterat*. Paris: Ettehadiyyeh-ye násherán-e irani dar Europa, 2000/1379, p. 94.
4. Quoted in Karbáschi, Gholam Husain. *Tárikh-e shafáhí-ye Enqelab*. Qom, 2001/1380, pp. 161–2.
5. Tavakoli-Targhi 2001/1380, p. 97.
6. Ibid., p. 90–1.
7. Ibid., p. 93.
8. Ibid., p. 91.
9. Sadri, Mahmoud. "Hojjatiya," in: *Encyclopædia Iranica*, vol. XII. Mazda Publishers, 2004.
10. Ghani, Mahdi. "Avvalin mo'menán-e secular," *Máhnámeh-ye jáme'e-ye nou*, 21, Tehran, 2004/1383.
11. Banisadr, Abol-Hasan. *Enqelab-e Islami dar Hejrat*. Paris, 1981/1360.
12. Sadri 2004.
13. Extracted from an interview with Mr Hashem Aqajari, about his involvement with Hojjatieh, Sadri 2004.
14. The late Bishop Dehqani Tafti recounted to the author that a few Iranian young men had embraced Christianity in Isfahan after attending meetings in the church. Two or three of them claimed that their friends and family had become very unfriendly as a result of their conversion to Christianity, and requested to be given some work in the office of the church. One of them became the telephone operator for the bishop's office. After the revolution, an attempt was made on the life of Bishop Dehqani by members of the Hojjatieh. Early one morning, two or three men climbed over the wall to his home, and while he and his British wife were still in bed, they fired a few shots at his head. Assuming that he had been killed, they left the house. The bullets had somehow only hit the pillow, and the bishop escaped death. He left the country immediately with his wife. A few days later, his son Bahram Tafti Yazdi was arrested, taken to the wild lands near Vanak, and was shot and killed. Bishop Dehqani had no doubt that the newly declared Christians were in fact all members of the Hojjatieh Society, and that their duty was to spy on the church and gather information about its activities, and that it was those same individuals who, despite his loving care and attention to them, attempted to kill him and who also murdered his son.
15. Sadri 2004.

16. Muhtashemi-pur, a member of the Central Council of the Association of Combatant Clerics, writes in this respect: "Young people, full of love for the *Imam-e Zaman* were recruited by the Hojjatieh Society, leading to a diversion [between religion and politics]. The condition for membership was that they do not enter politics under any circumstances. The ideology of religion without politics was a very strong one in the Hojjatieh Society, and they spread many rumours about those fighting for the revolution and Imam Khomeini." Muhtashemi-Pur adds: "After the Revolution, the Hojjatieh organization had no room for manoeuvre. They even announced the seeming disestablishment of the society on one occasion, although their organization continued as a secret and underground movement. They are presently actively functioning in many areas." *I'timad-e Melli* newspaper, published in Tehran, dated Tuesday 19 August 2008/29 Murdad 1387.
17. Adamiyat, Fereydun. *Amír Kabír va Iran, yá varaqí az táríkh-e síyasá-e Iran*. 8th edition, Tehran: Kharazmi, 1999/1378, p. 446.
18. Nateq 1988, p. 67, writes: "The British also pursued the matter, as they were backing the clergy, and they regarded the Babis as being on the government's side, and the clergy on their side."
19. For further information and documentation see Momen 1981, pp. 34–45.
20. Sura 17, The Night Journey/The Israelites (Al-Isra'), verse 104, and Sura 2, The Cow (Baqara), verse 47.
21. The recent book by A. Amanat and F. Vahman contains governmental documents and historical backgrounds of this exile: *Az Tehran Tá Akká: Bábíyán va Bahá'iyán dar asnád-e dourh-ye Qajar.* Copenhagen & New Haven: Áshkár Publishers, 2016.
22. *Sahife-ye Nur*, vol. 1, p. 277. Also see http://www.tebyan.net/index.aspx?pid=19673&ParentID=6171&Language=1
23. Mansuri, Firuz. *Negáhí Nou be Safar-námeh-ye Naṣer Khusrau*. Tehran: Chapakhsh, 1994/1372. pp. 168–9.
24. Saberi, Reza. "Sofalíneh-í bi arzesh," *Iranshenasi*, 16, 2. Meriland, 2004/1383, pp. 295–306.
25. 'Álikháni, 'Alinaqi (ed.) *Yad-dashthá-ye 'Alam*. Washington, DC: Ibex Publishers, 1995, p. 166.
26. Milani, Abbas. *The Persian Sphinx: Amir Abbas Hoveyda and the Riddle of the Iranian Revolution*. Washington, DC: Mage Publishers, 2000, p. 47; see also pp. 43–4, 266, 316, 337, 352.
27. *Rejál-e 'asr-e Pahlavi: Amir Abbas Hoveyda be raváyat-e SAVAK*, vol. 2, Tehran: Keyhan Publishers 2007/1386, p. 5.
28. Milani 2000, p. 44.
29. Shahbazi, 'Abdollah. *Zohour va soqut-e selseleh-ye Pahlavi*, vol. II. Tehran, 1991/1370, p. 388.
30. Milani 2000, p. 29.
31. Ibid.

32. Chehabi, Houchang E. "Anatomy of Prejudice: Reflections on Secular Anti-Baha'ism in Iran," in Brookshaw and Fazel, 2008, p. 190.
33. For more information about the conditions of this movement, the reader may refer to two noteworthy publications by Masha'alláh Ajúdaní: *Yá Marg, Ya Tajaddod, Daftarí dar she'r va adab-e mashrouteh* (*Either Death or Modernism*); and *Buf-e Kur va Nationalism* (*The Blind Owl and Nationalism*), an analysis of Sadeq Hedayat's novel. London: Fasl-e Ketab Publications.
34. Tavakoli-Targhi, Mohamad. "Refashioning Iran: Language and Culture during the Constitution Revolution," *Iranian Studies*, 23, 1–4. Taylor and Francis, 2001, p. 135.
35. Baha'u'llah, *Tablets of Bahá'u'lláh Revealed After the Kitáb-i-Aqdas*. Wilmette: Bahá'í Publishing Trust, USA, 1988, p. 138.
36. Browne, E. G. *The Persian Revolution of 1905–1909*. Cambridge: Cambridge University Press, 1910, p. 424.
37. Najafi, Muhammad Baqer. *Baháíyán*, Tehran: Tahouri, 1978/1357, p. 751.
38. Shoghi Effendi. *The World Order of Baha'u'llah*. Wilmette: Baha'i Publishing Trust USA, 1991, p. 41.
39. Baha'u'llah 1988, pp. 46, 47, 54.
40. Mottahedeh, Negar. "The Mutilated Body of the Modern Nation: Qurrat al-'Ayn Tahirah's Unveiling and the Iranian Massacre of the Babis," *Comparative Studies of South Asia, Africa, and the Middle East, The Emergence of Modernity and Nationalism in Iran*, XVIII, 2, Duck University Press, 1998, p. 27.
41. Sáber Tabrizi, 'Ali Akbar. *Hop-hop Námeh*. Baku, 1941, pp. 227–30.
42. Refer to Chapter 1.
43. Husain Amanat.
44. A section of the speech of Dr Abbas Milani, given at a gathering in San Francisco's Herbst Theater on 15 August 2009. This speech was given before an audience of around one thousand people who had gathered in solidarity with the Baha'is and in support of their most basic rights in Iran. The text of the talk was later published in the *New Republic* newspaper. The extract of the talk is quoted from *Payam-i-Baha'i*, issue 359, October 2009. The English extract is quoted from the *New Republic*, dated 15 August 2009.
45. Unfortunately, his premature death prevented him from completing and publishing his important final two books on linguistics that were in progress. Fo'ádi-Boshrou'i 2007, pp. 37–40.
46. Nateq 1988, p. 45.
47. Amanat, Abbas. *The Pivot of Universe, Naser al-Din Shah Qajar and the Iranian Monarchy 1831–1896*, University of California Press, Oakland, 1997, pp. 473–76 n. 113.
48. Adamiyat, Fereydun. *Amir Kabir va Iran ya varaqi az daftar-e siasi-ye Iran*, (1st edition), 1944/1323, pp. 241ff.
49. Conolly, Arthur. *Journey to the North of India, Overland from England, Through Russia, Persia, and Affghaunistaun*, 2 vols. London: Richard Bentley, 1834.

50. Momen, *Persian Heritage*, 9, 35, 2004, p. 29, fn. 13.
51. Amanat 1989, p. 439.
52. Adamiyat, *Andisheh-há ye Mirza Aqa Khan Kermani*, Tehran: Payam 1973/1352, p. 146, fn. 1.
53. Milani, Abbas. *Tajaddod va tajaddod satizí dar Iran.* Tehran: Nashr-e Átiyeh, 1999/1378, p. 342, fn. 10.
54. Nateq-Adamiyat. *Afkár-e ejtemá 'í va siyási va eqtesádi dar 'ásár-e montasher nashodeh-ye douran-e Qajar.* Germany: Navid Publishers, 1989, pp. 114–17.
55. Adamiyat, *Andísheh-ye taraqqí va hokoumat-e qánoon dar 'asr-e Sepahsalar.* Tehran: Kharazmi Publishers, 1972/1351, p. 348.
56. Kazemzadeh, Firuz. *Russia and Britain in Persia 1864–1914.* New Haven: Yale University Press, 1968, p. 108.

CHAPTER 5: THE SHAHRUD INCIDENT

1. For more information on the Kashan incident, see Chapter 6.
2. Naser Semino's great-grandfather, Barthélémy Antoine Semino, was an Italian officer in the service of Fath-Ali Shah who settled in Iran. Naser Semino was born in Tehran in 1918. In 1983 he emigrated with his family to Arizona, where he passed away in 1999. I am grateful to his family friend, Mrs Mona Mahmudi (Sana), who provided the information included here in her letter of November 4, 2010. See also http://www.iranicaonline.org/articles/semino-barthelemy.
3. Shahroudi, 'Abdollah, *Dasayes va Fetnehangizihaye Baha'iha* (*The Conspiracies and Sedition of the Baha'is*); publication of Religious Endowment of Nur, Tehran, n.d.
4. *Haqáyeq-e Guftani, Dar pírámun-e hadese-ye nangín-e Sahroud va koshtar-e Baha'iyan be daste Shi'ayan* (*About the shameful incident in Shahroud and the killings of the Baha'is by the Shi'is*), Tehran: Parcham Publication 1323/1944, p. 3.
5. Namdar, Habib. Private notes, 1993, p. 5.
6. *Haqáyeq-e Guftani*, p. 25.
7. Namdar, Habib, Vaqay'e Sahroud (unpublished manuscript), p. 5.
8. The lieutenant at the Gendarmerie who was sent to investigate described the incident in a letter to Semino, who was his friend. *Haqáyeq-e Guftani*, p. 33.
9. Ibid., p. 32.
10. Namdar, p. 6.
11. *Haqáyeq-e Guftani*, p. 34.
12. Ibid., p. 37.
13. *Baha'i World, 1944–46*, p. 42.
14. *Haqáyeq-e Guftani*, p. 41.
15. Namdar, p. 7–9.
16. After the Islamic Revolution, Yusef Subhani was imprisoned for his belief in the Baha'i faith and executed by firing squad.

17. *Haqáyeq-e Guftani*, p. 46.
18. Namdar, p. 9.
19. *Haqáyeq-e Guftani*, p. 47.
20. Namdar, p. 10.
21. *Haqáyeq-e Guftani*, p. 48.
22. Namdar, p. 10.
23. The book *The Baha'i World, 1944–46*, p. 41, does not give details of the storming of the office of the doctor by the mobs. Namdar states that the incident happened some one hundred meters from the police headquarters, and that the chief of police was personally observing the whole incident from the second floor balcony. The author of *Haqáyeq-e Guftani* writes that seeing the attackers, Jazbani fled into the home of Dr Mubarak, and the thugs followed him. They searched the rooms, some went to the second floor and found him there, attacking him with stones, clubs, and knives giving him blows on the head, neck, and face. They then lifted him and threw him out of the window to the street below. Hundreds of the inhabitants of Shahrud, including some constables of the municipal police were observing the incident. Jazbani died a few moments after hitting the ground. The assassins then left the office of Dr Mubarak and fell on the lifeless body again with clubs and knives. (*Haqáyeq-e Guftani*, pp. 48–9)
24. *Baha'i World, 1944–46*, p. 42.
25. *Baha'i World, 1944–46*, p. 41.
26. Namdar, p. 16.
27. Ibid., p. 11.
28. *Haqáyeq-e Guftani*, p. 50.
29. Ibid., p. 51.
30. *Haqáyeq-e Guftani*, p. 54. All existing reports confirm the splitting of Naderi's head with an axe.
31. *Baha'i World, 1944–46*, pp. 41–2.
32. *Baha'i World, 1944–46*, p. 42. *Haqáyeq-e Guftani* had counted him by mistake as one of the dead, and as such had determined the number of killed Baha'is to be four (p. 50).
33. *Haqáyeq-e Guftani*, p. 50.
34. *Baha'i World, 1944–46*, p. 42.
35. Namdar, p. 13.
36. *Haqáyeq-e Guftani*, p. 55.
37. Ibid., p. 61.
38. Namdar, p. 14.
39. *Haqáyeq-e Guftani*, p. 59.
40. *Haqáyeq-e Guftani*, p. 63.
41. Shahroudi, p. 100.
42. *Haqáyeq-e Guftani*, p. 42.
43. Shahroudi, p. 140.

CHAPTER 6: EIGHTY-ONE STAB WOUNDS: THE MURDER OF DR BERJIS IN KASHAN

1. In writing this section, I am indebted to Mr Naser Muhajer for his article entitled "A body thrust with knives: The case of Dr Berjis," published in *Baran Journal*, numbers 19 and 20, Sweden, 2008. I am also grateful to Mrs Nura Amanat (Samimi) who made available to me the notes of her late father, Mr Musa Amanat (*Baha'iyán-e Káshán*, published in 2012); and I thank Dr Naser Berjis who sent me two volumes of the manuscript of his valuable notes and memoirs to be used in this section. Other sources are a commentary written two weeks after the incident by Ruhollah Mehrabkhani, who had spoken to Baha'is who were present, and the memoir of the city judge Muhammad Taqi Dámghani, *A Stained Garment in the Sun* (*Jáme-ye Álúdeh dar Áftáb*). The documents and letters of the prime minister and the minister of justice are available in the *Baha'i News* (*Akhbar-e Amri*) (Issue 10, February 1950) published by the Baha'i Community of Iran.
2. Dámghani, Muhammad Taqi. *Jáme-ye Álúdeh dar Áftáb*. 2003/1382, p. 210.
3. Berjis, Naser. Shahid va Sháhed (private manuscripts and notes), 1996/1375, p. 90.
4. Mehrabkhani, Ruhollah. "Shahádat-e doctor Berjís," *Áhang-e Badi'*, 4. 17, Tehran, 1949/1328, p. 20.
5. Ibid., p. 20.
6. *Akhbar-e Amri* nr. 9420, 6 February 1950.
7. Berjis, p. 169.
8. *Ferdousi Journal*, number 32, 26 February 1950/ 7 Isfand 1328 SH.
9. Amanat, Musa. *Baha'iyán-e Káshán*. Madrid: Nehal Publishers, 2012, p. 213.
10. Ibid.
11. Fazel Mazandarani, Asadulláh. *Zuhúr al-Haq*, 8, Tehran, 1975/1354, p. 703.
12. In an article in *Payam Baha'i* (nr. 130, 1990. p. 17ff.) entitled "Forty Years after the Martyrdom of Dr Berjis," Mehrabkhani writes: "He was the only physician in town who was considered by the people as a true haven and refuge. Part of his time every day was dedicated to seeing poor and needy patients who used to come to his office without paying a fee. If they were bed-ridden, the doctor would go and visit them. It often happened that after visiting them and prescribing the medication, he would leave a sum of money under the pillow without anyone noticing. One day, I had gone to his home, a part of which consisted of his surgery. As it was the end of the day, I waited in his waiting room for him to finish for the day. His office door opened, and he guided the last patient out through the waiting room. I noticed that the patient turned to the doctor to thank him and apologize for not paying the fee; but the doctor had noticed my presence in the room, and quickly cut the conversation short, so that the subject of not affording to pay would not be mentioned in my presence."

13. Mehrabkhani 1990, p. 17.
14. Muhajer 2008, p. 21.
15. Berjis, p. 90.
16. Ibid., p. 91.
17. Mehrabkhani 1949/1328, p.7.
18. Berjis, p. 91.
19. Ja'fariyan, Rasoul. *Jarayán-há va sázmánhá-ye mazhabi-siasi-ye Iran 1320–1357*. Qom, 2006/1385, p. 116.
20. Amanat, Musa 2012, p. 214.
21. Berjis, p. 91.
22. The *Ettela'at* newspaper, Sunday 16 Bahman 1328 [5 February 1950]. Quotes here from Muhajer 2008, p. 14.
23. Mehrabkhani 1949/1328: 5; *The Baha'i World, 1950–1954*, p. 685.
24. *Ferdowsi Journal*, stated in *The Baha'i World* (ibid.)
25. Amanat 2012, p. 215; Berjis, p. 152.
26. Karbáschi 2001/1380, p. 296.
27. *Ferdowsi Journal* (ibid.).
28. Dámghani 2003/1382, p. 207.
29. Mehrabkhani 1949/1328, p. 5.
30. Muhajer 2008, p. 14.
31. Dámghani, pp. 206–8.
32. With reference to the *Ettela'at* newspaper, Sunday 5 and Monday 6 February/16 and 17 Bahman; Muhajer 2008, p. 15.
33. Mehrabkhani 1949/1328, p. 5.
34. Ibid.
35. Muhajer 2008, p. 15, quoting the *Ettela'at* newspaper, Sunday 5 and Monday 6 February (Sunday 16 and Monday 17 Bahman).
36. Muhajer 2008, p. 17.
37. Ibid., p. 16.
38. Nikusefat, Sohrab. *Kankáshi dar Bahá'i satízi*. Germany: Navid Publishers, 2006/1385, p. 38.
39. A letter dated 17/11/1328 [6 February 1950] addressed to the prime minister, Mr Sá'ed and his entire Cabinet; a letter on that same date to Gen. Zahedi, Head of the National Police (gendarmerie); and a letter dated 24/11/1328 [13 February 1950] addressed to the Shah. I clearly remember the incident as I was 17 years old. The National Assembly of Baha'is of Iran did its best to give the incident wide coverage. I myself wrote an article and sent it to one of the more friendly journals, but it was never published.
40. *Akhbar-e Amri* 1328, p. 12.
41. Gulsurkhi, Reza. *Khaterat-e Ayatollah Golsorkhi*. Tehran, 1991/1370, p. 183.
42. Dámghani, p. 209.
43. For more documents regarding this murder, see Nikisufat 2006/1385, pp. 43–50.

44. Muhajer, p. 17.
45. Ibid., p. 18.
46. Dámghani, p. 209.
47. Muhajer, p. 20.
48. Amanat, Musa, p. 217.
49. Muhajer, p. 20.
50. Amanat, pp. 215–16.
51. Dámghani, p. 209.
52. Ibid., p. 210.
53. Muhajer, p. 21.
54. Dámghani, p. 206.
55. Tavakoli-Targhi 2001/1380, p. 114.

CHAPTER 7: TRUE CRIME: THE INCIDENT AT ABARQU

This chapter is based on the book *The Innocent Ones* (Afnan, Muhammad Taqi, no date), circulated as a typed manuscript of 280 pages and drawn from the author's personal observations, newspaper articles, and documents provided to the author by the defense lawyers and the head of the court. Other than the events in Abarqu, it recounts similar incidents in which the Baha'is of Yazd were persecuted.

Afnan's account has been supplemented by four articles recently published on the internet, after the Islamic Republic's media once again publicized the case.

The article by Behyar Nikravan published in: http://www.goftman-iran1.info/-othermenu-13/1228, entitled "A New Conspiracy; the Review of an Incident in Abarqu" (*Taute'eh-ye tazeh, bar-rasi-ye vaqe'e-ye Abarqu*). The article relates the main happenings, and specifies the innocence of the Baha'is.

An article by Tooraj Amini, http://www.goftman-iran1.info/-othermenu-13/1228, entitled "Framing the Baha'is during the Pahlavi Regime" (*Parvandih sazi 'alayh-i Baha'iyan dar douriye Pahlavi*). The article recounts the Abarqu incident; provides the text of the prosecutor's indictment; includes a section of the report of the National Assembly of Iran (as cited in the Persian Baha'i News of the time); and reviews several instances of defects in the files as well as brutal incriminations. Amini also examines the cases of murders that were falsely blamed on the Baha'is in Zahedan and Yazd. Such frame-ups had bloody outcomes such as the lootings and destruction of the homes of the Baha'is, and having them beaten up and dismembered.

An article by Shinto, entitled "Criminal Charges Against the Baha'is; The Review of a File" (*Etteham-e jenayat be Baha'iyan; bazkhani-ye yek parvandeh*) in http://www.khandaniha.eu/items.php?id=683. This article provides a detailed account of the involvement of the Umidsalar family in this crime, and explains the motives for framing the Baha'is. It portrays a vivid image of the conditions of the court and its surroundings. The article also includes the texts of some of the announcements that were being distributed among the public during the trial.

An essay penned by Bahram Choubineh, entitled "Dr Muhammad Mossadegh and the Baha'is," published in http://www.memory-and-history.blogfa.com/post-42aspx. This paper examines the religious and political conditions of Iran between 1941–51, provides a detailed account of the persecution inflicted on the Baha'i community during that period (including the Abarqu incident and the role of the Salari brothers), and throws light on the critical state of the country and the impotence of the government in confronting the clergy's conspiracies against the Baha'is. The paper also presents a well-documented description of Mossaddeq's unbiased and compassionate attitude towards the Baha'is and other religious minorities.

I wish to express my gratitude to all five of these authors, without access to whose articles the writing of this chapter would not have been possible.

1. Afnan, Muhammad Taqi. *Bigunahan* (*The Innocent Ones*). Unpublished manuscript, n.d., p. 61.
2. Tooraj Amini (http://www.goftman-iran1.info/-othermenu-13/1228) writes: Haj Mirza Hasan Shamsi Isfandabadi was convicted of murder in the Abarqu case and was sentenced to ten years' imprisonment. Khakpur (the head of the Abarqu gendarmerie) had threatened him that if he were to refuse the payment requested by him, the latter would make sure that he was accused of murder and convicted. Haj Mirza Hasan replied, "There is absolutely no way that you can accuse me of such a murder!" The course of events, however, showed that anything is possible when the foundation is rotten. Hasan Shamsi lost everything he had through his imprisonment. He died in jail.
3. Afnan, p. 160.
4. For more information on this forged booklet, see Chapter 4, p. 64.
5. Bahram Choubineh (http://memory-and-history.blogfa.com/post-42.aspx) writes: "Following the victory of the Islamic Revolution, all his services to the clergy were disregarded and he had a grim fate." The London issue of *Keyhan* published the following on page 11 of its 677 issue dated Thursday 9 October 1997 [17 Mehr 1376]:

   "Abul-Hasan 'Amidi Nuri, the editor of the *Dad* newspaper, a distinguished court attorney, and a member of the consultative parliament was executed by the Islamic Republic. His family was subsequently informed that the execution was carried out in error. As such the verdict for the confiscation of his belongings was annulled."
6. Mirza Taqi Khan Farahani, also known as Amir Kabir, Atabak, and Amir Nezam, served as prime minister under Naser al-Din Shah from 1948–1951. He was put to death in Kashan by the order of the shah in January 1952.
7. Choubineh, p. 72.

CHAPTER 8: THE EVENTS OF 1955: HOJJAT AL-ISLAM FALSAFI, THE RAMADAN BROADCASTS, AND THE MILITARY OCCUPATION OF THE BAHA'I CENTER

1. Tavakoli-Targhi regards the assassination of Hazhir as "yet another sign of the onset of violence against the Baha'is"; rumors of him being a Baha'i had been circulated, and the followers of Ayatollah Kashani considered the opposition to Hazhir to be tantamount to "defending the Religion and the Quran." (Tavakoli-Targhi 2001/1380, pp. 104–5.)
2. [17 Esfand 1329/ 8 March 1951]. For background and details of the activities of the *Fada'iyan-e Islam*, see: Kazemi, F. "The *Fada'iyan-e Islam*: Fanaticisms, Politics and Terror," in *From Nationalism to Revolutionary Islam*, ed. S. Amir Arjomand. Albany: State University of New York Press, 1984, p. 158.
3. Tavakoli-Targhi 2001/1380, p. 105.
4. See Chapter 6.
5. Falsafi, Muhammad Taqi. *Khátérát va mobarezát-e hojjat al-Islam Falsafi*, ed. 'Ali Davani. Tehran: Markaz-e setád-e enqelab-e Islami, 2003/1382, p. 133.
6. Quoting *Ettehad-e Melli*, issue number 365, page 1: "The most comprehensive flow of activities that led to the siege of the Baha'i Center (*Haziratul-Quds.*)"; Falsafi 2003/1382, p. 191; Tavakoli-Targhi 2001/1380, p. 105.
7. Akhavi, S. *Religion and Politics in Contemporary Iran: Clergy–State Relations in the Pahlavi Period*. Albany: State University of New York Press, 2001/1380, p. 77.
8. Mahdavi, 'Abd al-Reza Hushang. *Guftuguhá-ye man bá Shah, khaterát-e mahramáneh-ye Asadolláh 'Alam* (*My Conversations with the Shah, the Secret Memoirs of Asadollah 'Alam*), 3rd edn. Tehran: Tarh-e Nou Publications, 1992, pp. 66–7. Translated in Iran Human Rights Documentation Center (2007). "*A Faith Denied: The Persecution of the Baha'is of Iran*". Iran Human Rights Documentation Center. http://www.iranhrdc.org/english/publications/reports/3149-a-faith-denied-the-persecution-of-the-baha-is-of-iran.html?p=8
9. *Khandaniha*, 15, 67, 13 May 1955/22 Urdibehesht 1334 SH. The reference made to the private affairs of the shah is an allusion to the objection made by Falsafi to the shah's doctor being a Baha'i.
10. This report is based on a complaint filed on 3 August 1955/11 Murdad 1334SH by Mrs Manzar Amiri, the sister of two of the deceased (Hedayatollah and Amanollah), addressed to the governor of Yazd and the public prosecutor of that city; as well as an account of the upheaval in Hurmuzak including the photographs of the martyrs, written by Muhammad Labib. (Labib, M. *The Seven Martyrs of Hurmuzak*, trans. M. Momen. Oxford: George Ronald, 1981.)
11. Extracted from a report from Mashhad dated 25 January 1956/5 Bahman 1334 SH. addressed to the National Spiritual Assembly of the Baha'is of Iran.
12. *Keyhan*, 8 May 1955/17 Urdibehesht 1334 SH.

13. *Ettela'at*, 10 May 1955/19 Urdibehesht 1334 SH.
14. *Ettela'at*, 10 May 1955/19 Urdibehesht 1334 SH., p. 12
15. *Keyhan*, 5 May 1955/14 Urdibehesht 1334SH. Quran 61:13.
16. "The governor-general of Fars replaced", *Setarey-e Islam* dated 16 July 1955/24 Tir 1334 SH.
17. Akhavi, p. 77; translation quoted from Iran Human Rights Documentation Center: *A Faith Denied: The Persecution of the Baha'is of Iran.*
18. *Ettela'at*, 18 May 1955/27 Urdibehesht 1334 SH.
19. *Taraqqi*, 26 May 1955/4 Khurdad 1334 SH. Quran 48: 15–16.
20. Davani, 'Ali. *Zendegi-námeh-ye za'im-e bozorg-e 'alam-e tashayo 'Ayatuolláh Boroujerdi.* Tehran: printed by Motayyar, 1991/1370, p. 210.
21. 'Álikháni. *Yad-dashthá-ye 'Alam.* Washington, DC: Ibex Publishers, 1992, p. 162.

PART TWO: THE ISLAMIC REPUBLIC IN CONFRONTATION WITH THE BAHA'I FAITH

1. Sanasarian, Eliz. *Religious Minorities in Iran.* Cambridge: Cambridge University Press, 2000, p. 57.
2. Ibid., p. 53.

CHAPTER 9: BAHA'I PERSECUTION DURING THE LAST DAYS OF THE SHAH'S REGIME

1. The information in this section has been extracted from numerous reports written by both Baha'i and Muslim eyewitnesses. These reports have been made available by the archives office of the Baha'i World Centre, at the request of the author.
2. Katoozian, Muhammad Ali Homayoun. *Mehregan Journal*, II, 4. Printed in US, 1993/1372, p. 55; Afnan, Abu al-Qasem. *Payam Baha'i*, 20, 224 and 225, 1998/1377, p. 104.
3. For a more detailed eyewitness account of the Sa'diyeh incident see Mahingostar, Iraj. *Khoon va gol-e sorkh, baláyá-ye várdedeh bar Bahá'iyán-e Iran, 1320–1368.* California: Shrkat-e Ketab, 2008, pp. 95–162.
4. *The Baha'i World, 1979–1983.*
5. Ibid., pp. 271–4.

CHAPTER 10: THE BAHA'IS—THE FIRST VICTIMS OF OPPRESSION IN THE ISLAMIC REPUBLIC

1. Professor James Cockroft of Rutgers University in December 1978, published in the US journal of public affairs, *Seven Days*, 23 February 1979,

p. 20. The transcript of the interview was approved by the Ayatollah and his aide, Dr Ebrahim Yazdi, February 13, 1979.

2. "U.S. Jews Hold Talks With Khomeini Aide on Outlook For Rights," *The New York Times*, February 13, 1979.
3. Afshari, Reza. *Human Rights in Iran: The Abuse of Cultural Relativism*. Philadelphia: University of Pennsylvania Press, 2001, p. 132.
4. Sanasarian 2000, pp. 40–54, 114–23.
5. English translation of the Constitution is from: http://www.iranchamber.com/government/laws/constitution_ch01.php#sthash.ek4ZTilp.dpuf
6. *The Jewish Chronicle*, 18 May 1979, p. 1; *Los Angeles Times*, 23 May 1979, p.1.
7. Sanasarian 2000, pp. 64–71.
8. Khubruy-Pák, Manuchehr. "Tahavolat-e qavánín-e Iran dar báreh-ye aqalyyathá-ye díní az dourh-ye Qajar tá emrouz," *Khoosheh-ha'i az khaman-e adab va honar*, 16. Darmstadt: 'Asr-e jadíd, 2008, p. 250.
9. Malikiyan. *Hafteh-nameh-ye Nimruz*, 619, London, 1379, p. 18.

CHAPTER 11: THE PERSECUTION OF BAHA'IS UNDER BAZARGAN AND THE REVOLUTIONARY COUNCIL

1. Martin, Douglas. "The Persecution of the Baha'is of Iran 1844–1984," *Baha'i Studies*, 12 & 13, Ottawa, Canada, Association for Baha'i Studies, 1984, p. 37ff.
2. Extract of a statement by Dr Husain Naji, member of the National Assembly of the Baha'is of Iran. *A Faith Denied*: http://www.iranhrdc.org/english/publications/reports/3149-a-faith-denied-the-persecution-of-the-baha-is-of-iran.htm 1368, pp. 29–31.
3. *The Baha'i World, 1979–1983*, p. 256
4. *A Faith Denied*, pp. 29–31.
5. Ibid., p. 21.
6. The information on the follow-up of the fate of the members of the National Assembly of the Baha'is of Iran is based on the statement of the Baha'i International Community at the United Nations, New York, addressed to "The Working Group on Enforced or Involuntary Disappearances", dated 31 January 1981.
7. *The Baha'i World, 1979–1983*, pp. 256–7.
8. For further information see: http://lab.noghtenazar2.info/node/111
9. Djazayeri, Ezzat. *Strangers in their Native Land*. Uppsala: Baha'i Publishing Trust of Sweden, 1987, p. 70.
10. *A Faith Denied*, p. 30.
11. The following account is based on a report given by Mr Lutfí.
12. *The Baha'i World, 1979–1983*, p. 279.

CHAPTER 12: THE PRESIDENCIES OF BANISADR AND RAJA'I

1. *Inqelab-e Islami* newspaper, 21 June 1980/31 Khurdad 1359.
2. *Le Monde*, 24 June 1980.
3. Kravetz, M. *Irano Nox*, Paris: Edition Grasset et Fasquelle, 1982, p. 241.
4. Martin 1984, p. 53.
5. *The Baha'i World, 1979–1983*, p. 261.
6. Martin 1984, p. 54.
7. In a public press release, Kurush Niknam, the Zoroastrian delegate in the parliament severely criticized Jannaati's statement, following which he was arrested and imprisoned on the charge of spreading lies. "Iran Plans a Final Solution," *Sunday Times*, London, 20 September 1981. http://www.emrouz.info/archives/2005/11/005532.php; http://www.raha.gooya.name/politics/archives/038930.php

CHAPTER 13: ARRESTS AND EXECUTIONS OF THE BAHA'I ASSEMBLIES, 1981–85

1. Information on the Second National Assembly presented here is based on communications received from Mrs Gaiti Vahid (Qadimi), a member of that Assembly, and the testimony of Mrs Farideh Samímí who was arrested with her husband, Mr Kamran Samimi, secretary of the National Assembly.
2. *A Faith Denied*, pp. 31, 22.
3. Ibid.
4. Ibid., p. 32.
5. *Le Monde* published an article on January 5, 1982: "Tehran denies the execution of eight Baha'i leaders" (*Téhéran dement l'éxecution de huit responsables Bahá'is*).
6. *The Baha'i Question: Cultural Cleansing In Iran*. Geneva: Baha'i International Community, 2005, p. 79. Accessible at: http://question.bahai.org/001.php
7. For the full text of the original letter see *Payam-e Baha'i*, issue 50, December 1983.
8. *The Baha'i World, 1983–1986*, p. 194.
9. Ibid., p. 205.
10. Ibid., p. 208.
11. Ibid., p. 211.
12. *A Faith Denied*, p. 29.
13. Ibid.
14. Ibid.

15. *The Baha'i World, 1979–1983*, pp. 281–3.
16. Ibid., p. 284.
17. Press interview of the religious judge and the prosecutor of the Revolutionary Courts in Tehran, published in the *Keyhan* newspaper, number 11488, 19 February 1982 / 30 Bahman 1360 SH.
18. *A Faith Denied*, p. 26.
19. The report is available online at http://www.iranhrdc.org/httpdocs/persian/reports/htm
20. *A Community Under Siege: The Ordeal of the Baha'is of Shiraz* (*A Faith Denied*, and: http://www.iranhrdc.org/httpdocs/persian/reports/htm).
21. Idem, as well as the memoirs of his wife, Zhinus Afnan.
22. Issue number 782, dated 22 February 1984.
23. For a detailed account of the arrests, interrogations, tortures, and executions of the Baha'is of Shiraz see *A Faith Denied*: http://www.iranhrdc.org/english/publications/reports/3149-a-faith-denied-the-persecution-of-the-baha-is-of-iran.html.
24. For the names of all those arrested see *Payam-e Baha'i*, issue 47, September 1983 and subsequent issues.

CHAPTER 14: THE DESTRUCTION OF BAHA'I HOLY SITES AND COMMUNITY RESOURCES

1. Ishraq-Khávari, A. *Mohazerát*, 3, ed. Vahid Ra'fati, Germany, 2009, pp. 341–8.
2. *A Faith Denied*, p. 40.
3. Memorandum, "Current Situation of the Baha'is in Iran, August 1994," issued by the Baha'i International Community, New York, addressed to the 49th session of the United Nation's General Assembly, September 1994.
4. Economic and Social Council of the United Nations, report: E/CN.4/2006/41/Add.2, dated March 21, 2006. See pp. 12 and 19.

CHAPTER 15: AFTER AYATOLLAH KHOMEINI: THE ESCALATION OF PERSECUTION

1. Moojan Momen, *Economic Strangulation of the Baha'i Community*, in: http://www.iranpresswatch.org/post/1578, 2 March 2009. This site includes various documents on the crackdown on the Baha'is.
2. "Iran Closes University Run Covertly by the Baha'is", *New York Times*, 29 October 1998, p. A7.
3. See: http://denial/bahai.org/004.php

4. Mehrpour, Husain. *Vazife-ye dushvar-e nezarat bar ejra-ye qanun-e asasi.* (*The Challenging Task of Monitoring the Implementation of Constitutional Law.*) Tehran: Nshr-e Thaleth, 2005/1384, p. 636.

CHAPTER 16: EFFORTS AT REFORM UNDER PRESIDENT KHATAMI

1. Mehrpour, p. 384.
2. Ibid., p. 597.
3. Ibid., p. 611.
4. Ibid., p. 626.
5. Letter number 43-20500, dated 21 February 2000 [2/12/1387 SH].
6. Mehrpour, p. 625.
7. http://info.bahai.org/pdf/iran_update2003-04.pdf. The statement and the news of the demolition of the Baha'i historic sites appeared on that same day in newspapers in Australia, Canada, France, Germany, Norway, the United States, and the United Kingdom, including the *New York Times*, the *Los Angeles Times*, the *Washington Post*, the London *Times*, and *Le Monde*, etc.

CHAPTER 17: ESCALATING REPRESSION UNDER PRESIDENT AHMADINEJAD (2005–13)

1. See Chapter 7.
2. For example the website of the Islamic Propaganda Organization in Kerman reported that one thousand copies of the book *Babism and Bahaism* was distributed in June 2010 among the attendees of the Friday prayer, lamentation and mourning gatherings, trade unions, etc. See: http://www.ido.ir/n.aspx?n=13890406335
3. See: http://ketabhayebahai.com/2009-03-30-13-37-10, http://ketabhayebahai.com/2009-03-30-13-38-44, Sohrab Nikusefat's book, *Kankáshi dar Bahá'i satízi* (*A Deliberation on anti-Baha'i Hostility*), the first in a series of books on *Clearing up Misconceptions* by S. Nikusefat, Germany: Payam Publications, 2006 [1385].
4. Momen, M. *Economic Strangulation of the Baha'i Community*, at: http://www.iranpresswatch.org/post/1578, 2 March 2009.
5. *Payam-e Baha'i*, issue number 345–6, August–September 2008, pp. 15–24.
6. For a detailed report on the daily harassment and persecution of the Baha'is of Iran, see: http://www.dipity.com/mideastyouth/Persecution_of_Baha_is/embed_list?skin. For a more detailed report on the demolition of the 50 houses of the Baha'is in Ayval, see: http://khabarnavard.blogspot.com/2010/06/50.html
7. *Payam-Baha'i*, June 2008. http://news-bahai.blogfa.com/post-9.aspx
8. http://www.iranpresswatch.org/fa/post/13#more-13

CHAPTER 18: AN OBSESSION WITH CONSPIRACY THEORIES IN THE ISLAMIC REPUBLIC

1. Shahbazi, 'Abdollah, *Justar ha-i az tarikh-e Bahaigari dar Iran*. Tehran, 1382, p. 21.
2. Shahbazi 2003/1382, p. 32; also see Aram Anahid, "Baha'is, the Sole Targets of Conspiracism?" at: http://iranpresswatch.org/post/1407/
3. The site of "The Scientific Society of Iranian Students" provides such an extended definition of the Iranian *Ánusim* that it can include almost all the clergy, the religious authorities, the teachers of the seminarian schools in Qom, the Prayer leaders, and many of the military and nation's officials in the Islamic Republic. For more information see: http://www.daneshju.ir/forum/f1522/t55285.html

CHAPTER 19: SYSTEMATIC HUMILIATION: BEING LABELED RITUALLY UNCLEAN (*NAJES*)

1. This debate was broadcast from the ILNA news site (Iran Labor News Agency). The original site was changed after the 2009 elections, and is no longer accessible. The article was moved to http://www.tasnimnews.com/Home/Single/195775 and the term 'homosexual' was changed to 'adulterer.'
2. Afshari 2001.
3. *Raha* was a pseudonym for the author of the book *Haqiqat-e Sadeh* (*Simple Truth*). This book is now published under the author's name, Munireh Baradaran. It has also been translated into German by Bahrám Chúbínih. See Baradaran 1998.
4. Azadi 1987, p. 168.
5. Raha 1992, p. 199.
6. Afshari 2001, p. 51.
7. *Risalih Ajwabat al Istifta'at*; available at: http://leader.ir/ar/book/12; for the English version see: http://www.islam-pure.de/imam/books/ajvab.pdf
8. T.N.: The original states 'my dear children'; the translation reads 'my dear friends.'
9. Ibid.
10. Taken from the English website: http://www.jannaati.com/eng/index.php?page=6. An alternative translation of the second phrase would be: . . . "And if they stay away from the things that are considered as impure (*najes*) by Muslims, they would not even be considered unintentionally unclean."
11. Other rulings of Mr Jannaati are also interesting, for example: "It is not necessary that a Mojtahed who is followed for Taqlid should be a man." Also, he was asked if he agreed that some views that are presented in society as views of Islam are in fact totally contrary to and loathed by Islam. He replied affirmatively stating that: "Yes, we agree. Unfortunately some views

are presented in the Islamic society as views of Islam, and are treated as the Law of God, whereas it is not so, and there are many such examples. These are elements that have inflicted great blows upon Islam throughout history. These views and rulings clothe the stature of Islamic jurisprudence with an inverse cover and sheathe; a cover that creates hatred and loathing in healthy minds." http://www.jannaati.com/eng/index.php?page=6.

12. Malcolm 1908, pp. 45–6.

CHAPTER 20: THE PERSPECTIVES OF IRAN'S GRAND AYATOLLAHS ON THE BAHA'I FAITH

1. For details of this *fatwa* see: http://www.shahrvanemruz.com/content/3986/default.aspx
2. Cooper R. *The Baha'is of Iran*. London: Minority Rights Group Ltd., 1982, p. 15.
3. *Keyhan* newspaper 8/3/1362–5/29/1083 (speech of the Imam on his visit with the authorities on the occasion of the celebration of the anniversary of the birth of Imam Mahdi); English translation: Iran Human Rights Document Center (2014), p. 26.
4. Afshari, Reza. "The Discourse and Practice of Human Rights Violation of the Iranian Baha'is in the Islamic Republic of Iran," in *The Bahá'is of Iran, Socio-Historical Studies*, ed. Dominic Parviz Brookshaw and Seena B. Fazel. London and New York: Routledge, 2008, pp. 238, 241.
5. Afshari 2008, p. 238. During the first four years of the regime, 12,800 political prisoners were hung or executed by firing squad, two thirds of whom were members of the Mujahedin Organization or their supporters (Abrahamian, E. *The Iranian Mujahedin*. New Haven: Yale University Press, 1989, p. 223.)
6. *The Baha'i World: 1983–1986*, p. 332. Although the harassment of the Baha'is of *Sangesar* was halted at that time, a few years later the persecutions rose to such heights that hundreds of families in that area lost their lands, farms, homes, and belongings and had to leave their homeland and take refuge in other countries.
7. The original term is *mahqun al-dam* : Him whose shedding of blood is not permissible.
8. Hashemi, Kamran. *Religious Legal Traditions, International Human Rights Law and Muslim States*. Brill, 2008, p. 194, fn. 210.
9. Based on a letter written by Ruhi Roushani's wife at the request of the author, about the mentioned meeting.
10. See Chapter 17.
11. See Chapter 4 regarding the memoirs of Ayatollah Montazeri's youth years.
12. Radio Zamaneh site: radiozamaaneh.com/idea/2008/06/post_320.html; radiozamaaneh.com/idea/2008/06/post_321.html
13. This interview is available on: http://www1.rfi.fr/actufa/articles/101/article_2372.asp

14. See: Radio France 9 June 2009; http://www.rfi.fr/actufa/articles/114/article_6817.asp
15. Mr Karrubí and Mr Mussavi, another reformist presidential candidate, are under house arrest since the widespread protest called The Green Movement following the 2009 election.

CHAPTER 21: THE APPEALS OF INTERNATIONAL ORGANIZATIONS AND THE IRANIAN DIASPORA

1. https://www.bic.org and http://question.bahai.org
2. Ghanea 2002.
3. Martin 1984, p. 41.
4. See Chapter 10 regarding Articles 13 and 14 of the Constitutional Law, and how the Islamic Republic has mutilated these two articles.
5. For the full interview see: http://www.radiozamaaneh.com/seraj/2009/01/post_12.html
6. See: http://khandaniha.eu/items.php?id=682
7. English translation taken from Iran Press Watch.
8. This article was first published in the Shahrgon online journal in September 2008, available at: http://www.shahrgon.com/index.php?news=1959; it was later published in several journals outside Iran. The English translation is by Dr Ahang Rabbani.
9. These six women who are active under the banner of Nobel Women's Initiative consist of: Betty Williams and Mairead Corrigan Maguire, founders of the Peace People in Northern Ireland and winners of the Nobel Peace Prize in 1976; Rigoberta Menchu Tum, a leading advocate of ethno-cultural reconciliation in her native Guatemala and Nobel winner in 1992; Professor Jody Williams, international campaigner for the banning of land mines, winner in 1997; Iranian human rights lawyer Dr Shirin Ebadi, winner in 2003; Kenyan environmental activist Professor Wangari Muta Maathai, Nobel winner in 2004.

EPILOGUE

1. See Chapter 15 for how the BIHE came into being.
2. The Baha'is involved in the BIHE who suffered or are suffering five years' imprisonment are:
   Ms Negin Ghadamian (imprisoned in December 2017)
   Mr Hasan Momtaz (imprisoned in November 2017)
   Mr Peyman Koushk-Baghi (imprisoned in February 2016)
   Mr Amanollah Mostaghim (imprisoned in May 2013, and released in November 2015 due to ill-health)

Mr Kayvan Rahimian (imprisoned in September 2012)
Mr 'Azizollah Samandarí (imprisoned in July 2012)
Mr Foad Moghaddam (imprisoned in June 2012)
Mr Kamran Mortezaie (imprisoned in 2011)
Mr Vahid Mahmoudi (imprisoned in October 2011, but released in January 2012 after his sentence was reportedly suspended).
The following Bahá'ís affiliated with the BIHE suffered or are suffering four years' imprisonment:
Ms Azita Rafizadeh (imprisoned in October 2015)
Ms Nasim Bagheri Tari (imprisoned in April 2014)
Mr Shahin Negari (imprisoned in January 2013)
Ms Faran Hesami (imprisoned in 2012)
Mr Kamran Rahimian (imprisoned in September 2011)
Mr Riaz Sobhani (arrested in June 2011)
Mr Farhad Sedghi (arrested in May 2011)
Mr Mahmoud Badavam (imprisoned in May 2011)
Ms Nooshin Khadem (arrested in May 2011)
Mr Ramin Zibaie (imprisoned in 2011).
More information about some of these individuals can be found at the following website: http://news.bahai.org/human-rights/iran/education/profiles. (Source: The Baha'i International Community, Geneva, Switzerland.)

3. Mr Rezvani's cousin, Navid Aqdasi, was arrested at his home on November 15, 2015, by agents of the "Drug Squad." He has not been heard from since then. This could be a plot to extract a forced confession to baseless drug possession offences that carry the death penalty in Iran. It seems that Mr Aqdasi's real "crime" is demanding justice for the execution-style murder of his cousin. Compare this incident with a similar case in France, when an eighty-five-year-old Jewish lady named Mireille Knoll was murdered, in an anti-Semitic attack, in her flat in late March 2018; thousands took to the streets in cities throughout France in protest at this crime.
4. These include: Reports of the Special Rapporteur on the situation of human rights in the Islamic Republic of Iran; Reports of the United Nations Secretary-General on the situation of human rights in Iran; Universal Periodic Review; and Resolutions on the situation of human rights in the Islamic Republic of Iran (although the Human Rights Council resolutions are not substantive and therefore do not mention the Bahá'ís, or any other issue for that matter).
5. Booklet produced in October 2016 by the Bahá'í International Community called *The Bahá'í Question Revisited: Persecution and Resilience in Iran*: https://www.bic.org/sites/default/files/pdf/thebahaiquestionrevisited_final_160930e.pdf

   Infographic produced in January 2018 on the situation of the Baha'is in Iran: https://www.bic.org/sites/default/files/pdf/iran/infographic_january_2018.pdf

Website of the archives of the persecution of the Baha'is in Iran across the decades: https://iranbahaipersecution.bic.org/

Website of the Baha'is of Iran: https://www.bahaisofiran.org/

https://en.wikipedia.org/wiki/Statements_about_the_persecution_of_Bah%C3%A1%27%C3%ADs.

6. The talks at this conference are available at: http://www.sitenama.net.
7. See the trailer: https://vimeo.com/ondemand/thegardener.
8. See: http://www.jamnews.com/detail/news/213183.
9. See: http://mehdikhalaji.com/archives/1368.
10. See: https://iranbahaipersecution.bic.org/fa/node.

Index

References to images are indicated by *italics*.